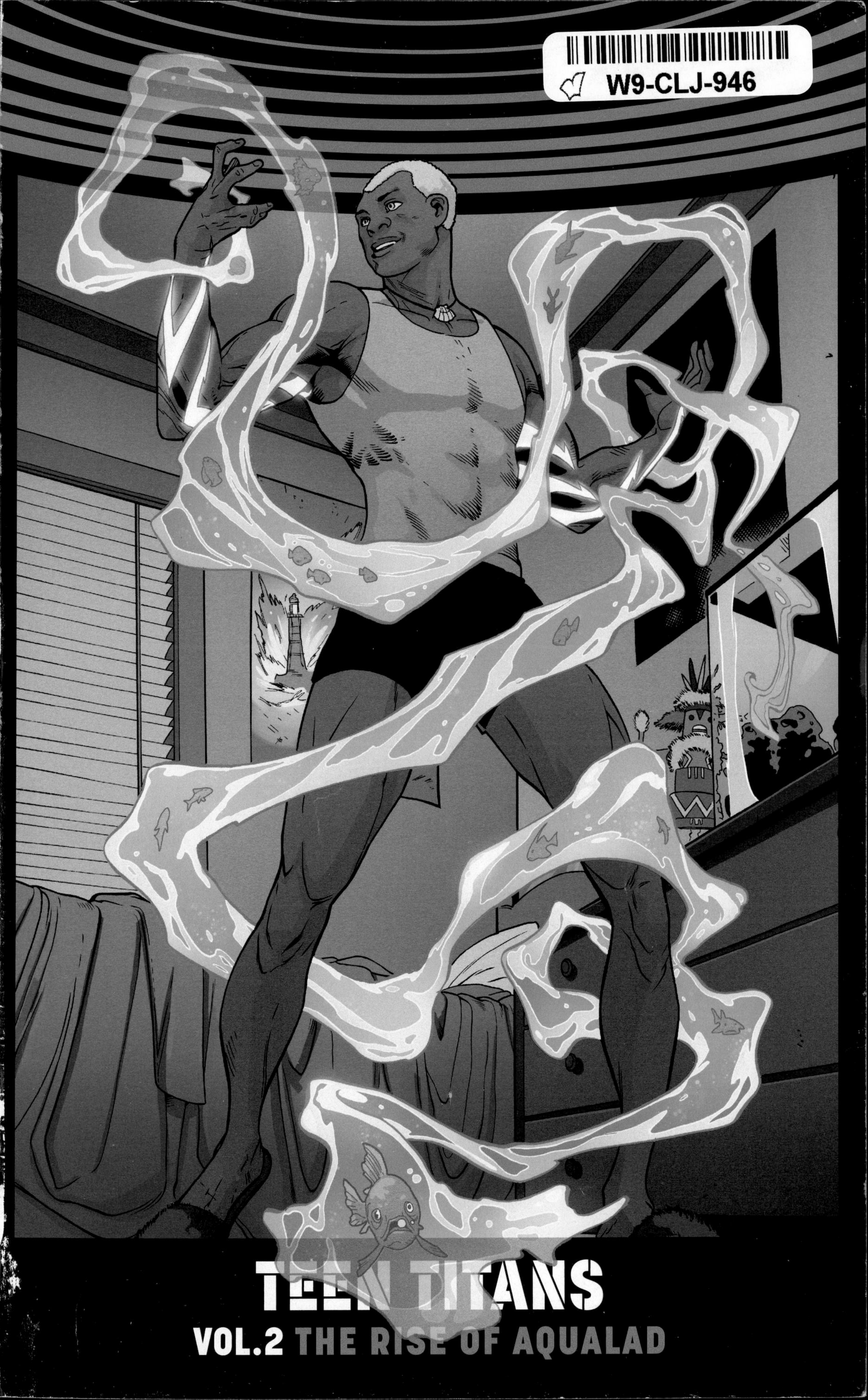

TEEN TITANS
VOL.2 THE RISE OF AQUALAD

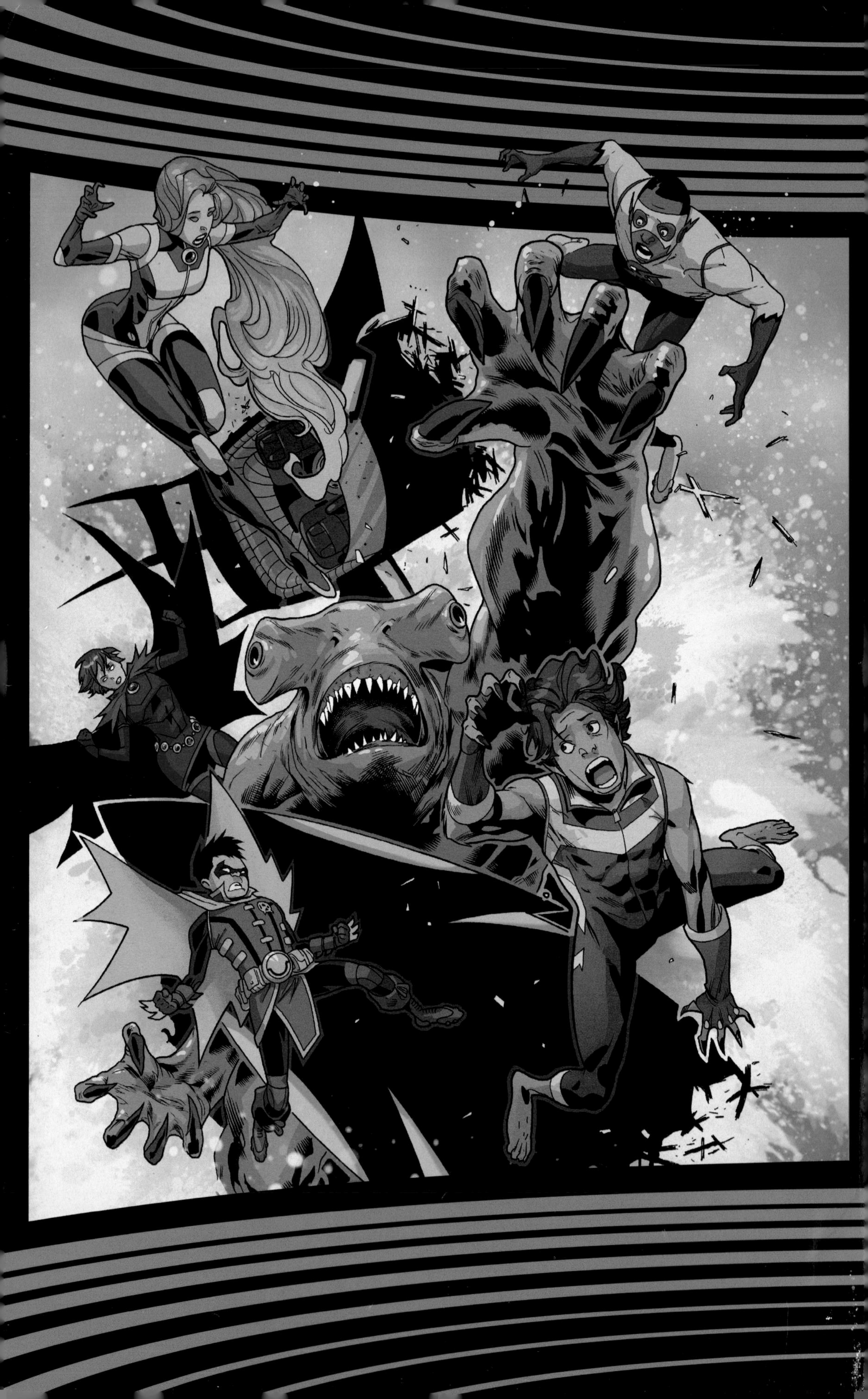

TEEN TITANS

VOL.2 THE RISE OF AQUALAD

BENJAMIN PERCY
writer

KHOI PHAM
POP MHAN
pencillers

PHIL HESTER
breakdowns

TREVOR SCOTT
WADE VON GRAWBADGER * POP MHAN * CRAIG YEUNG
inkers

JIM CHARALAMPIDIS
colorist

COREY BREEN
letterer

KHOI PHAM and JIM CHARALAMPIDIS
collection cover artists

BLACK MANTA created by **BOB HANEY**

ALEX ANTONE Editor - Original Series ✻ **BRITTANY HOLZHERR** Associate Editor - Original Series
JEB WOODARD Group Editor - Collected Editions ✻ **ROBIN WILDMAN** Editor - Collected Edition
STEVE COOK Design Director - Books ✻ **MONIQUE NARBONETA** Publication Design

BOB HARRAS Senior VP - Editor-in-Chief, DC Comics
PAT McCALLUM Executive Editor, DC Comics

DIANE NELSON President ✻ **DAN DiDIO** Publisher ✻ **JIM LEE** Publisher ✻ **GEOFF JOHNS** President & Chief Creative Officer
AMIT DESAI Executive VP - Business & Marketing Strategy, Direct to Consumer & Global Franchise Management
SAM ADES Senior VP & General Manager, Digital Services ✻ **BOBBIE CHASE** VP & Executive Editor, Young Reader & Talent Development
MARK CHIARELLO Senior VP - Art, Design & Collected Editions ✻ **JOHN CUNNINGHAM** Senior VP - Sales & Trade Marketing
ANNE DePIES Senior VP - Business Strategy, Finance & Administration ✻ **DON FALLETTI** VP - Manufacturing Operations
LAWRENCE GANEM VP - Editorial Administration & Talent Relations ✻ **ALISON GILL** Senior VP - Manufacturing & Operations
HANK KANALZ Senior VP - Editorial Strategy & Administration ✻ **JAY KOGAN** VP - Legal Affairs ✻ **JACK MAHAN** VP - Business Affairs
NICK J. NAPOLITANO VP - Manufacturing Administration ✻ **EDDIE SCANNELL** VP - Consumer Marketing
COURTNEY SIMMONS Senior VP - Publicity & Communications ✻ **JIM (SKI) SOKOLOWSKI** VP - Comic Book Specialty Sales & Trade Marketing
NANCY SPEARS VP - Mass, Book, Digital Sales & Trade Marketing ✻ **MICHELE R. WELLS** VP - Content Strategy

TEEN TITANS VOL. 2: THE RISE OF AQUALAD

DC Comics, 2900 West Alameda Ave., Burbank, CA 91505
Printed by LSC Communications, Kendallville, IN, USA. 1/26/18. First Printing.
ISBN: 978-1-4012-7504-4

Library of Congress Cataloging-in-Publication Data is available.

PEFC Certified
Printed on paper from
sustainably managed
forests, controlled
sources
PEFC/29-31-337   www.pefc.org

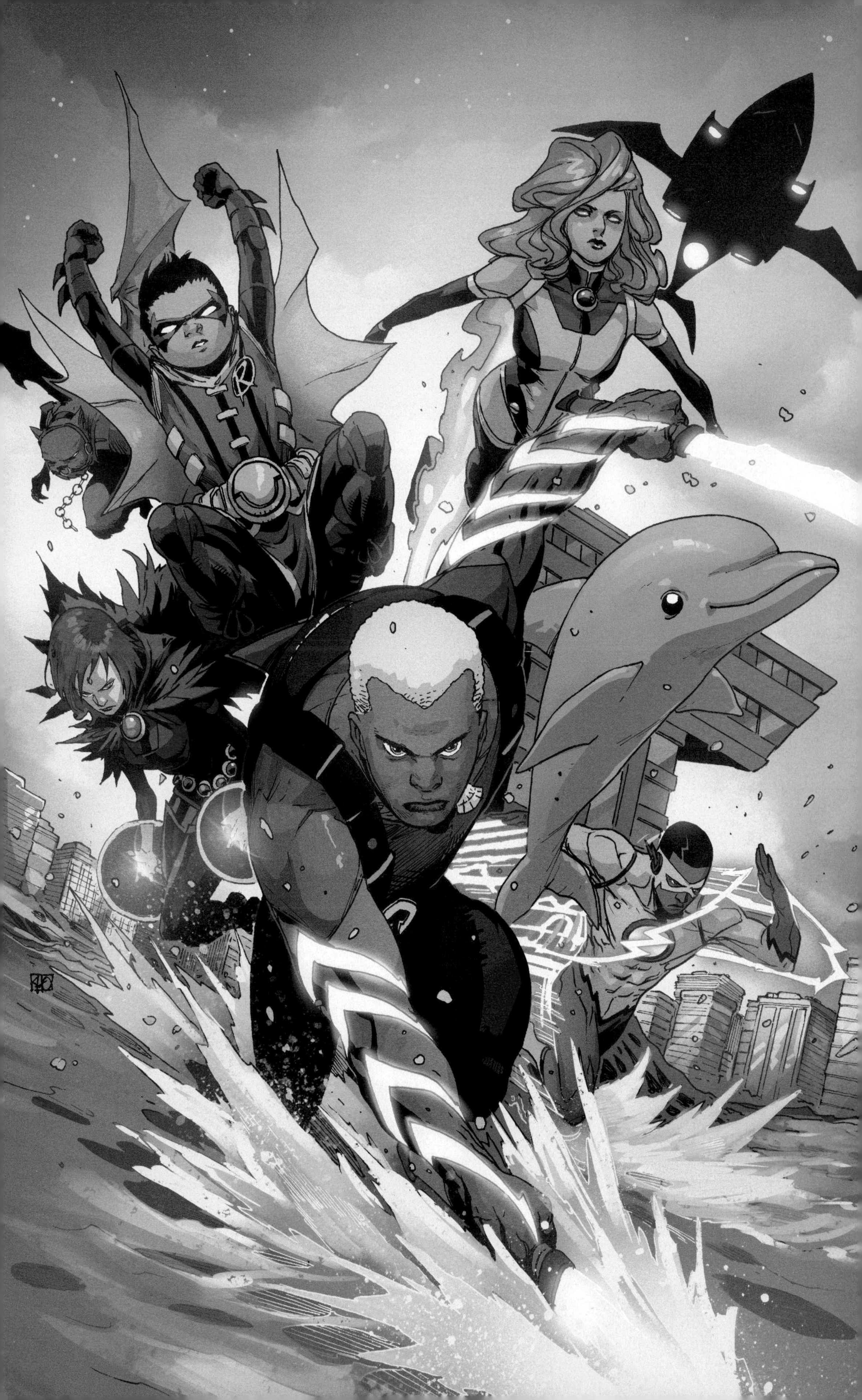

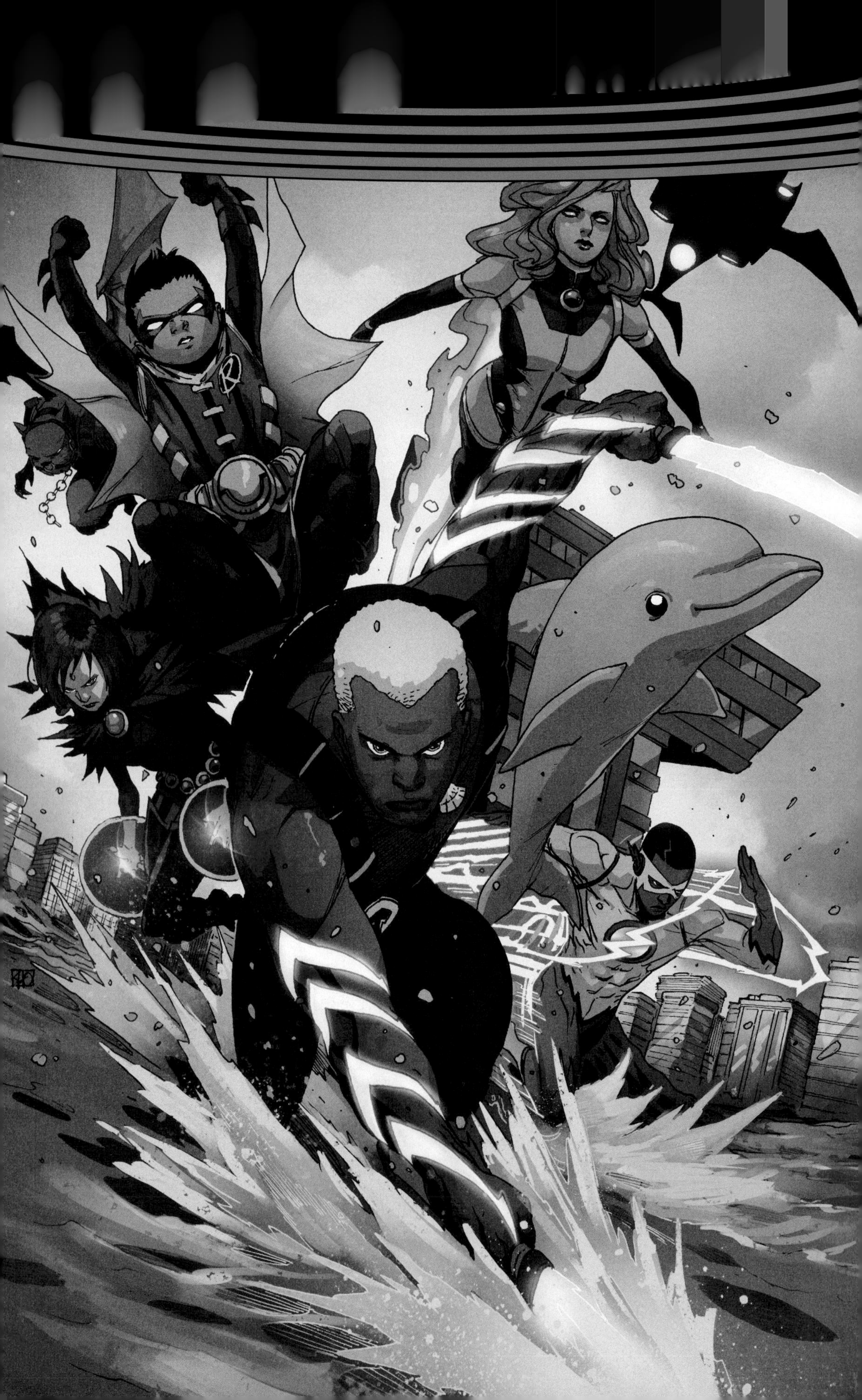

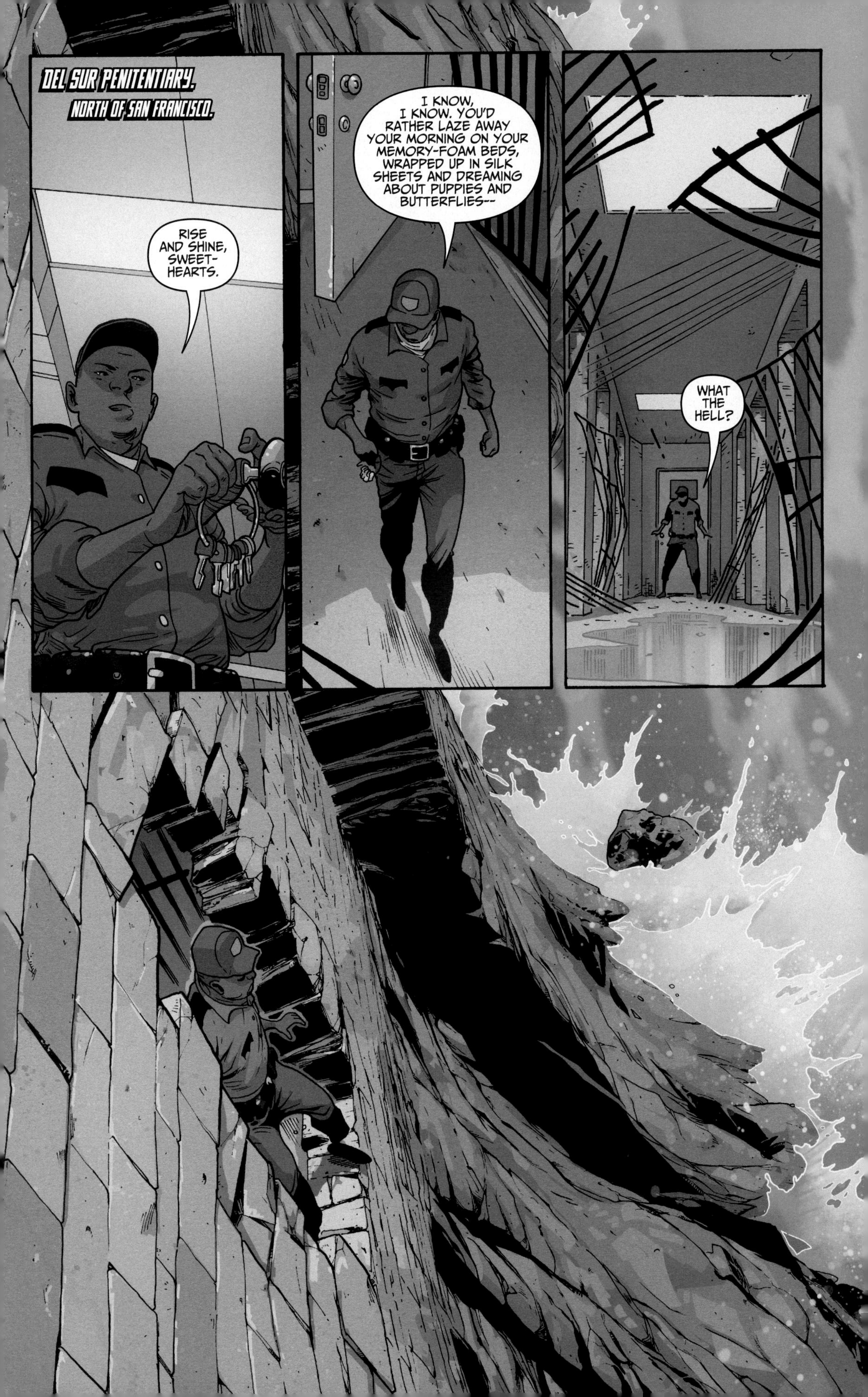
DEL SUR PENITENTIARY.
NORTH OF SAN FRANCISCO.
RISE AND SHINE, SWEET-HEARTS.
I KNOW, I KNOW. YOU'D RATHER LAZE AWAY YOUR MORNING ON YOUR MEMORY-FOAM BEDS, WRAPPED UP IN SILK SHEETS AND DREAMING ABOUT PUPPIES AND BUTTERFLIES--
WHAT THE HELL?

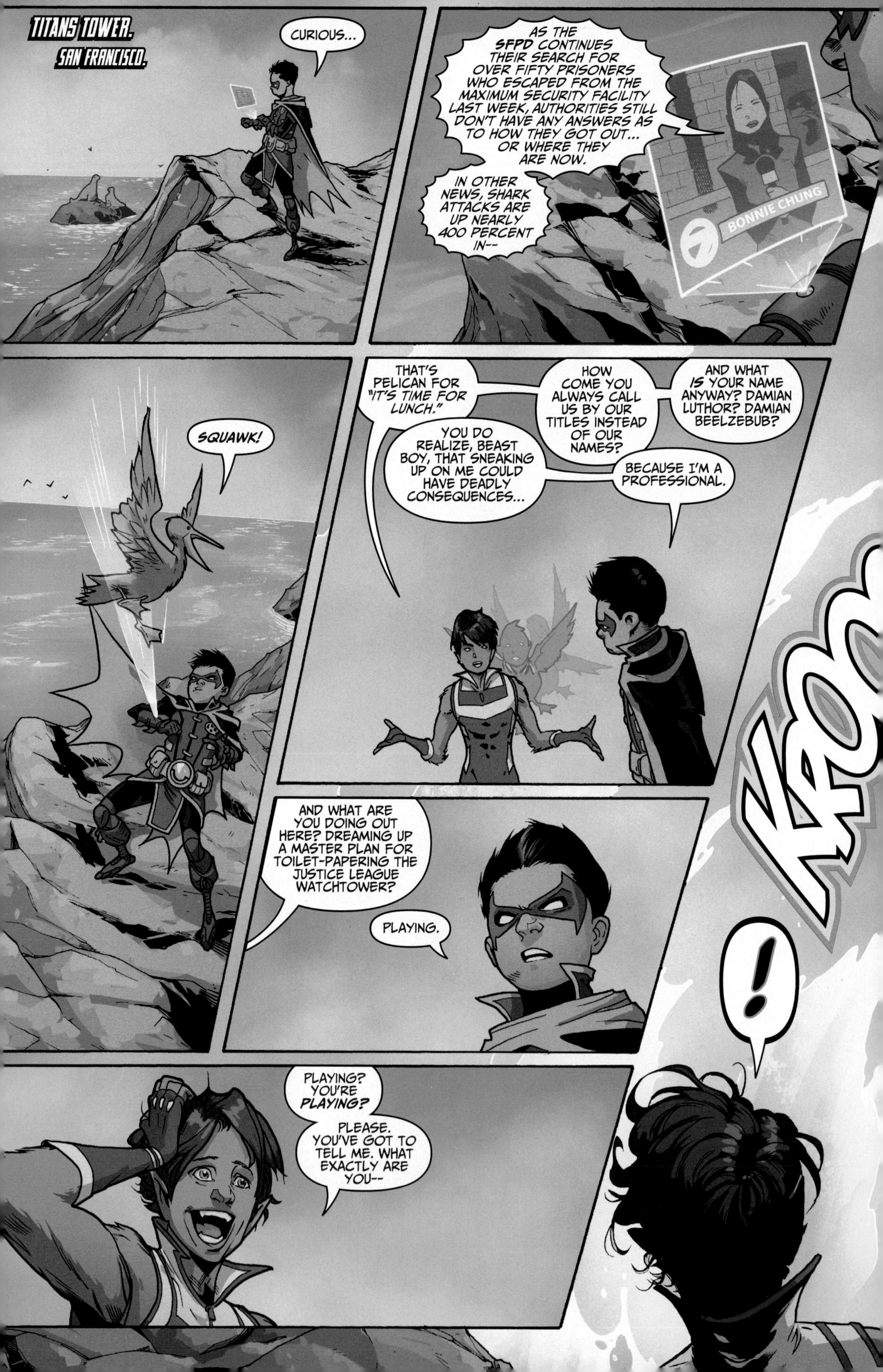
TITANS TOWER.
SAN FRANCISCO.
CURIOUS...
AS THE SFPD CONTINUES THEIR SEARCH FOR OVER FIFTY PRISONERS WHO ESCAPED FROM THE MAXIMUM SECURITY FACILITY LAST WEEK, AUTHORITIES STILL DON'T HAVE ANY ANSWERS AS TO HOW THEY GOT OUT... OR WHERE THEY ARE NOW.
IN OTHER NEWS, SHARK ATTACKS ARE UP NEARLY 400 PERCENT IN--
BONNIE CHUNG
SQUAWK!
THAT'S PELICAN FOR "IT'S TIME FOR LUNCH."
YOU DO REALIZE, BEAST BOY, THAT SNEAKING UP ON ME COULD HAVE DEADLY CONSEQUENCES...
HOW COME YOU ALWAYS CALL US BY OUR TITLES INSTEAD OF OUR NAMES?
BECAUSE I'M A PROFESSIONAL.
AND WHAT IS YOUR NAME ANYWAY? DAMIAN LUTHOR? DAMIAN BEELZEBUB?
AND WHAT ARE YOU DOING OUT HERE? DREAMING UP A MASTER PLAN FOR TOILET-PAPERING THE JUSTICE LEAGUE WATCHTOWER?
PLAYING.
PLAYING? YOU'RE PLAYING?
PLEASE. YOU'VE GOT TO TELL ME. WHAT EXACTLY ARE YOU--
!

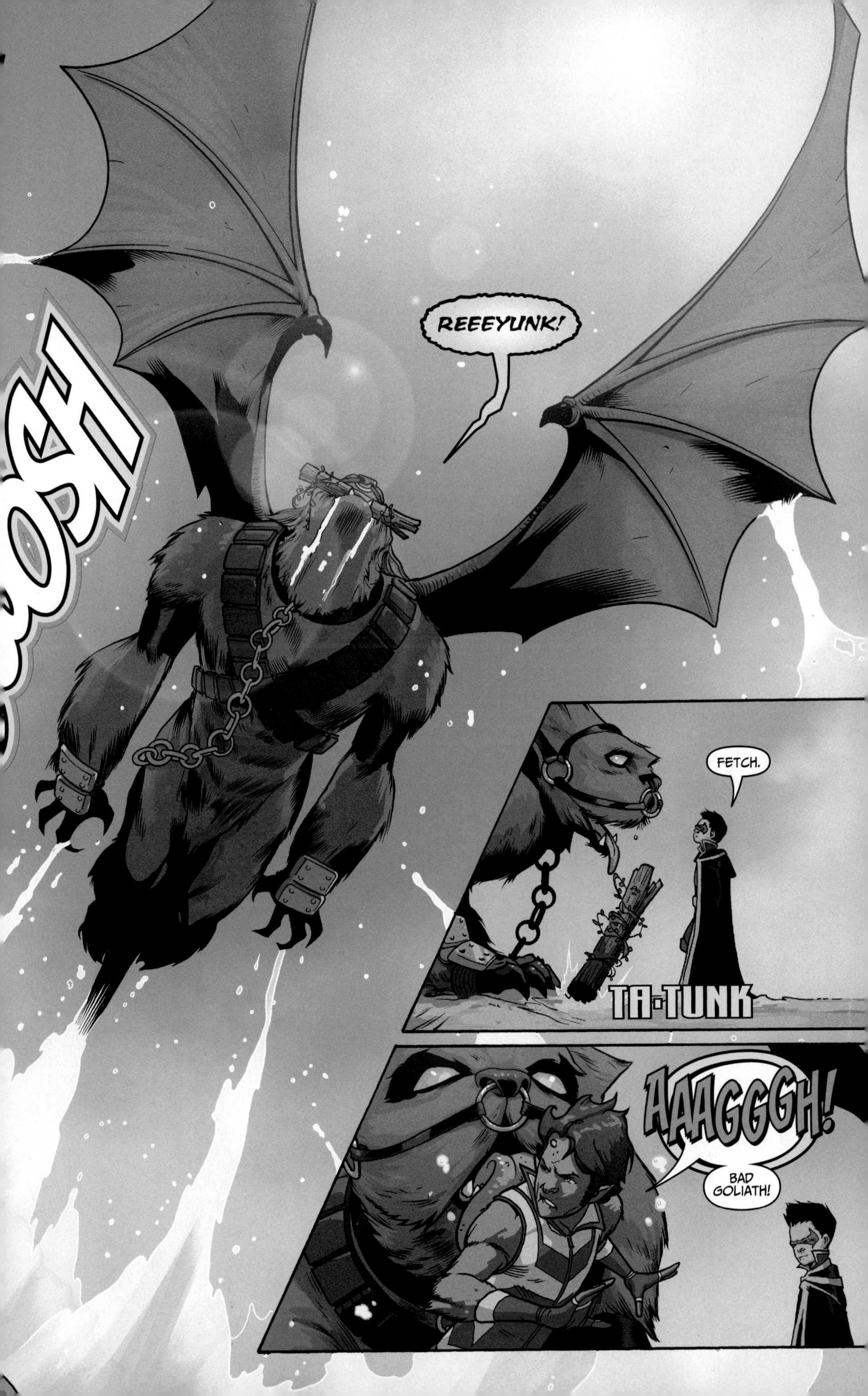
REEEYUNK!
FETCH.
TA-TUNK
AAAGGGH!
BAD GOLIATH!

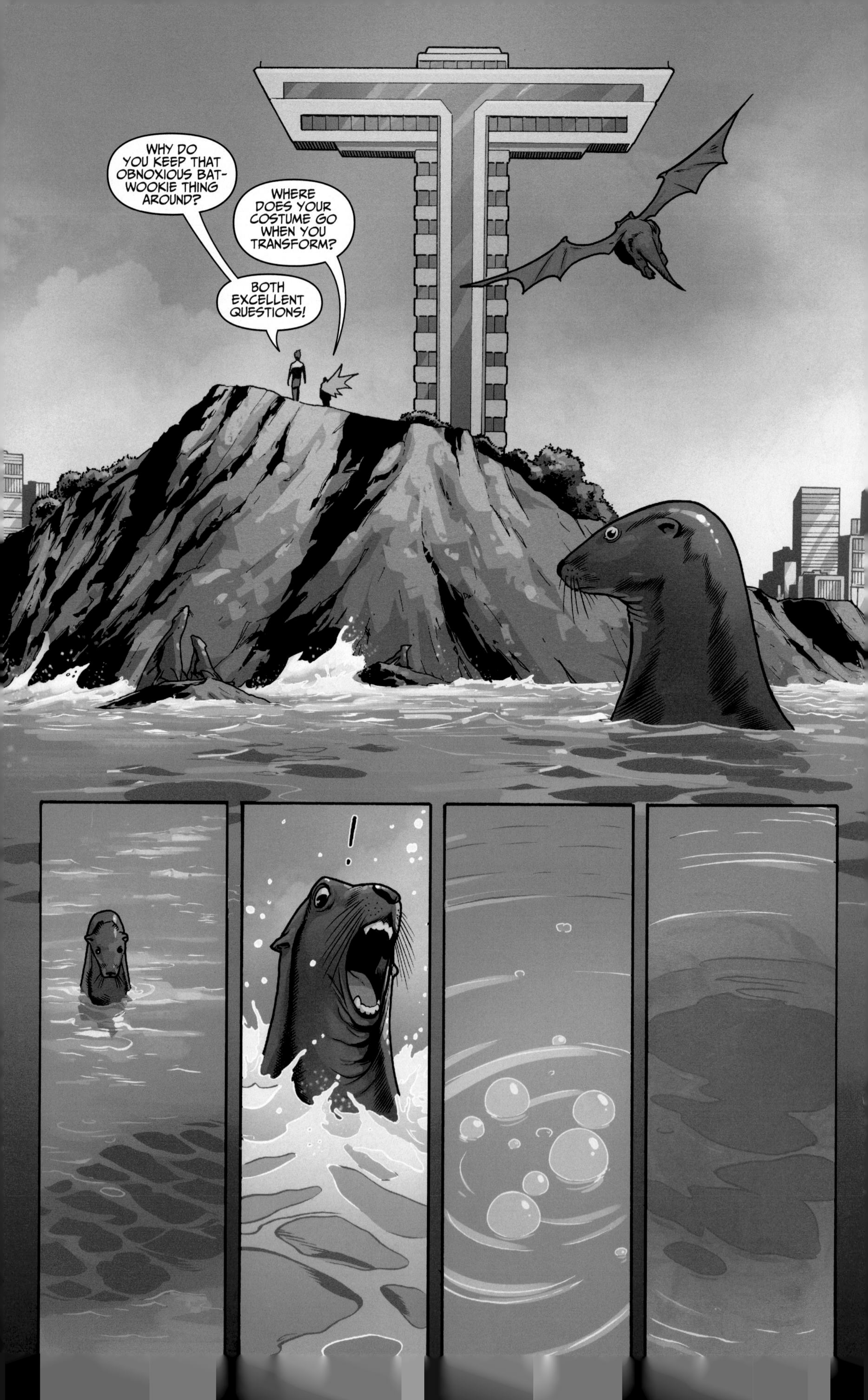
WHY DO YOU KEEP THAT OBNOXIOUS BAT-WOOKIE THING AROUND?
WHERE DOES YOUR COSTUME GO WHEN YOU TRANSFORM?
BOTH EXCELLENT QUESTIONS!
!

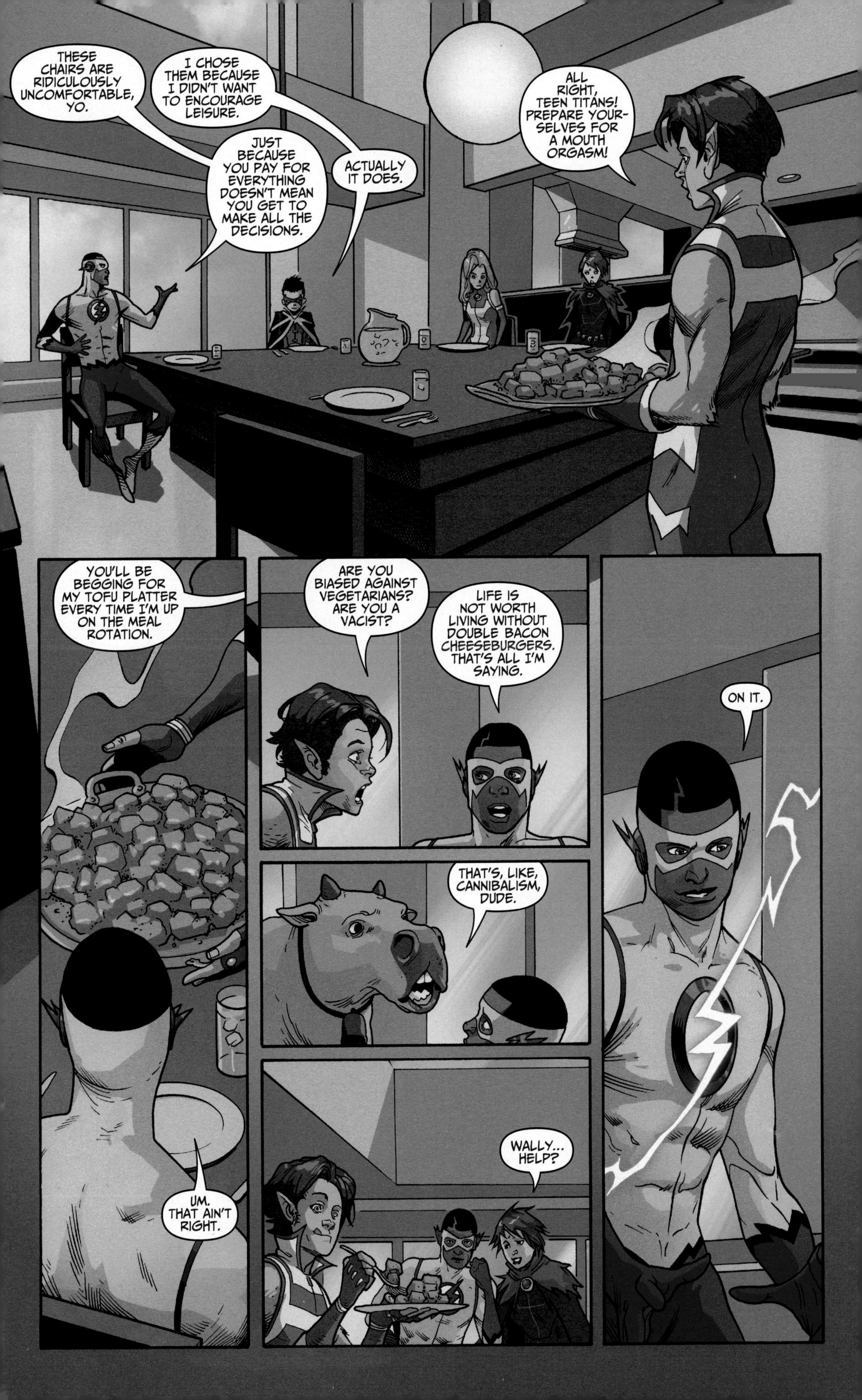
THESE CHAIRS ARE RIDICULOUSLY UNCOMFORTABLE, YO.
I CHOSE THEM BECAUSE I DIDN'T WANT TO ENCOURAGE LEISURE.
JUST BECAUSE YOU PAY FOR EVERYTHING DOESN'T MEAN YOU GET TO MAKE ALL THE DECISIONS.
ACTUALLY IT DOES.
ALL RIGHT, TEEN TITANS! PREPARE YOUR-SELVES FOR A MOUTH ORGASM!
YOU'LL BE BEGGING FOR MY TOFU PLATTER EVERY TIME I'M UP ON THE MEAL ROTATION.
UM. THAT AIN'T RIGHT.
ARE YOU BIASED AGAINST VEGETARIANS? ARE YOU A VACIST?
LIFE IS NOT WORTH LIVING WITHOUT DOUBLE BACON CHEESEBURGERS. THAT'S ALL I'M SAYING.
THAT'S, LIKE, CANNIBALISM, DUDE.
WALLY... HELP?
ON IT.

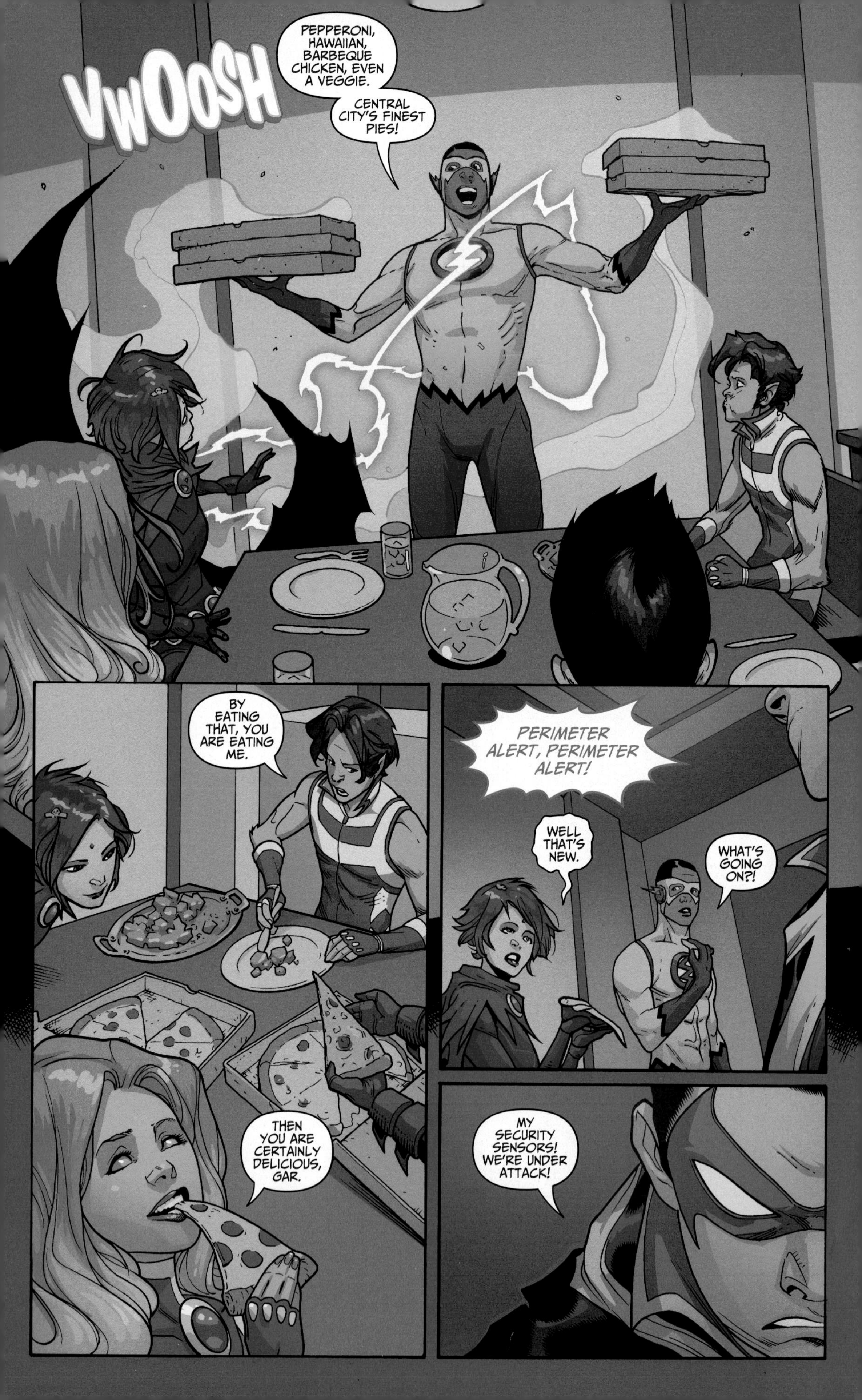
VWOOSH
PEPPERONI, HAWAIIAN, BARBEQUE CHICKEN, EVEN A VEGGIE.
CENTRAL CITY'S FINEST PIES!
BY EATING THAT, YOU ARE EATING ME.
THEN YOU ARE CERTAINLY DELICIOUS, GAR.
PERIMETER ALERT, PERIMETER ALERT!
WELL THAT'S NEW.
WHAT'S GOING ON?!
MY SECURITY SENSORS! WE'RE UNDER ATTACK!

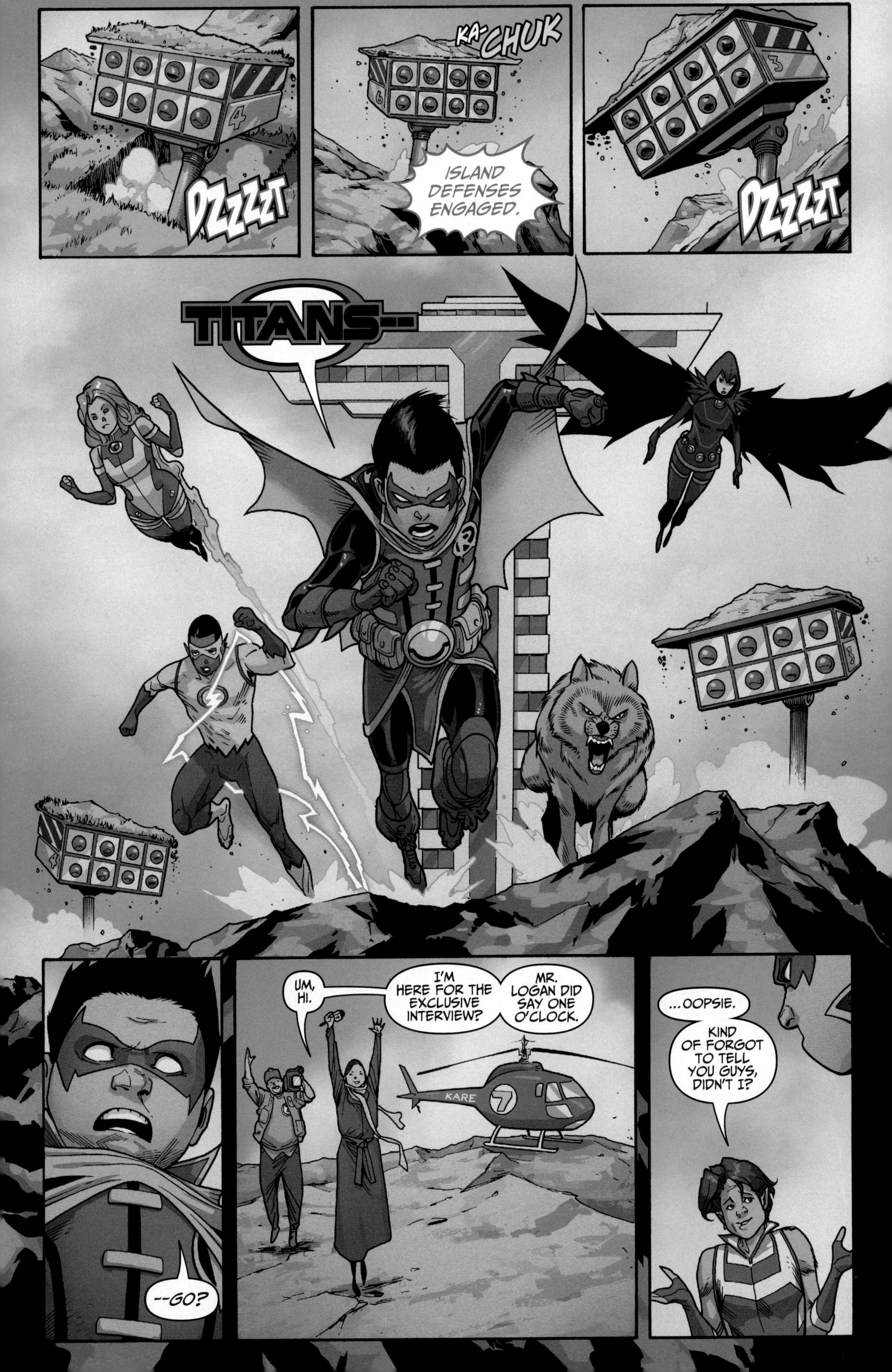
DZZZZT
KA-CHUK
ISLAND DEFENSES ENGAGED.
DZZZZT
TITANS--
--GO?
UM, HI.
I'M HERE FOR THE EXCLUSIVE INTERVIEW?
MR. LOGAN DID SAY ONE O'CLOCK.
KARE 7
...OOPSIE.
KIND OF FORGOT TO TELL YOU GUYS, DIDN'T I?

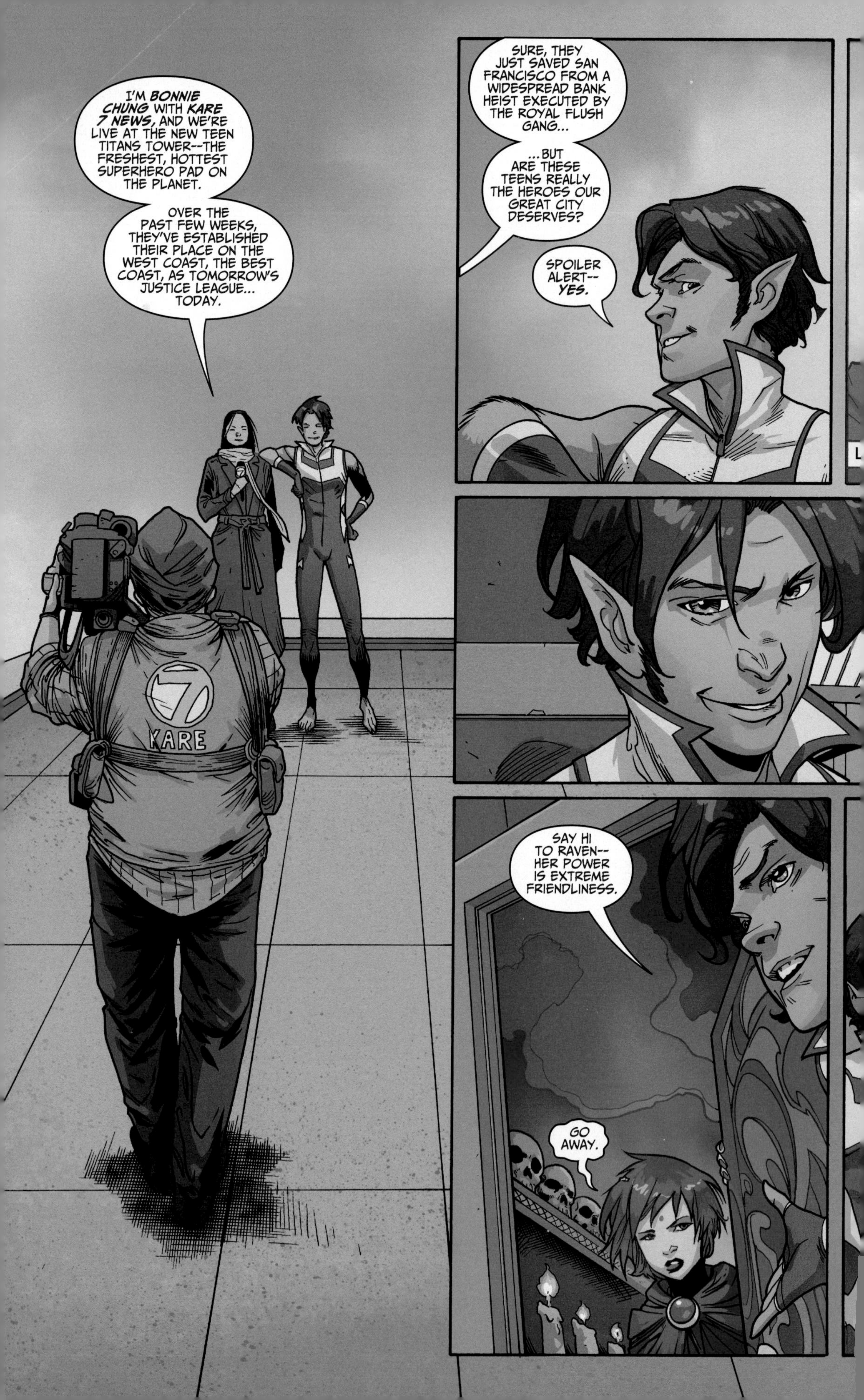

I'M BONNIE CHUNG WITH KARE 7 NEWS, AND WE'RE LIVE AT THE NEW TEEN TITANS TOWER--THE FRESHEST, HOTTEST SUPERHERO PAD ON THE PLANET.
OVER THE PAST FEW WEEKS, THEY'VE ESTABLISHED THEIR PLACE ON THE WEST COAST, THE BEST COAST, AS TOMORROW'S JUSTICE LEAGUE... TODAY.
KARE
SURE, THEY JUST SAVED SAN FRANCISCO FROM A WIDESPREAD BANK HEIST EXECUTED BY THE ROYAL FLUSH GANG...
...BUT ARE THESE TEENS REALLY THE HEROES OUR GREAT CITY DESERVES?
SPOILER ALERT-- YES.
SAY HI TO RAVEN-- HER POWER IS EXTREME FRIENDLINESS.
GO AWAY.

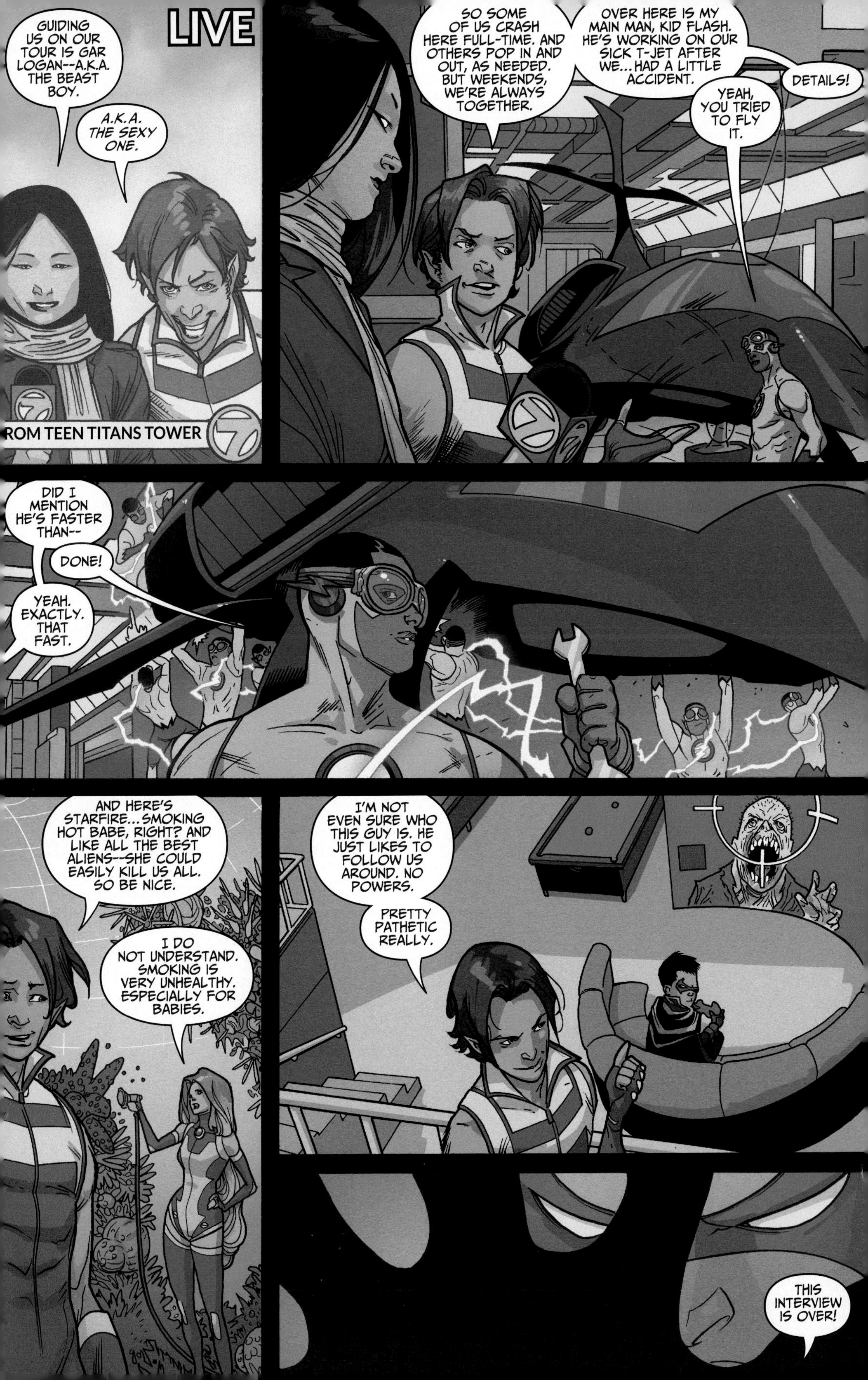
LIVE
GUIDING US ON OUR TOUR IS GAR LOGAN--A.K.A. THE BEAST BOY.
A.K.A. THE SEXY ONE.
ROM TEEN TITANS TOWER
SO SOME OF US CRASH HERE FULL-TIME. AND OTHERS POP IN AND OUT, AS NEEDED. BUT WEEKENDS, WE'RE ALWAYS TOGETHER.
OVER HERE IS MY MAIN MAN, KID FLASH. HE'S WORKING ON OUR SICK T-JET AFTER WE...HAD A LITTLE ACCIDENT.
DETAILS!
YEAH, YOU TRIED TO FLY IT.
DID I MENTION HE'S FASTER THAN--
DONE!
YEAH. EXACTLY. THAT FAST.
AND HERE'S STARFIRE...SMOKING HOT BABE, RIGHT? AND LIKE ALL THE BEST ALIENS--SHE COULD EASILY KILL US ALL. SO BE NICE.
I DO NOT UNDERSTAND. SMOKING IS VERY UNHEALTHY. ESPECIALLY FOR BABIES.
I'M NOT EVEN SURE WHO THIS GUY IS. HE JUST LIKES TO FOLLOW US AROUND. NO POWERS.
PRETTY PATHETIC REALLY.
THIS INTERVIEW IS OVER!

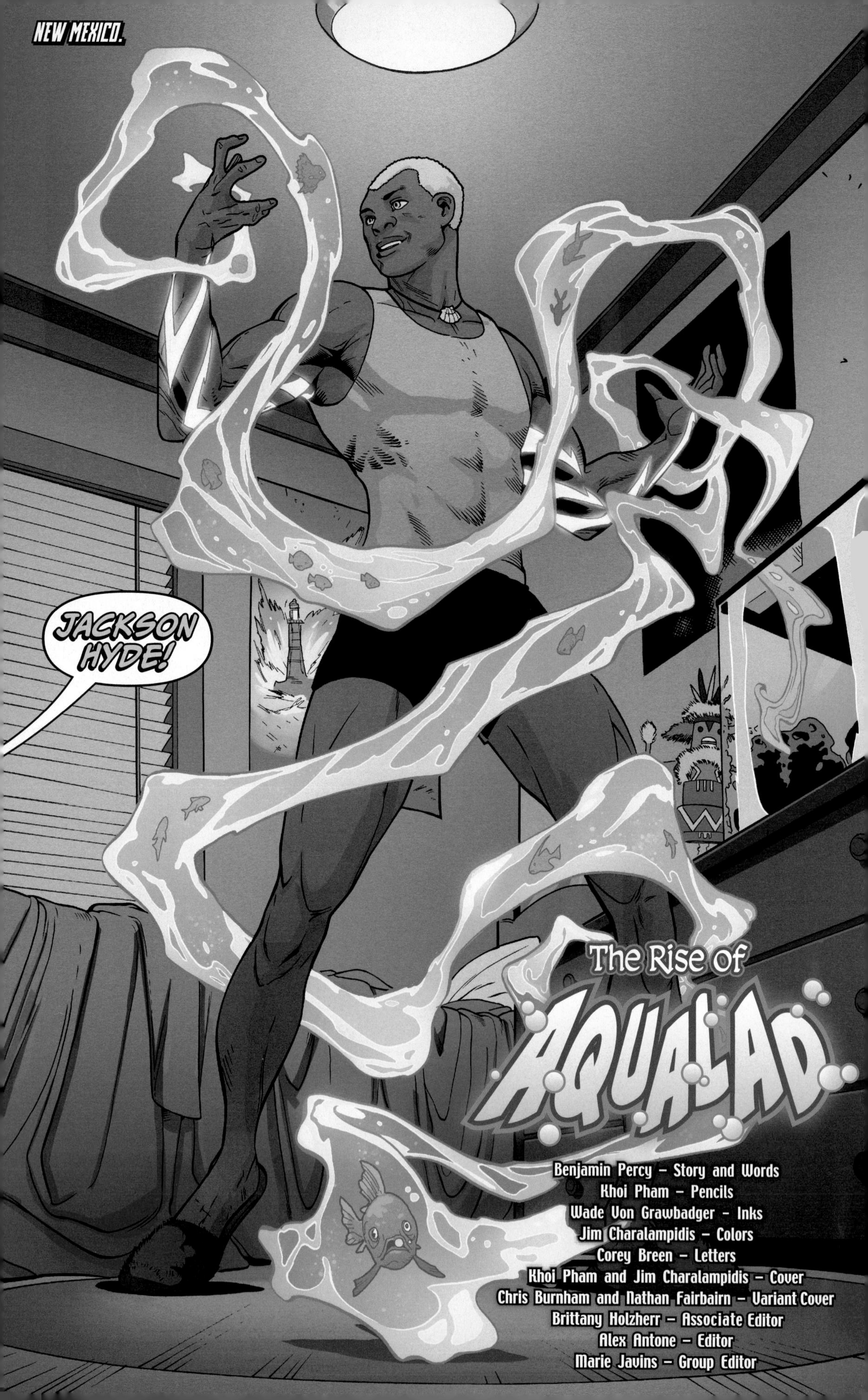
NEW MEXICO.
JACKSON HYDE!
The Rise of
AQUALAD
Benjamin Percy – Story and Words
Khoi Pham – Pencils
Wade Von Grawbadger – Inks
Jim Charalampidis – Colors
Corey Breen – Letters
Khoi Pham and Jim Charalampidis – Cover
Chris Burnham and Nathan Fairbairn – Variant Cover
Brittany Holzherr – Associate Editor
Alex Antone – Editor
Marie Javins – Group Editor

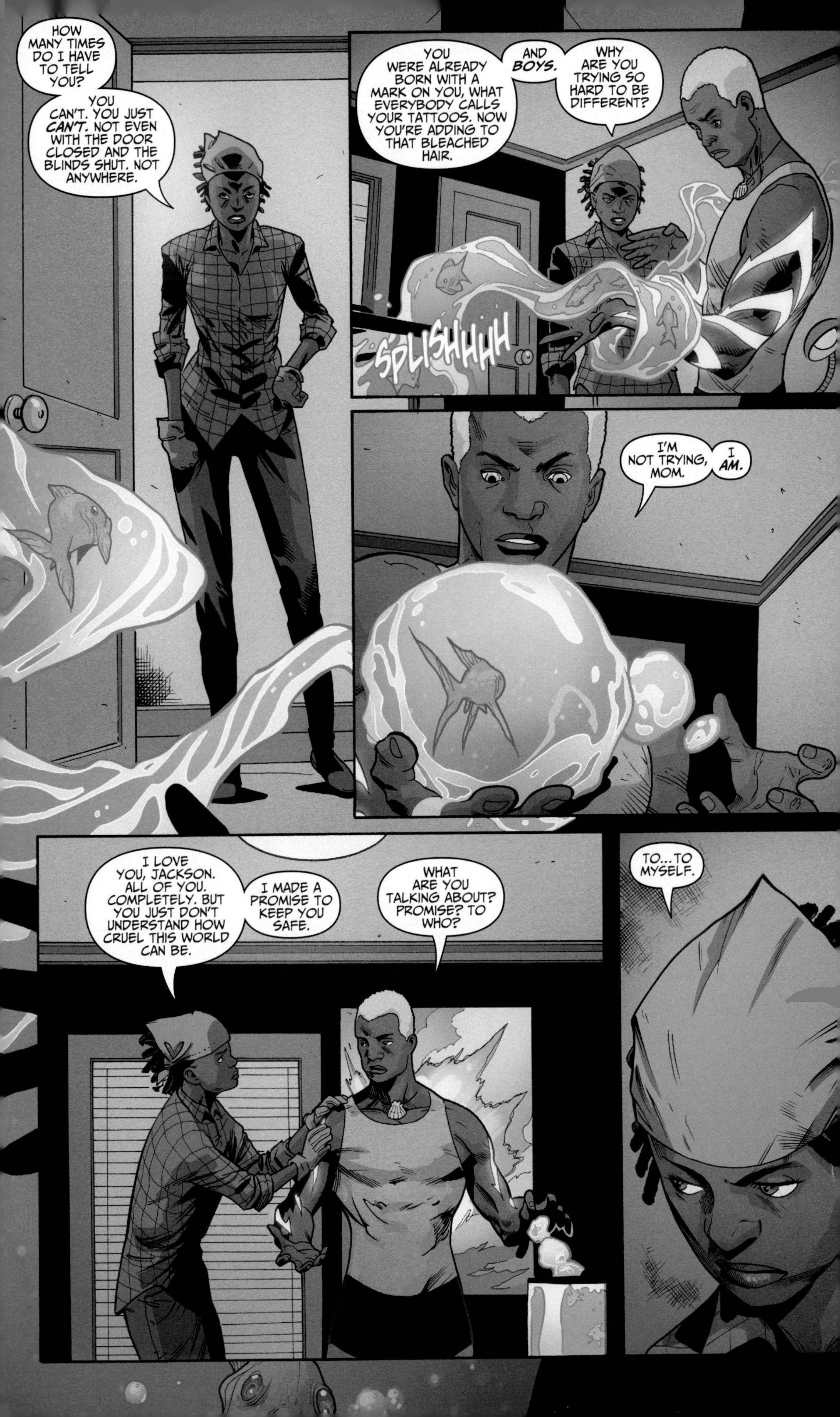

HOW MANY TIMES DO I HAVE TO TELL YOU?
YOU CAN'T. YOU JUST *CAN'T.* NOT EVEN WITH THE DOOR CLOSED AND THE BLINDS SHUT. NOT ANYWHERE.
YOU WERE ALREADY BORN WITH A MARK ON YOU, WHAT EVERYBODY CALLS YOUR TATTOOS. NOW YOU'RE ADDING TO THAT BLEACHED HAIR.
AND *BOYS.*
WHY ARE YOU TRYING SO HARD TO BE DIFFERENT?
SPLISHHHH
I'M NOT TRYING, MOM.
I *AM.*
I LOVE YOU, JACKSON. ALL OF YOU. COMPLETELY. BUT YOU JUST DON'T UNDERSTAND HOW CRUEL THIS WORLD CAN BE.
I MADE A PROMISE TO KEEP YOU SAFE.
WHAT ARE YOU TALKING ABOUT? PROMISE? TO WHO?
TO...TO MYSELF.

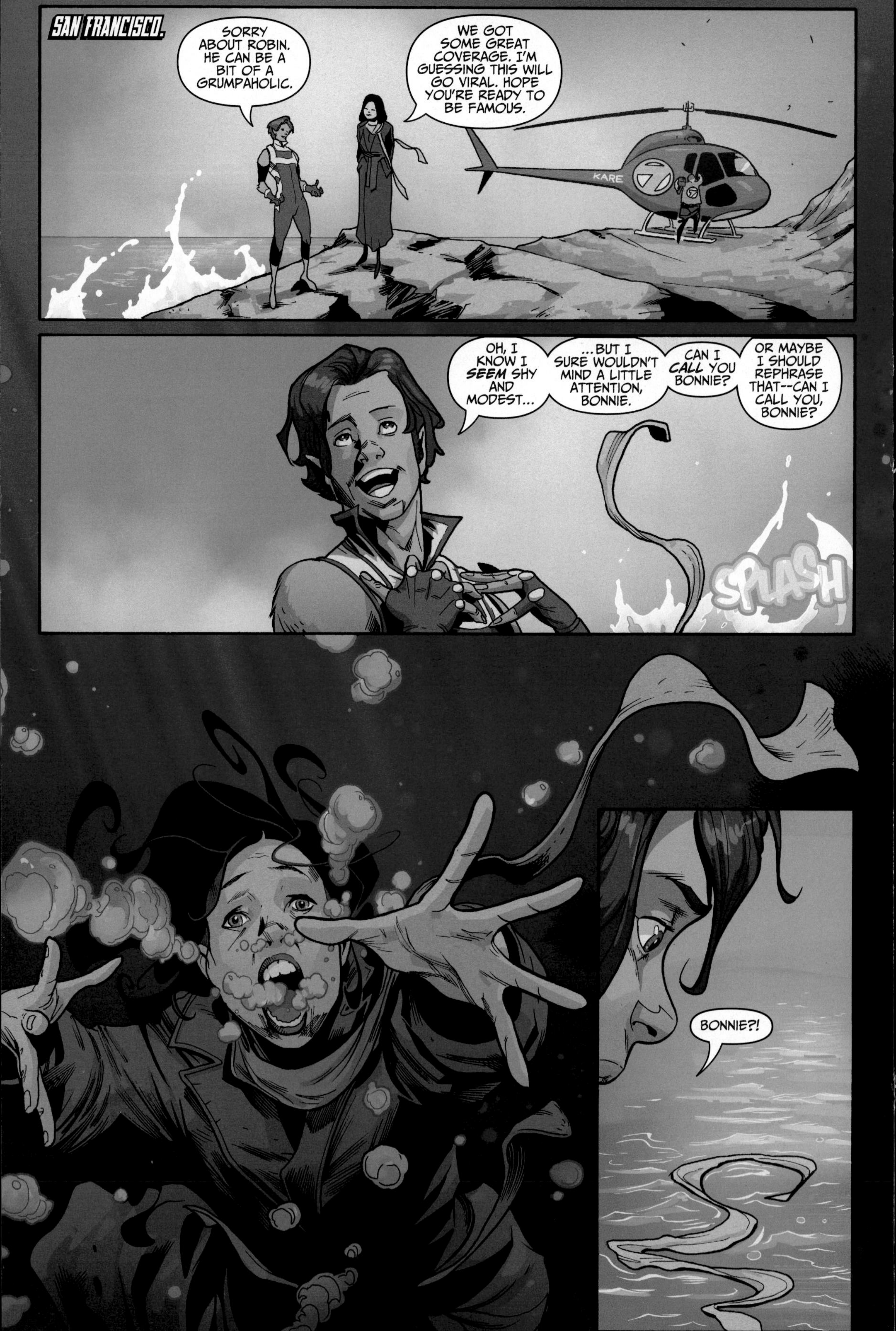
SAN FRANCISCO.
SORRY ABOUT ROBIN. HE CAN BE A BIT OF A GRUMPAHOLIC.
WE GOT SOME GREAT COVERAGE. I'M GUESSING THIS WILL GO VIRAL. HOPE YOU'RE READY TO BE FAMOUS.
KARE
OH, I KNOW I SEEM SHY AND MODEST...
...BUT I SURE WOULDN'T MIND A LITTLE ATTENTION, BONNIE.
CAN I CALL YOU BONNIE?
OR MAYBE I SHOULD REPHRASE THAT--CAN I CALL YOU, BONNIE?
SPLASH
BONNIE?!

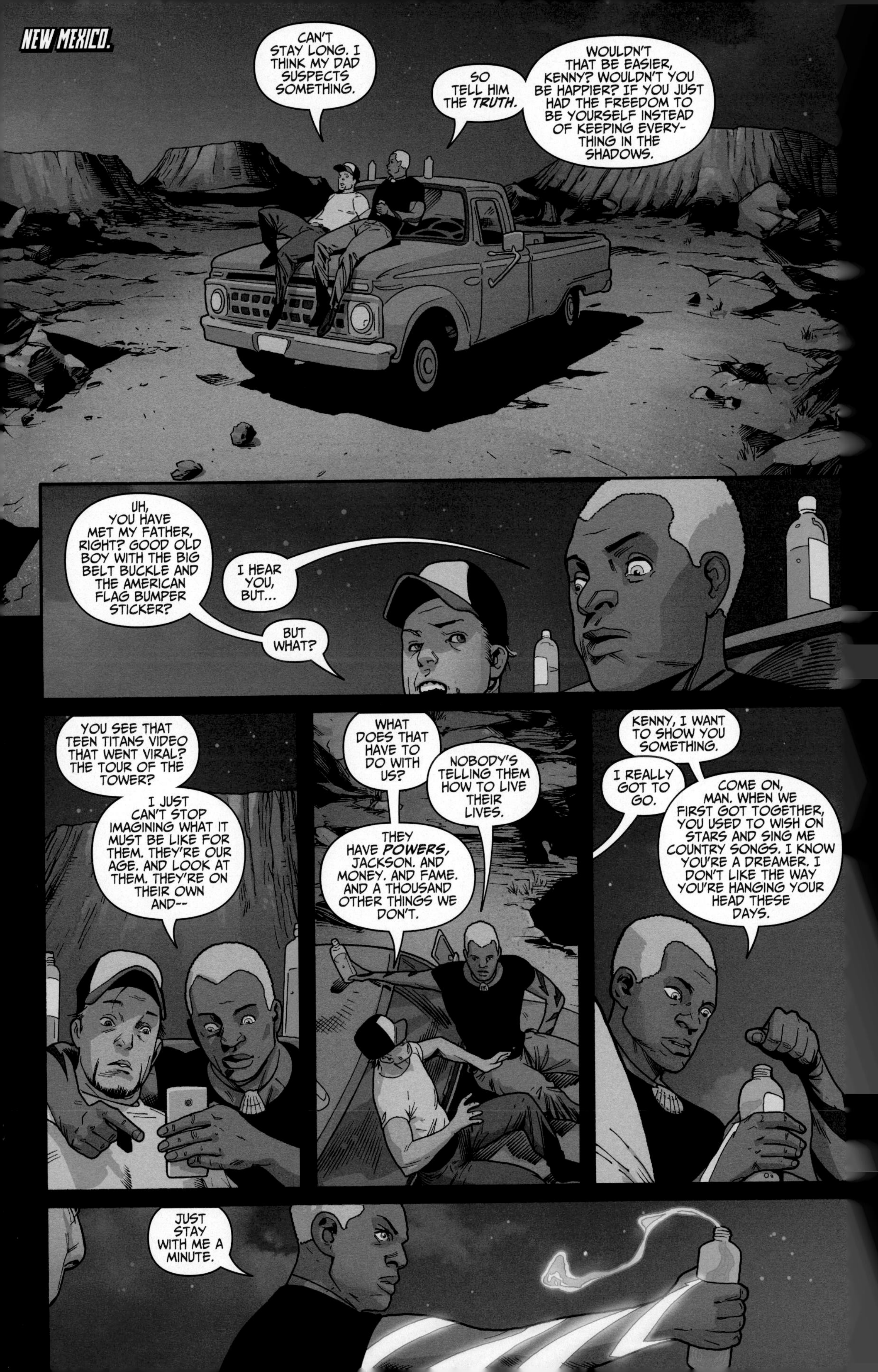
NEW MEXICO.
CAN'T STAY LONG. I THINK MY DAD SUSPECTS SOMETHING.
SO TELL HIM THE *TRUTH.*
WOULDN'T THAT BE EASIER, KENNY? WOULDN'T YOU BE HAPPIER? IF YOU JUST HAD THE FREEDOM TO BE YOURSELF INSTEAD OF KEEPING EVERY-THING IN THE SHADOWS.
I HEAR YOU, BUT...
UH, YOU HAVE MET MY FATHER, RIGHT? GOOD OLD BOY WITH THE BIG BELT BUCKLE AND THE AMERICAN FLAG BUMPER STICKER?
BUT WHAT?
YOU SEE THAT TEEN TITANS VIDEO THAT WENT VIRAL? THE TOUR OF THE TOWER?
I JUST CAN'T STOP IMAGINING WHAT IT MUST BE LIKE FOR THEM. THEY'RE OUR AGE. AND LOOK AT THEM. THEY'RE ON THEIR OWN AND--
WHAT DOES THAT HAVE TO DO WITH US?
NOBODY'S TELLING THEM HOW TO LIVE THEIR LIVES.
THEY HAVE *POWERS,* JACKSON. AND MONEY. AND FAME. AND A THOUSAND OTHER THINGS WE DON'T.
KENNY, I WANT TO SHOW YOU SOMETHING.
I REALLY GOT TO GO.
COME ON, MAN. WHEN WE FIRST GOT TOGETHER, YOU USED TO WISH ON STARS AND SING ME COUNTRY SONGS. I KNOW YOU'RE A DREAMER. I DON'T LIKE THE WAY YOU'RE HANGING YOUR HEAD THESE DAYS.
JUST STAY WITH ME A MINUTE.

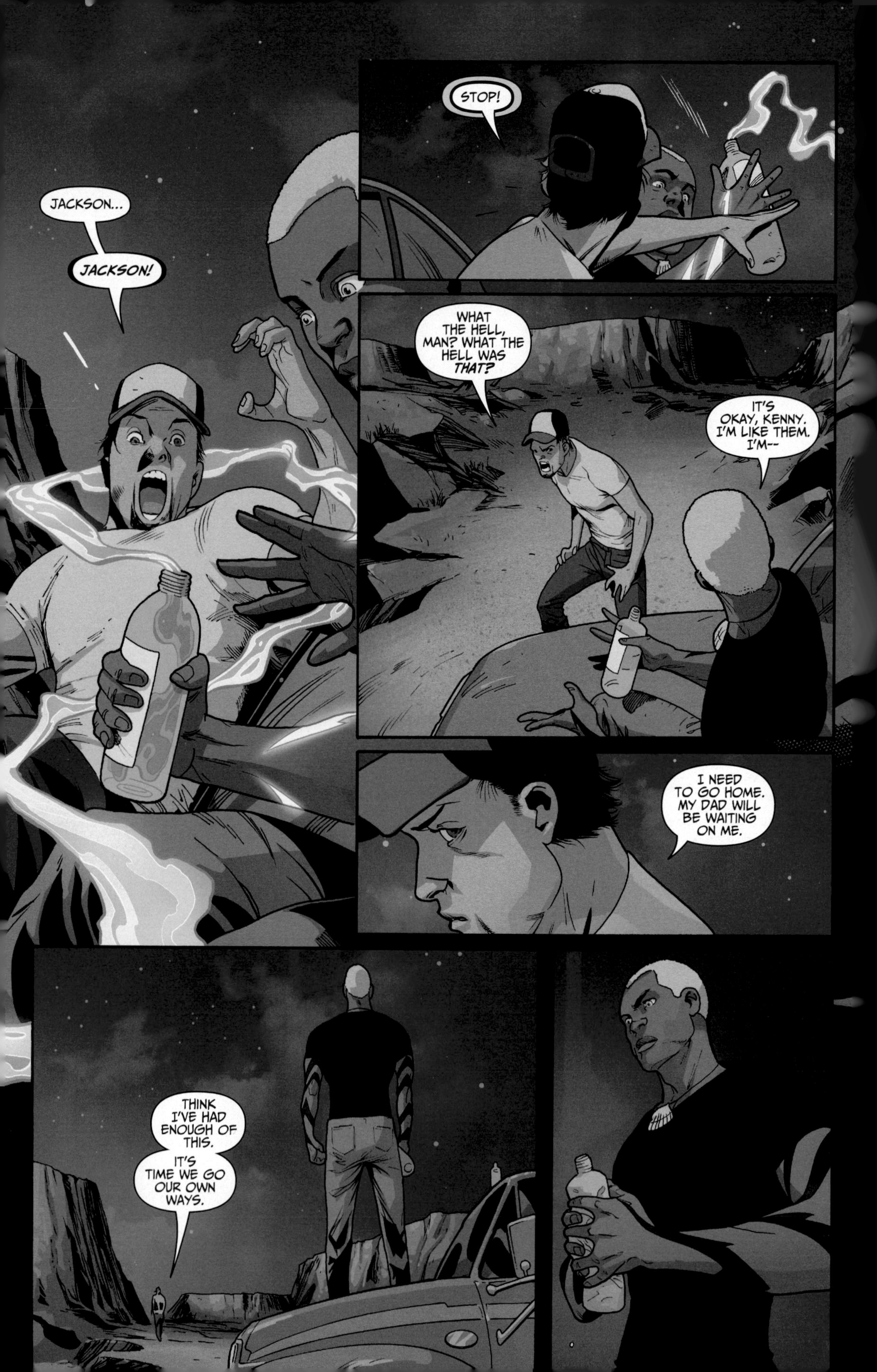
JACKSON...
JACKSON!
STOP!
WHAT THE HELL, MAN? WHAT THE HELL WAS THAT?
IT'S OKAY, KENNY. I'M LIKE THEM. I'M--
I NEED TO GO HOME. MY DAD WILL BE WAITING ON ME.
THINK I'VE HAD ENOUGH OF THIS.
IT'S TIME WE GO OUR OWN WAYS.

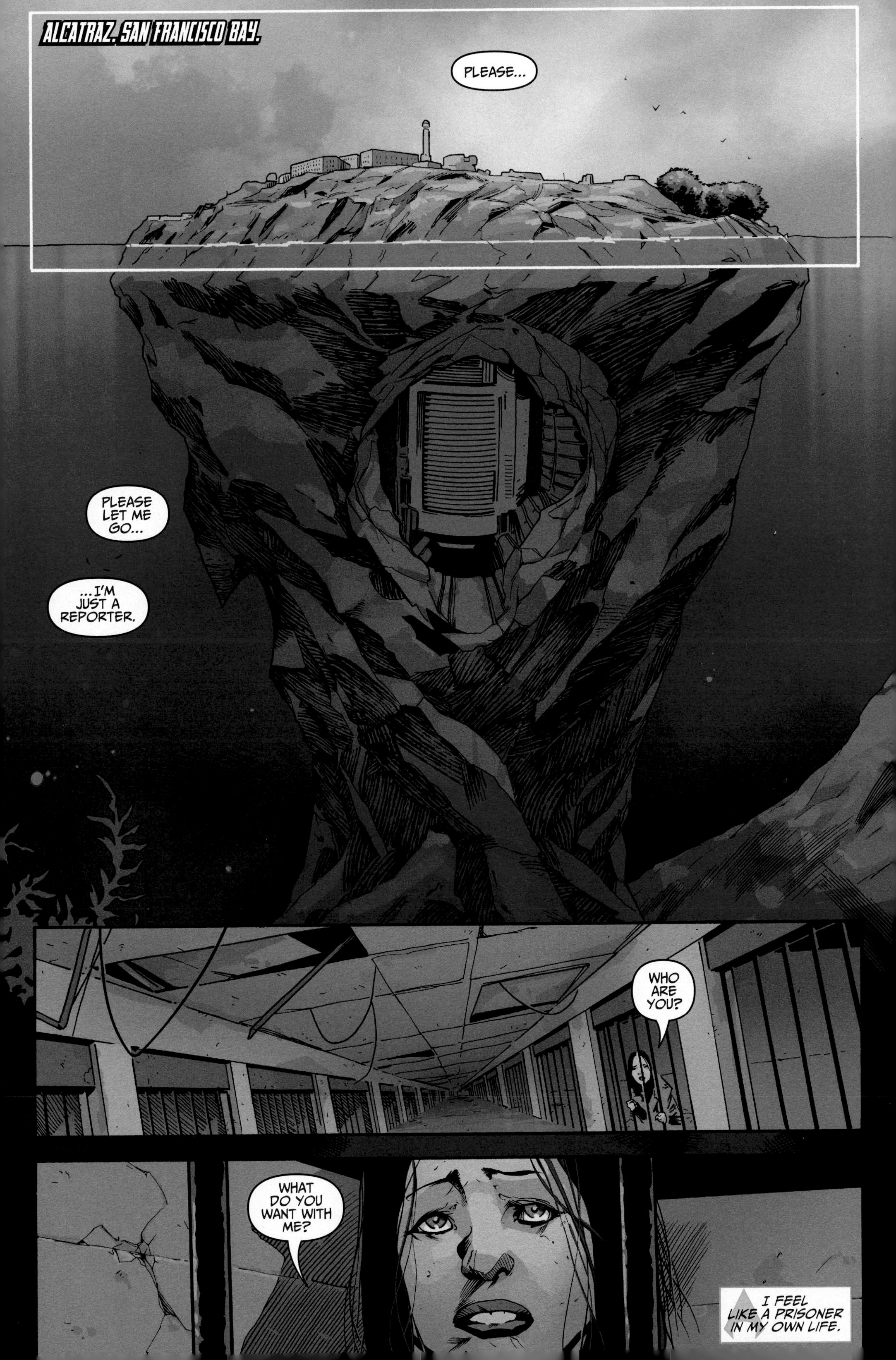
ALCATRAZ. SAN FRANCISCO BAY.
PLEASE...
PLEASE LET ME GO...
...I'M JUST A REPORTER.
WHO ARE YOU?
WHAT DO YOU WANT WITH ME?
I FEEL LIKE A PRISONER IN MY OWN LIFE.

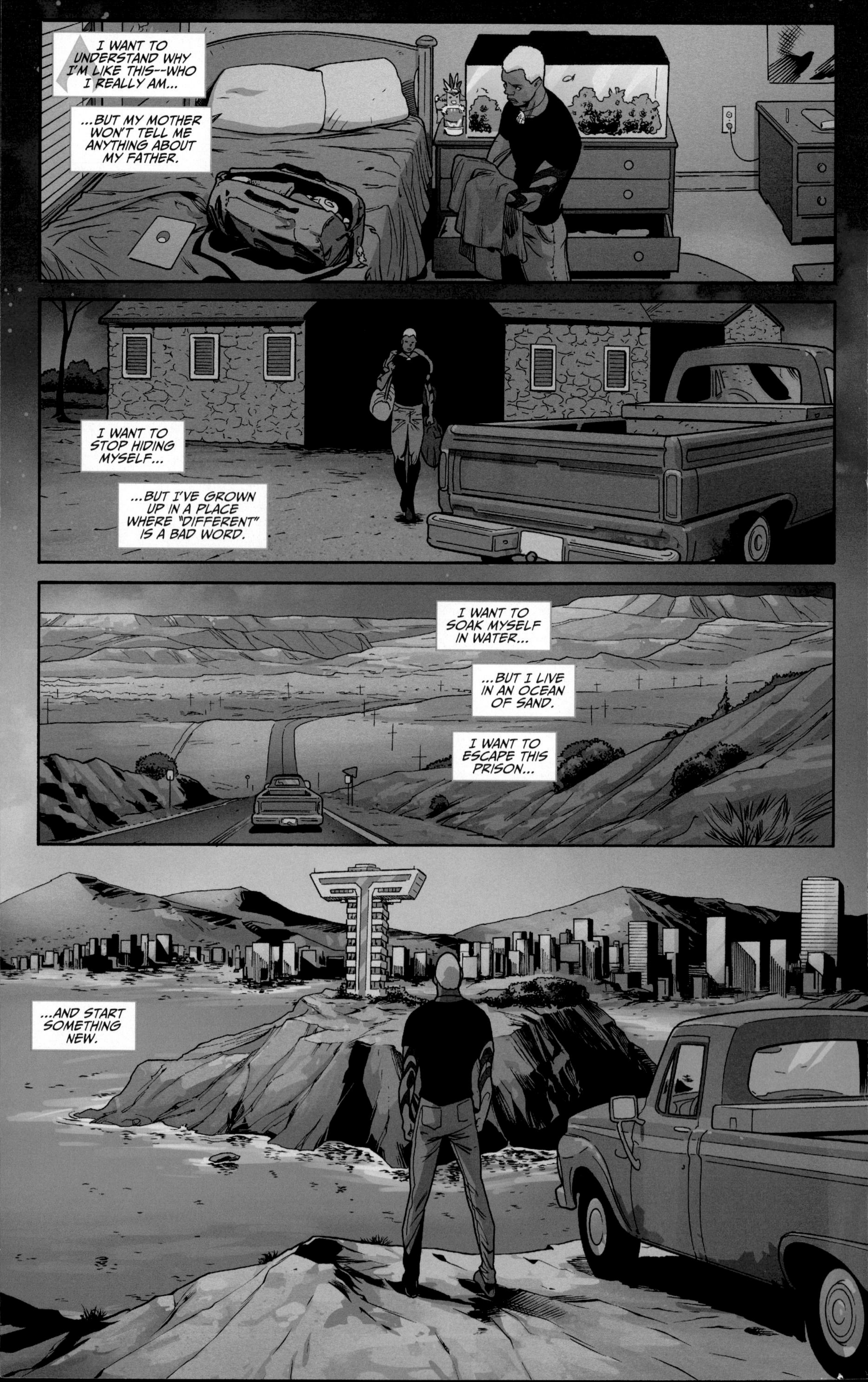

I WANT TO UNDERSTAND WHY I'M LIKE THIS--WHO I REALLY AM...
...BUT MY MOTHER WON'T TELL ME ANYTHING ABOUT MY FATHER.
I WANT TO STOP HIDING MYSELF...
...BUT I'VE GROWN UP IN A PLACE WHERE "DIFFERENT" IS A BAD WORD.
I WANT TO SOAK MYSELF IN WATER...
...BUT I LIVE IN AN OCEAN OF SAND.
I WANT TO ESCAPE THIS PRISON...
...AND START SOMETHING NEW.

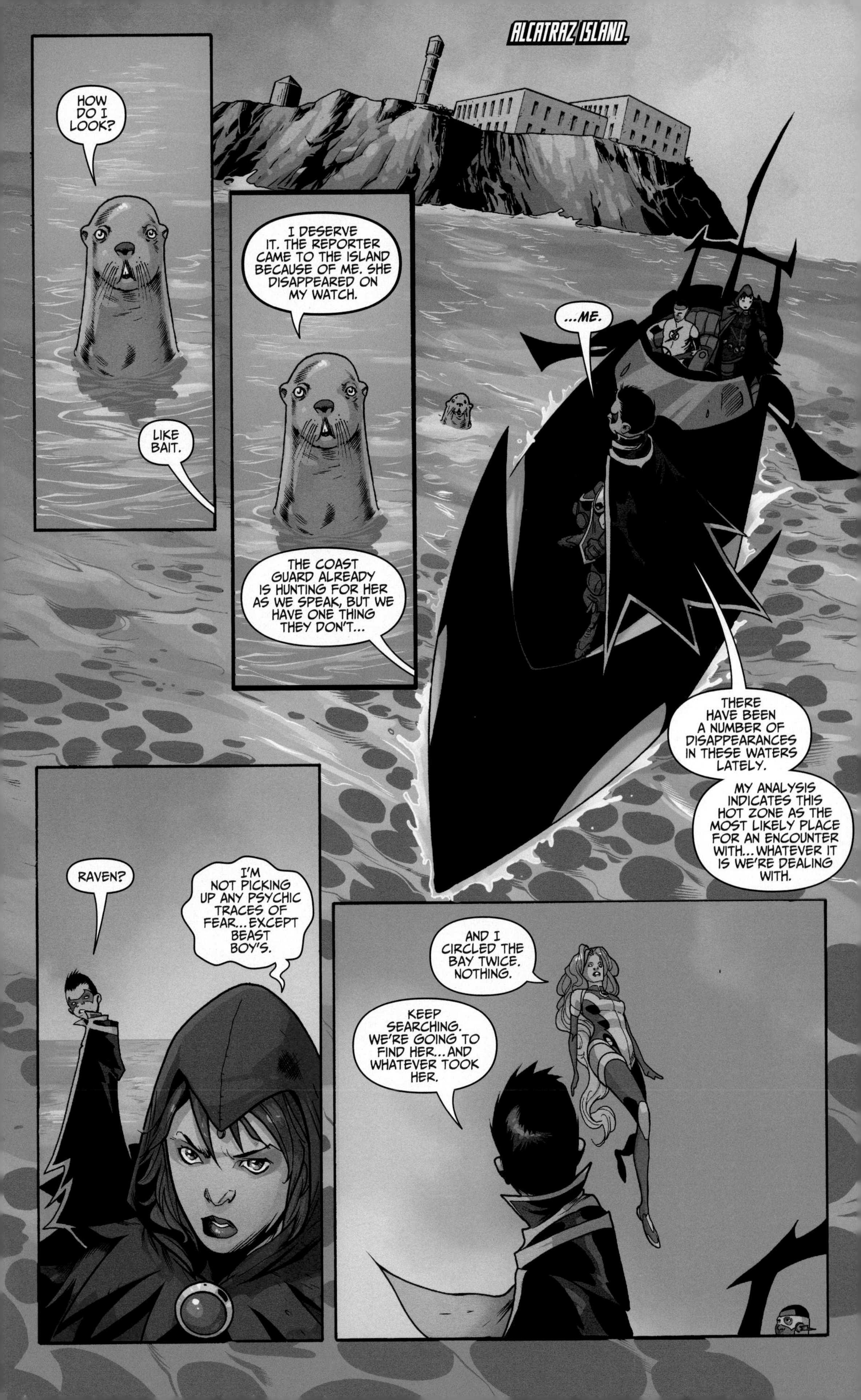
ALCATRAZ ISLAND.
HOW DO I LOOK?
LIKE BAIT.
I DESERVE IT. THE REPORTER CAME TO THE ISLAND BECAUSE OF ME. SHE DISAPPEARED ON MY WATCH.
THE COAST GUARD ALREADY IS HUNTING FOR HER AS WE SPEAK, BUT WE HAVE ONE THING THEY DON'T...
...ME.
THERE HAVE BEEN A NUMBER OF DISAPPEARANCES IN THESE WATERS LATELY.
MY ANALYSIS INDICATES THIS HOT ZONE AS THE MOST LIKELY PLACE FOR AN ENCOUNTER WITH...WHATEVER IT IS WE'RE DEALING WITH.
RAVEN?
I'M NOT PICKING UP ANY PSYCHIC TRACES OF FEAR...EXCEPT BEAST BOY'S.
AND I CIRCLED THE BAY TWICE. NOTHING.
KEEP SEARCHING. WE'RE GOING TO FIND HER...AND WHATEVER TOOK HER.

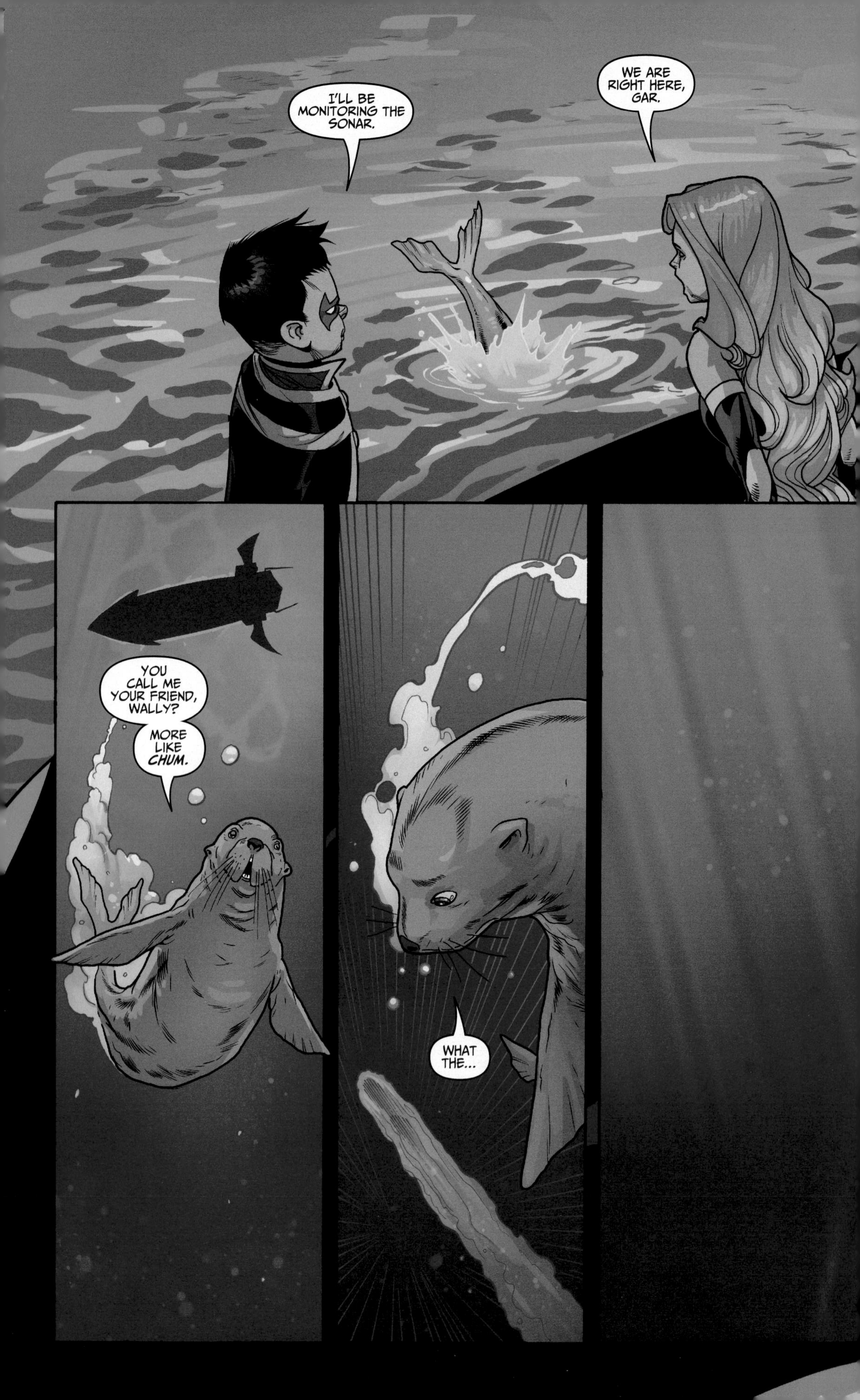
I'LL BE MONITORING THE SONAR.
WE ARE RIGHT HERE, GAR.
YOU CALL ME YOUR FRIEND, WALLY?
MORE LIKE *CHUM*.
WHAT THE...

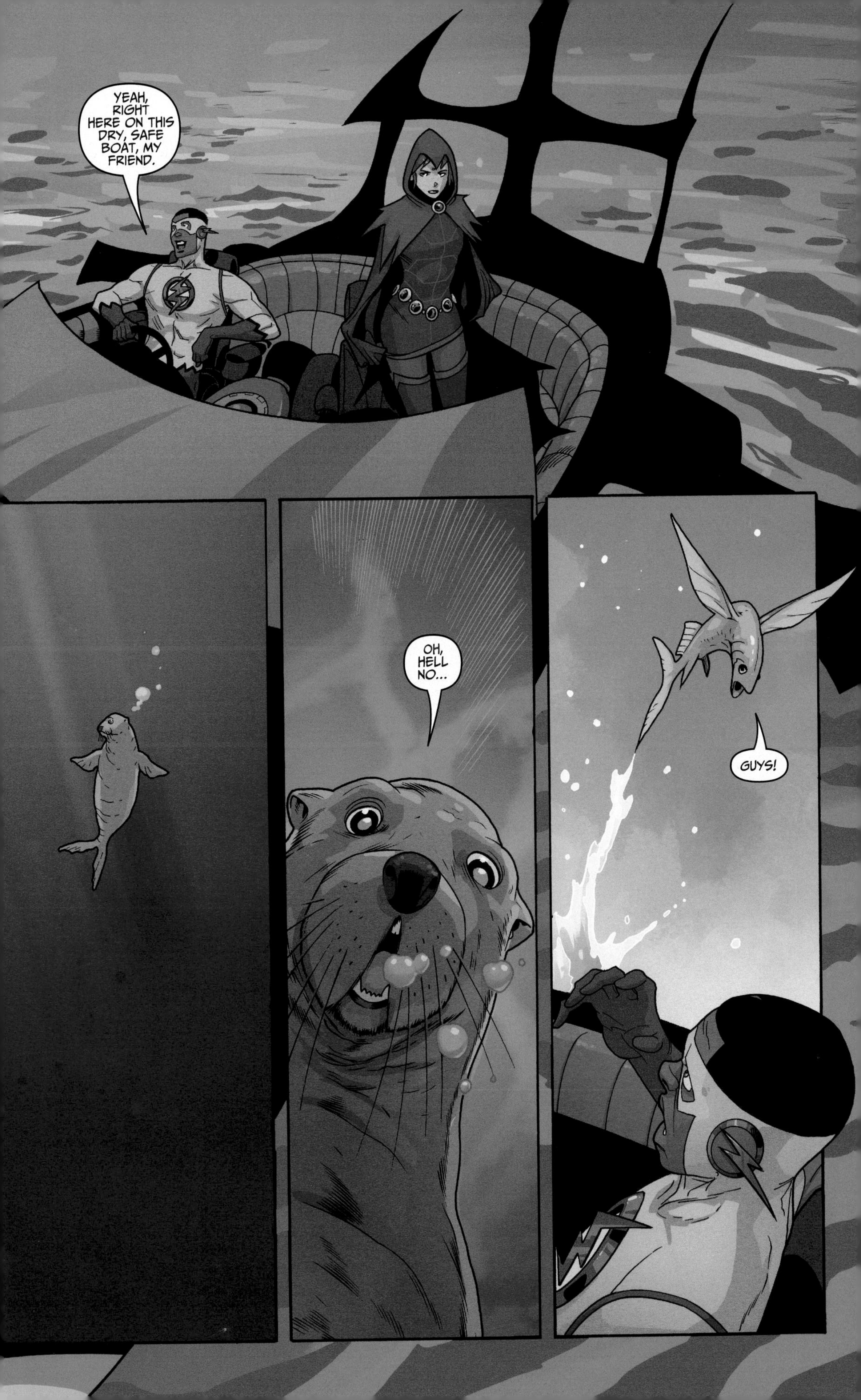
YEAH, RIGHT HERE ON THIS DRY, SAFE BOAT, MY FRIEND.
OH, HELL NO...
GUYS!

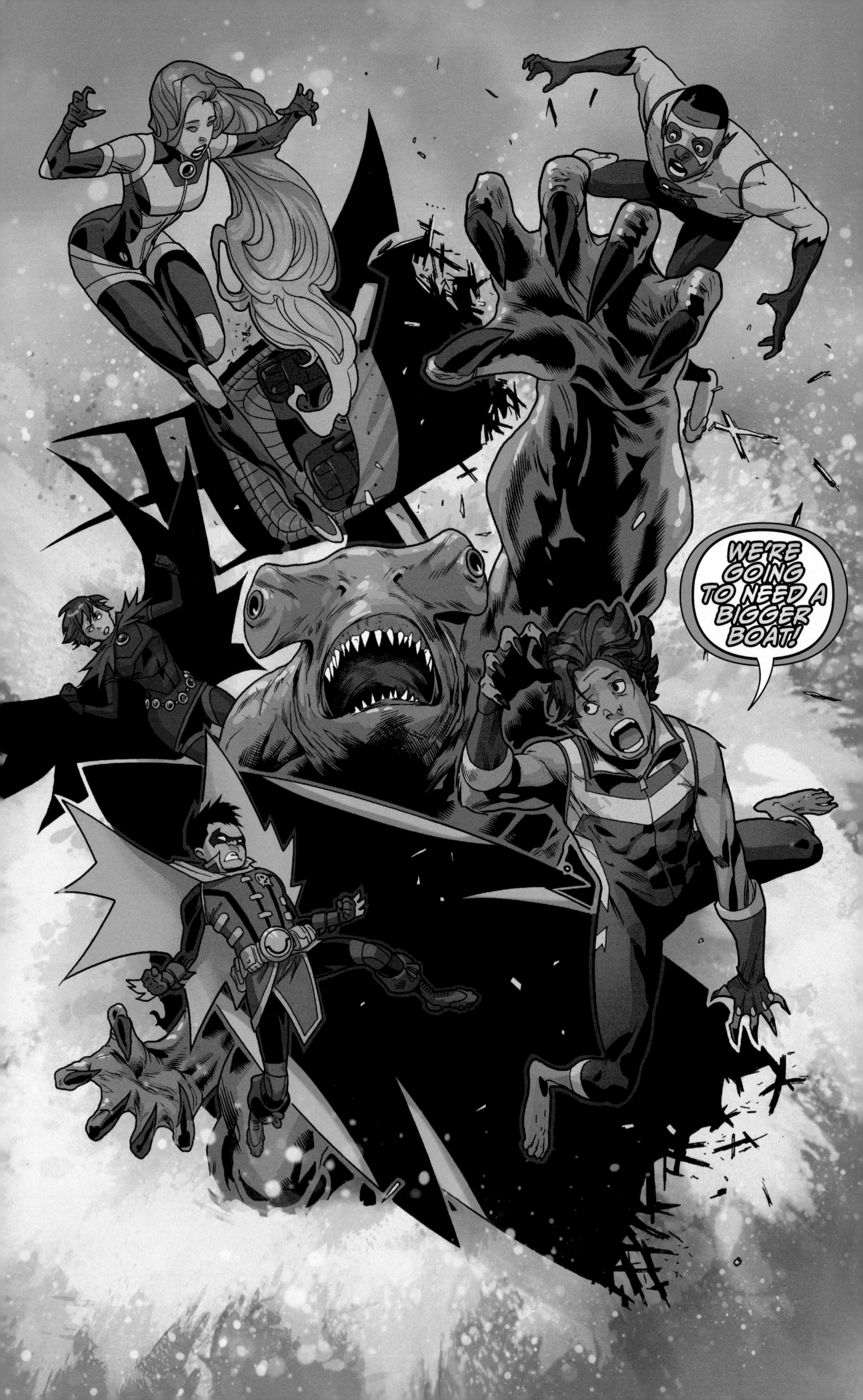
WE'RE GOING TO NEED A BIGGER BOAT!

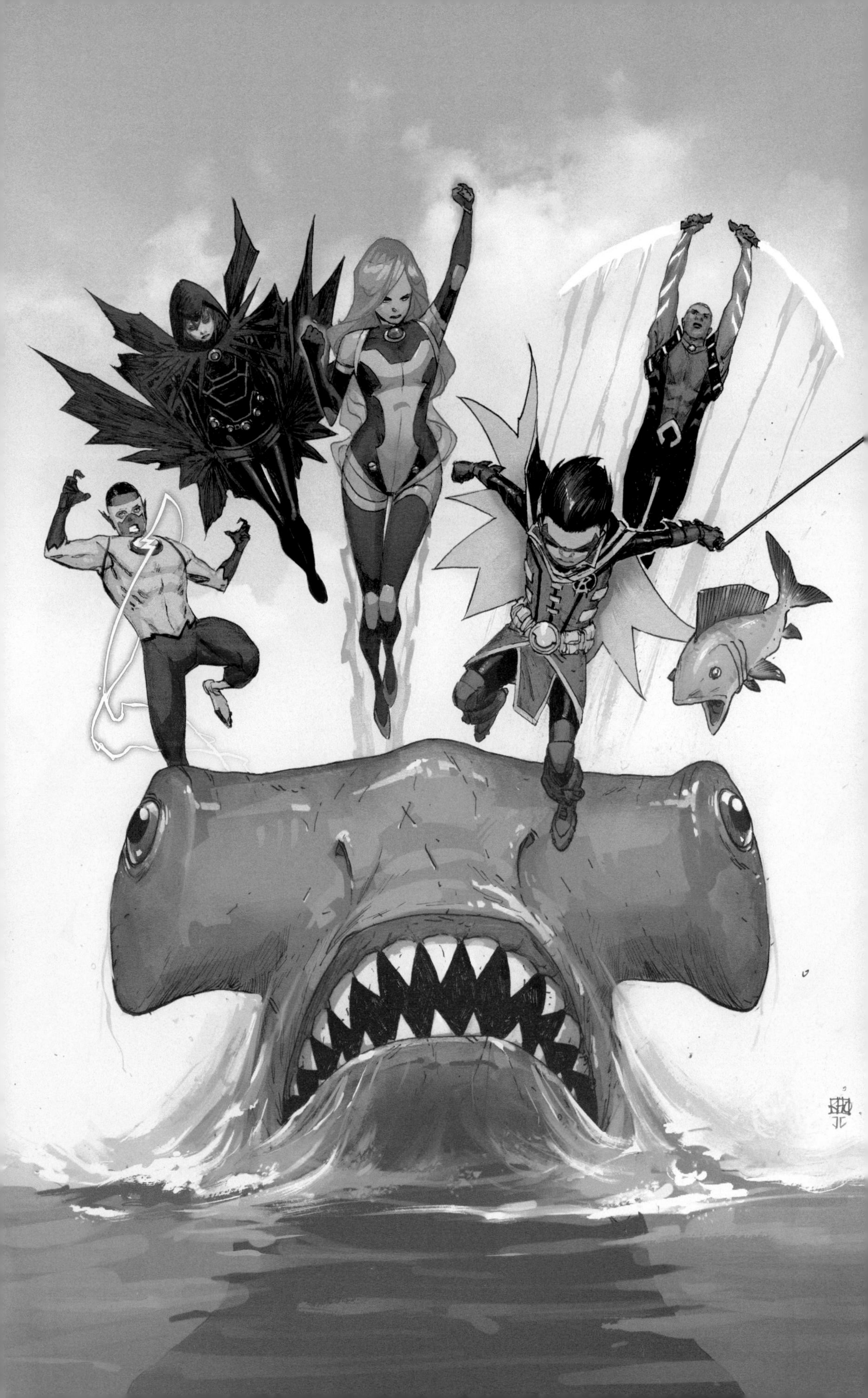

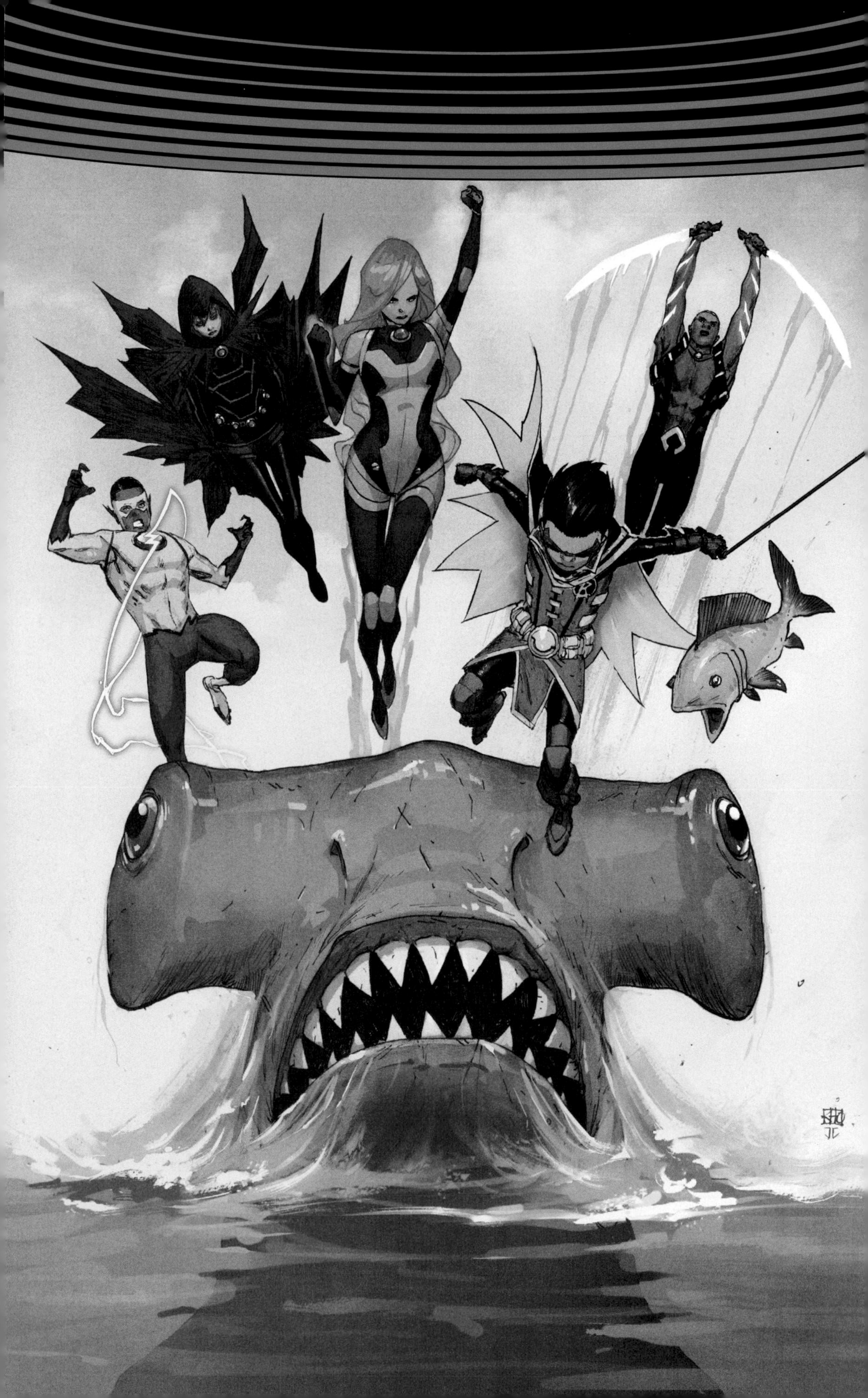

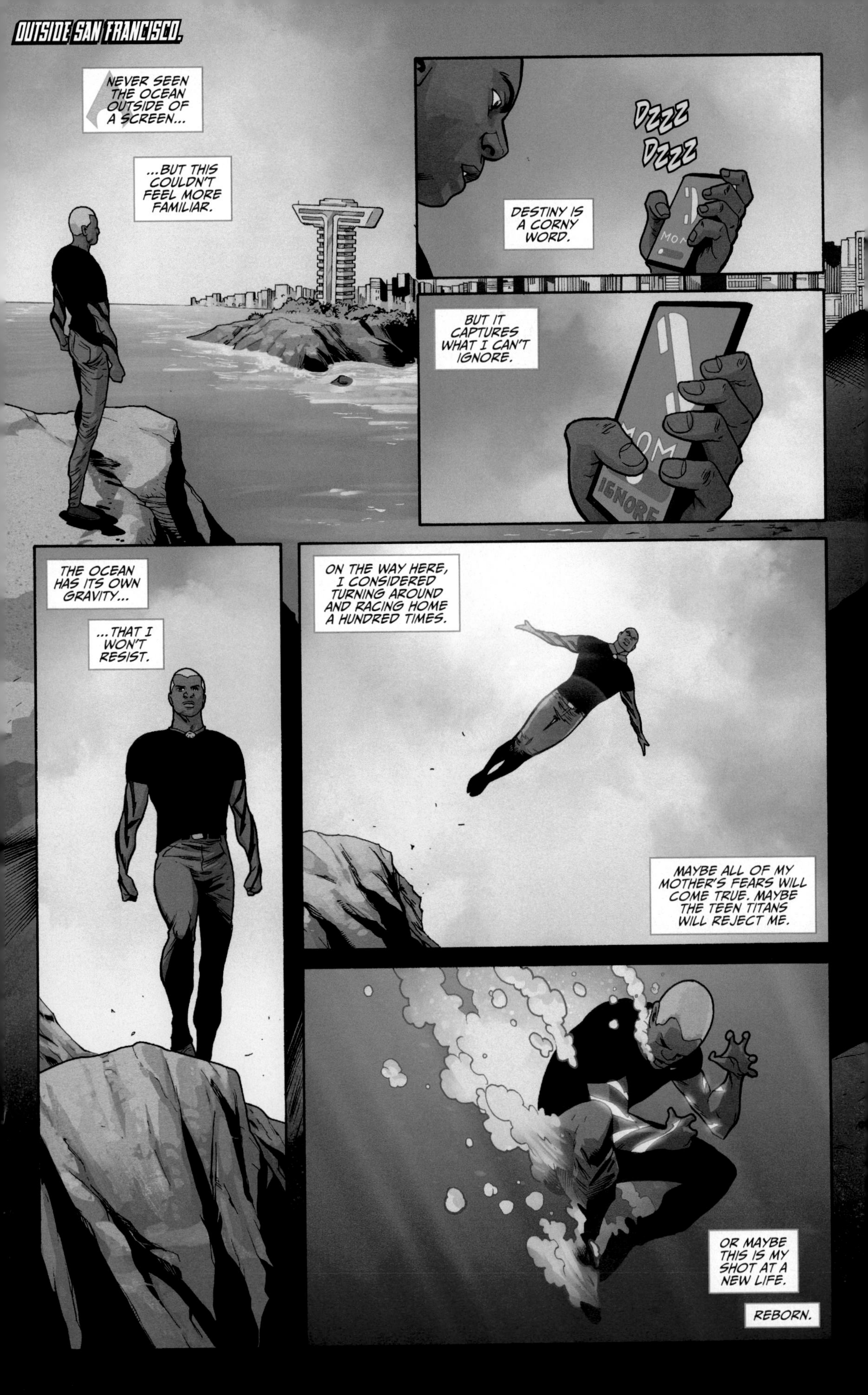
OUTSIDE SAN FRANCISCO.
NEVER SEEN THE OCEAN OUTSIDE OF A SCREEN...
...BUT THIS COULDN'T FEEL MORE FAMILIAR.
DZZZ DZZZ
MOM
DESTINY IS A CORNY WORD.
BUT IT CAPTURES WHAT I CAN'T IGNORE.
MOM
IGNORE
THE OCEAN HAS ITS OWN GRAVITY...
...THAT I WON'T RESIST.
ON THE WAY HERE, I CONSIDERED TURNING AROUND AND RACING HOME A HUNDRED TIMES.
MAYBE ALL OF MY MOTHER'S FEARS WILL COME TRUE. MAYBE THE TEEN TITANS WILL REJECT ME.
OR MAYBE THIS IS MY SHOT AT A NEW LIFE.
REBORN.

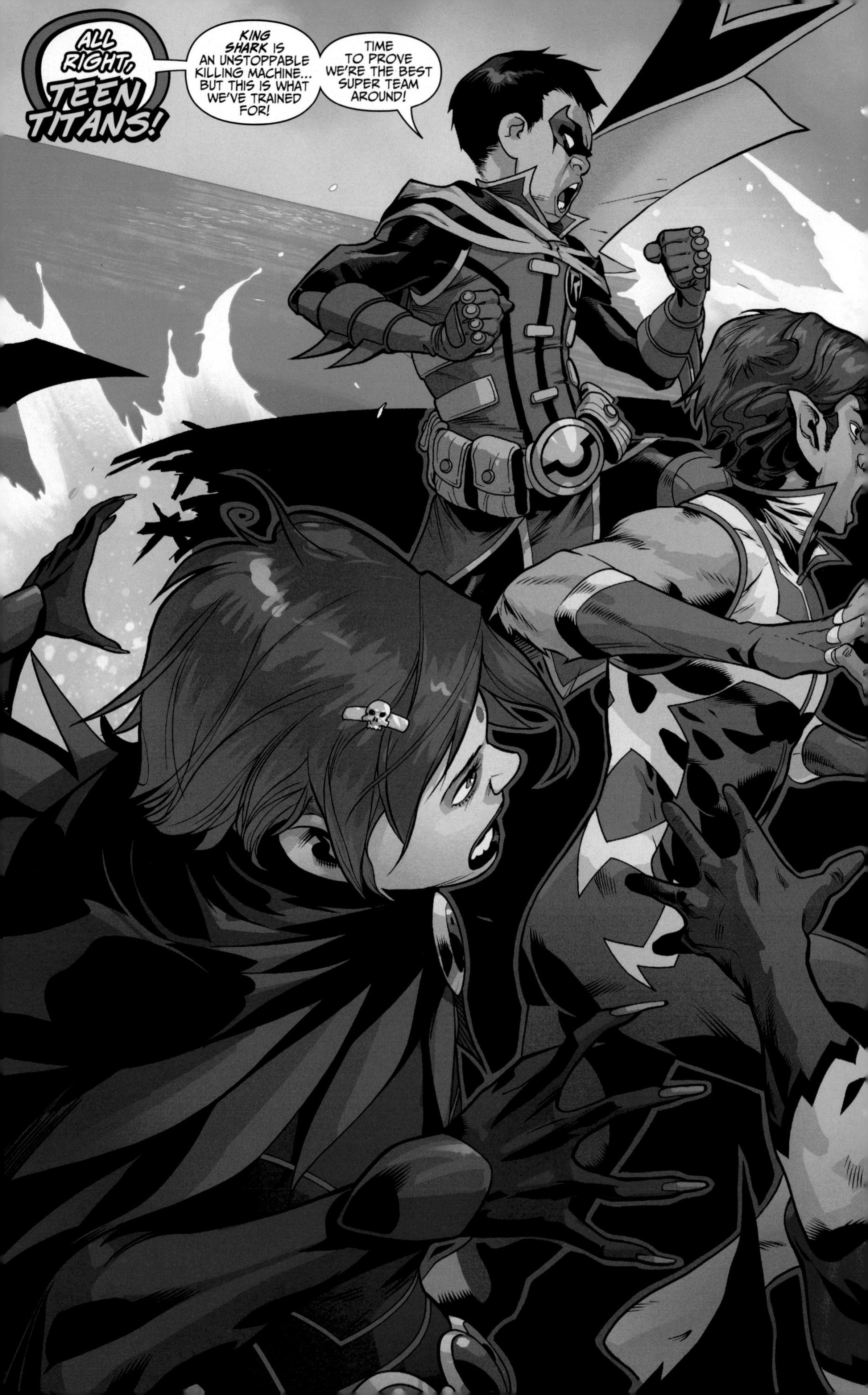
ALL RIGHT, TEEN TITANS!
KING SHARK IS AN UNSTOPPABLE KILLING MACHINE... BUT THIS IS WHAT WE'VE TRAINED FOR!
TIME TO PROVE WE'RE THE BEST SUPER TEAM AROUND!

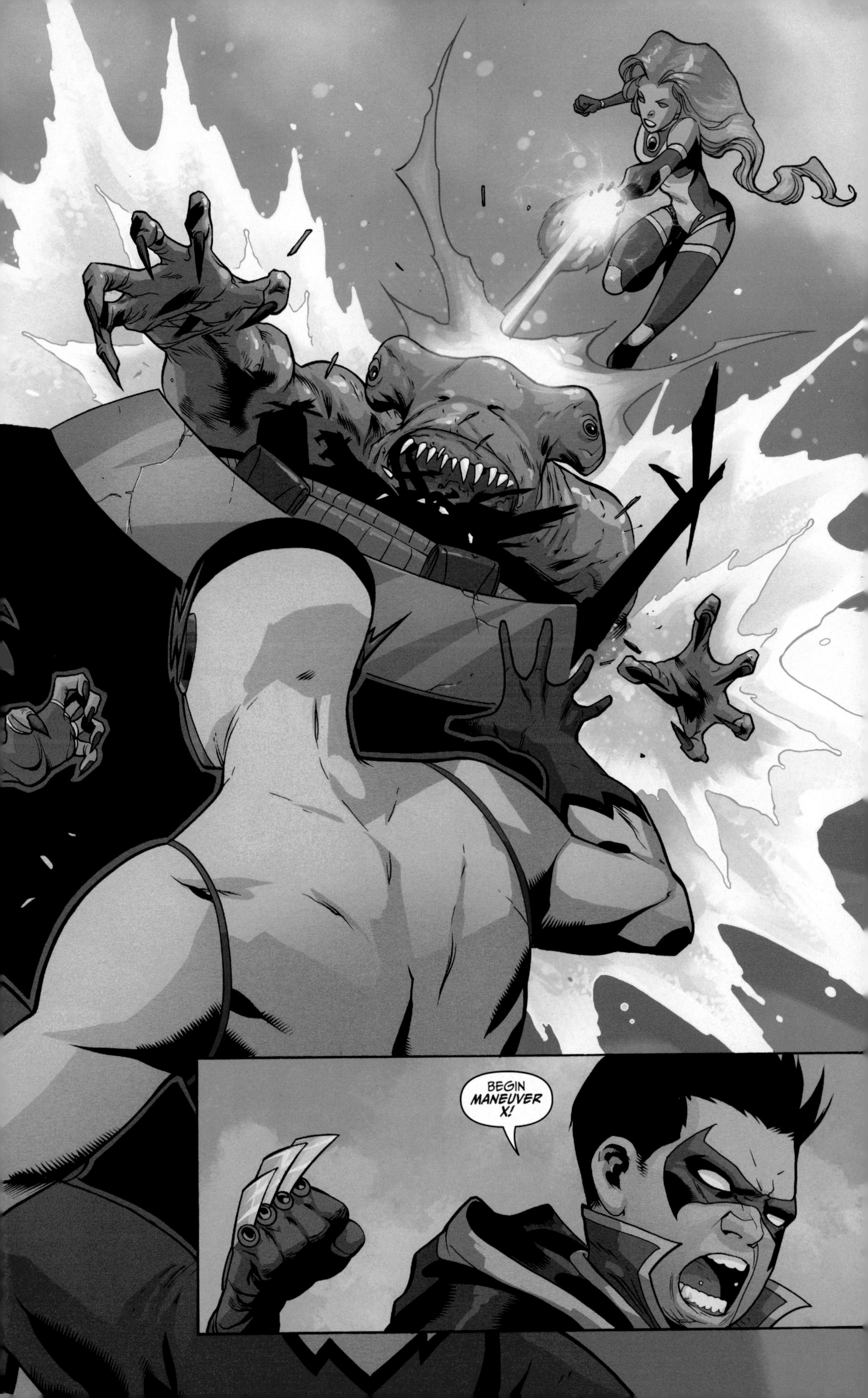
BEGIN MANEUVER X!

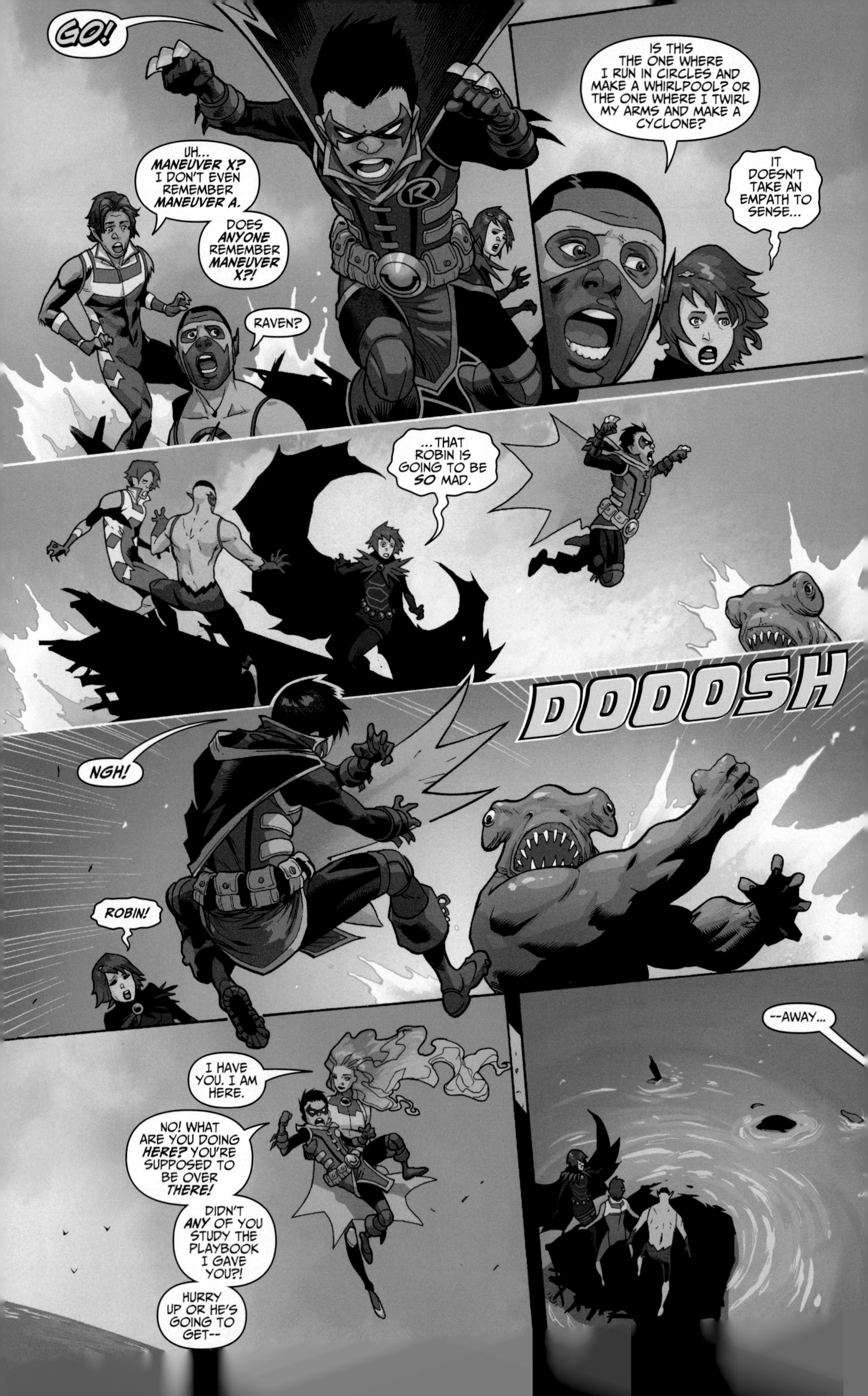
GO!
UH... MANEUVER X? I DON'T EVEN REMEMBER MANEUVER A.
DOES ANYONE REMEMBER MANEUVER X?!
RAVEN?
IS THIS THE ONE WHERE I RUN IN CIRCLES AND MAKE A WHIRLPOOL? OR THE ONE WHERE I TWIRL MY ARMS AND MAKE A CYCLONE?
IT DOESN'T TAKE AN EMPATH TO SENSE...
...THAT ROBIN IS GOING TO BE SO MAD.
DOOOSH
NGH!
ROBIN!
I HAVE YOU. I AM HERE.
NO! WHAT ARE YOU DOING HERE? YOU'RE SUPPOSED TO BE OVER THERE!
DIDN'T ANY OF YOU STUDY THE PLAYBOOK I GAVE YOU?!
HURRY UP OR HE'S GOING TO GET--
--AWAY...

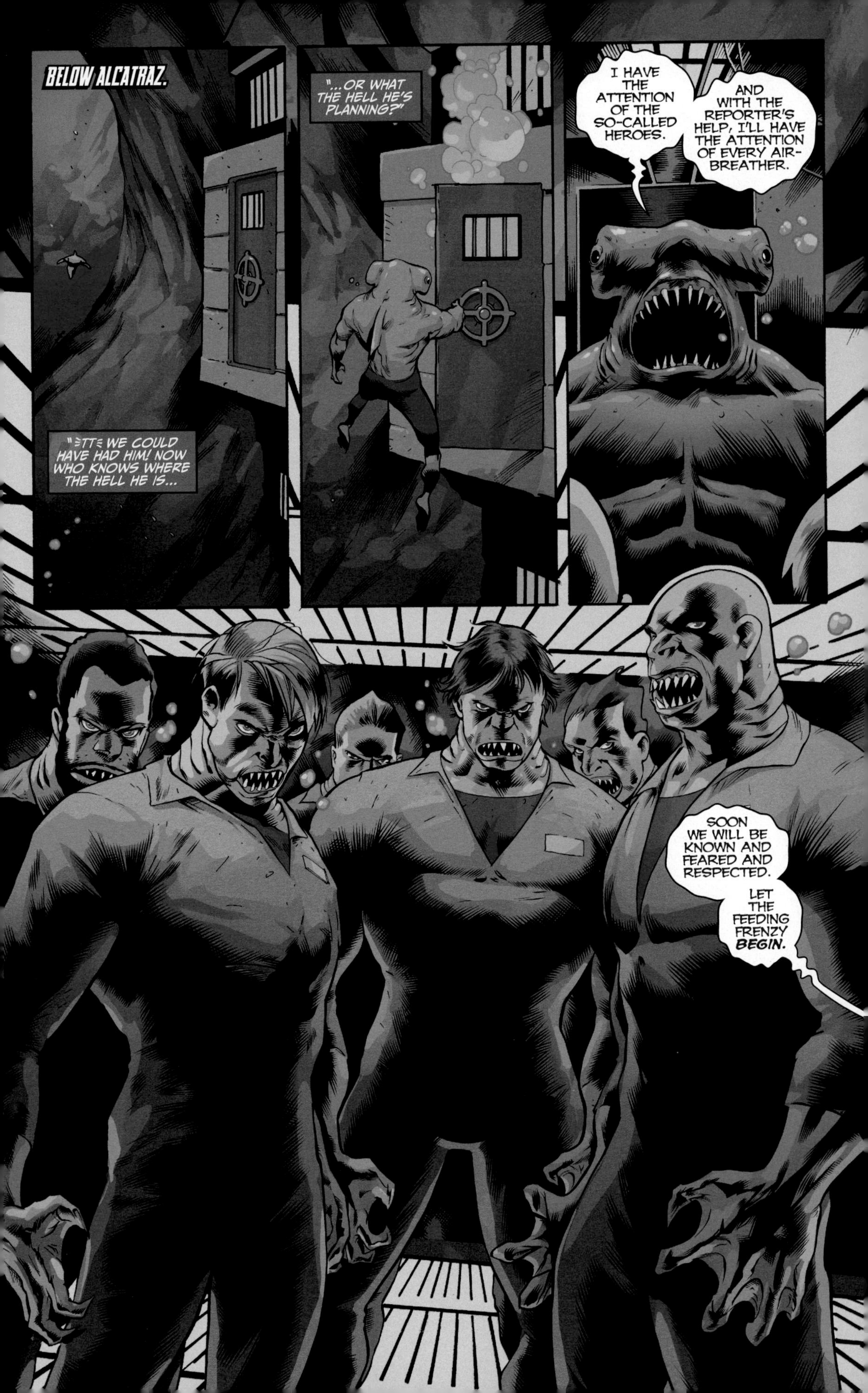
BELOW ALCATRAZ.
"WE COULD HAVE HAD HIM! NOW WHO KNOWS WHERE THE HELL HE IS...
"...OR WHAT THE HELL HE'S PLANNING?"
I HAVE THE ATTENTION OF THE SO-CALLED HEROES.
AND WITH THE REPORTER'S HELP, I'LL HAVE THE ATTENTION OF EVERY AIR-BREATHER.
SOON WE WILL BE KNOWN AND FEARED AND RESPECTED.
LET THE FEEDING FRENZY BEGIN.

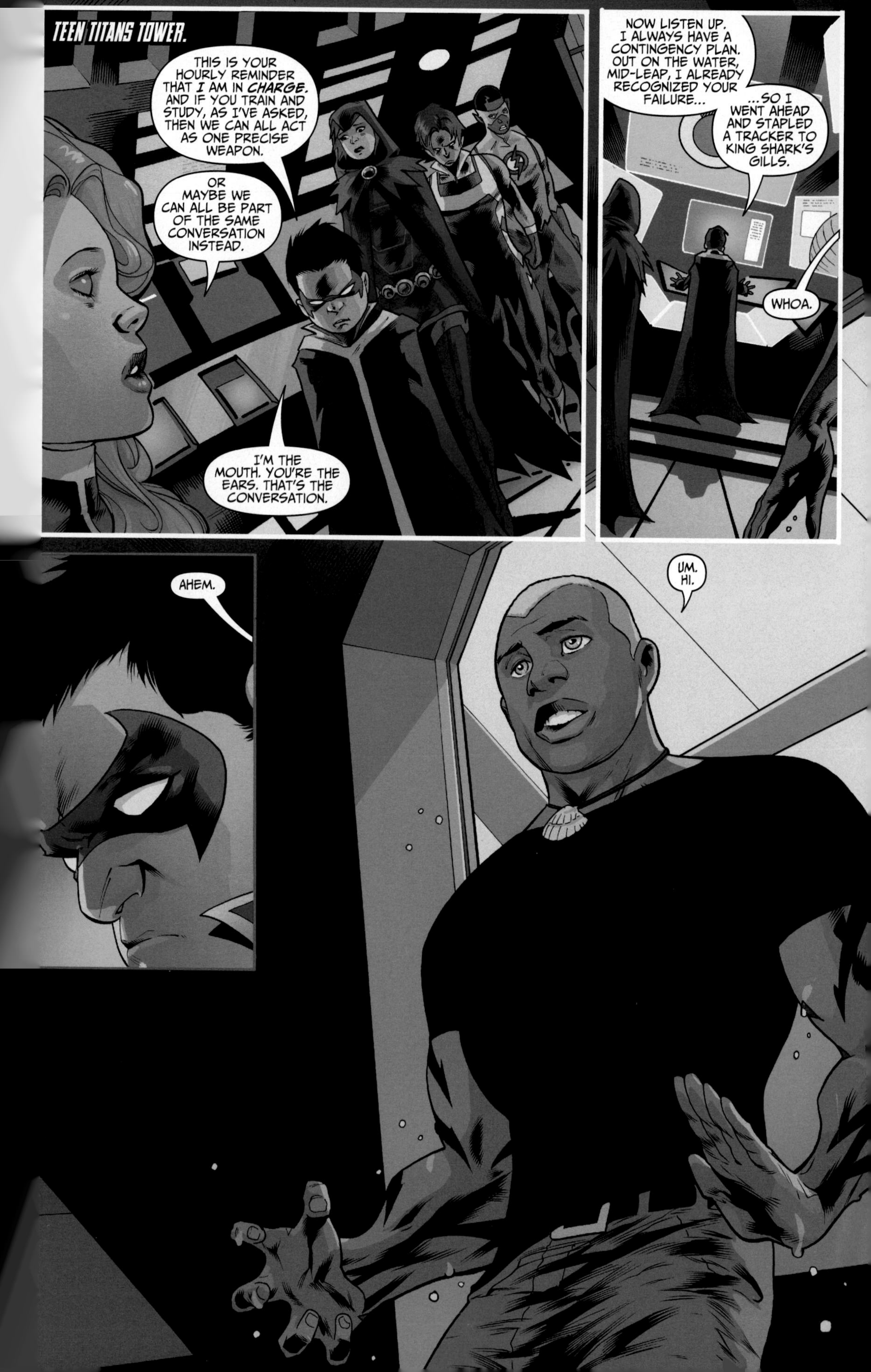
TEEN TITANS TOWER.
THIS IS YOUR HOURLY REMINDER THAT I AM IN CHARGE. AND IF YOU TRAIN AND STUDY, AS I'VE ASKED, THEN WE CAN ALL ACT AS ONE PRECISE WEAPON.
OR MAYBE WE CAN ALL BE PART OF THE SAME CONVERSATION INSTEAD.
I'M THE MOUTH. YOU'RE THE EARS. THAT'S THE CONVERSATION.
NOW LISTEN UP. I ALWAYS HAVE A CONTINGENCY PLAN. OUT ON THE WATER, MID-LEAP, I ALREADY RECOGNIZED YOUR FAILURE...
...SO I WENT AHEAD AND STAPLED A TRACKER TO KING SHARK'S GILLS.
WHOA.
AHEM.
UM. HI.

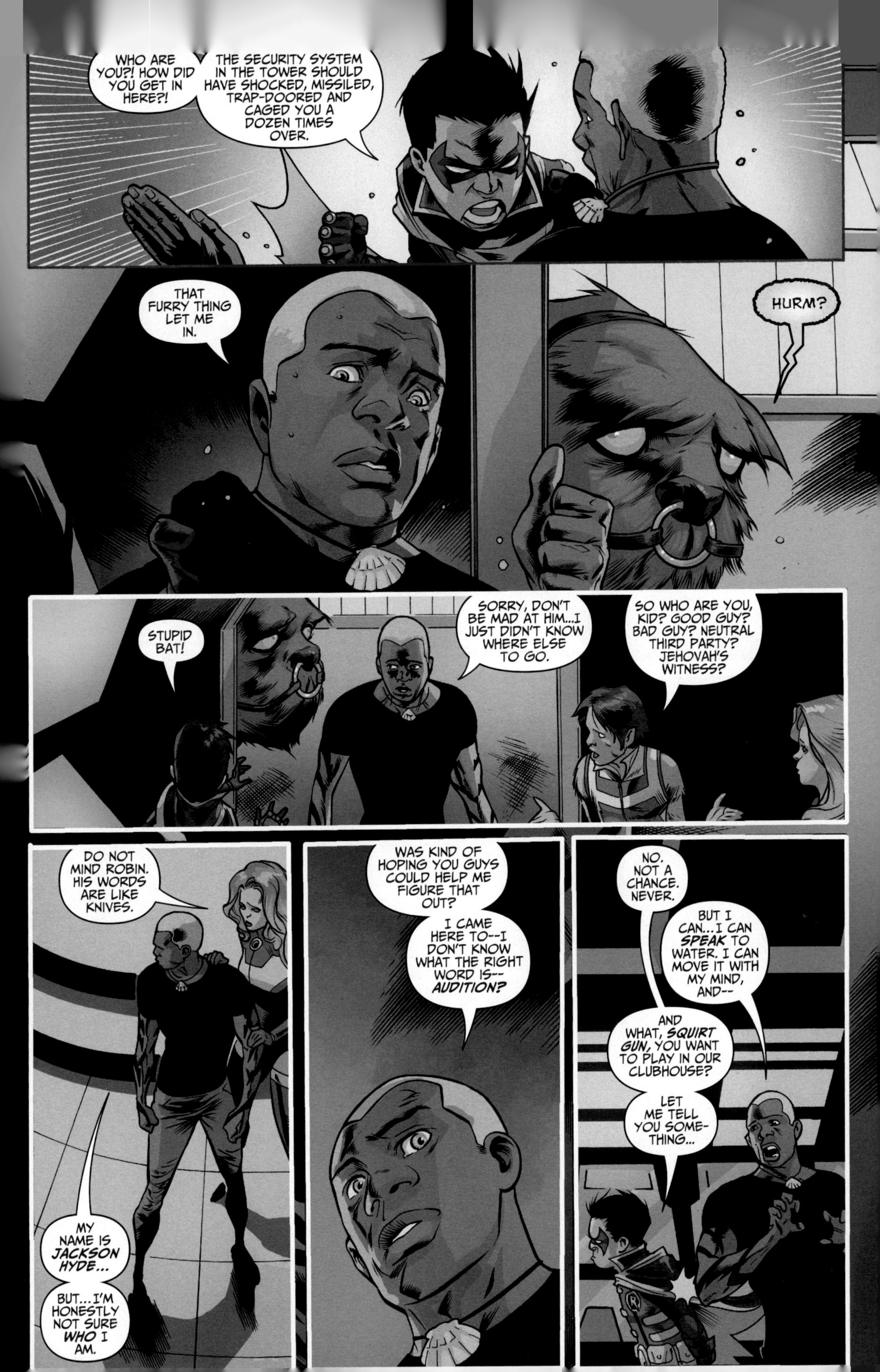
WHO ARE YOU?! HOW DID YOU GET IN HERE?!
THE SECURITY SYSTEM IN THE TOWER SHOULD HAVE SHOCKED, MISSILED, TRAP-DOORED AND CAGED YOU A DOZEN TIMES OVER.
THAT FURRY THING LET ME IN.
HURM?
STUPID BAT!
SORRY, DON'T BE MAD AT HIM...I JUST DIDN'T KNOW WHERE ELSE TO GO.
SO WHO ARE YOU, KID? GOOD GUY? BAD GUY? NEUTRAL THIRD PARTY? JEHOVAH'S WITNESS?
DO NOT MIND ROBIN. HIS WORDS ARE LIKE KNIVES.
MY NAME IS JACKSON HYDE...
BUT...I'M HONESTLY NOT SURE WHO I AM.
WAS KIND OF HOPING YOU GUYS COULD HELP ME FIGURE THAT OUT?
I CAME HERE TO--I DON'T KNOW WHAT THE RIGHT WORD IS--AUDITION?
NO. NOT A CHANCE. NEVER.
BUT I CAN...I CAN SPEAK TO WATER. I CAN MOVE IT WITH MY MIND, AND--
AND WHAT, SQUIRT GUN, YOU WANT TO PLAY IN OUR CLUBHOUSE?
LET ME TELL YOU SOME-THING...

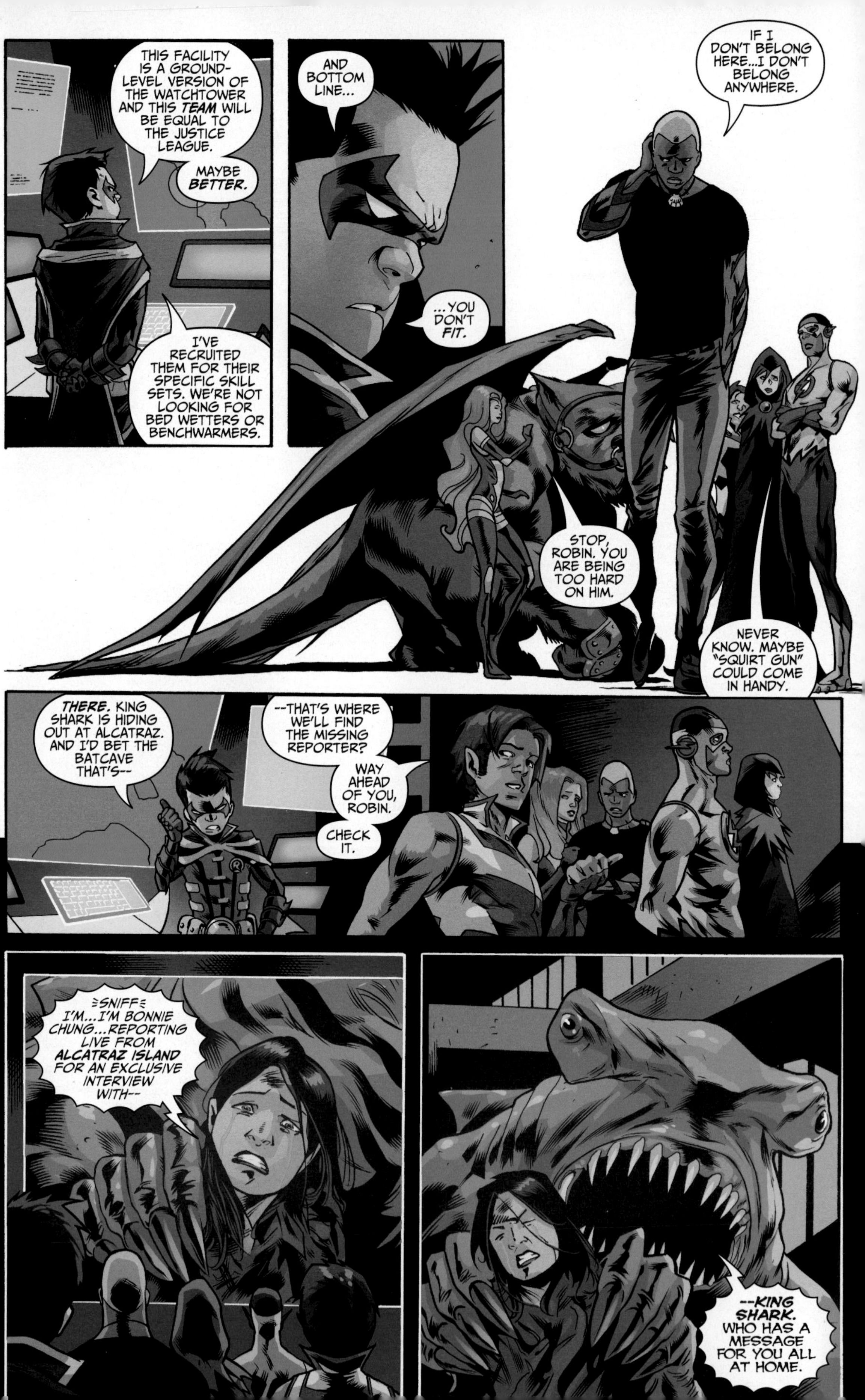
THIS FACILITY IS A GROUND-LEVEL VERSION OF THE WATCHTOWER AND THIS TEAM WILL BE EQUAL TO THE JUSTICE LEAGUE.
MAYBE BETTER.
I'VE RECRUITED THEM FOR THEIR SPECIFIC SKILL SETS. WE'RE NOT LOOKING FOR BED WETTERS OR BENCHWARMERS.
AND BOTTOM LINE...
...YOU DON'T FIT.
IF I DON'T BELONG HERE...I DON'T BELONG ANYWHERE.
STOP, ROBIN. YOU ARE BEING TOO HARD ON HIM.
NEVER KNOW. MAYBE "SQUIRT GUN" COULD COME IN HANDY.
THERE. KING SHARK IS HIDING OUT AT ALCATRAZ. AND I'D BET THE BATCAVE THAT'S--
--THAT'S WHERE WE'LL FIND THE MISSING REPORTER?
WAY AHEAD OF YOU, ROBIN.
CHECK IT.
≥SNIFF≤ I'M...I'M BONNIE CHUNG...REPORTING LIVE FROM ALCATRAZ ISLAND FOR AN EXCLUSIVE INTERVIEW WITH--
--KING SHARK. WHO HAS A MESSAGE FOR YOU ALL AT HOME.

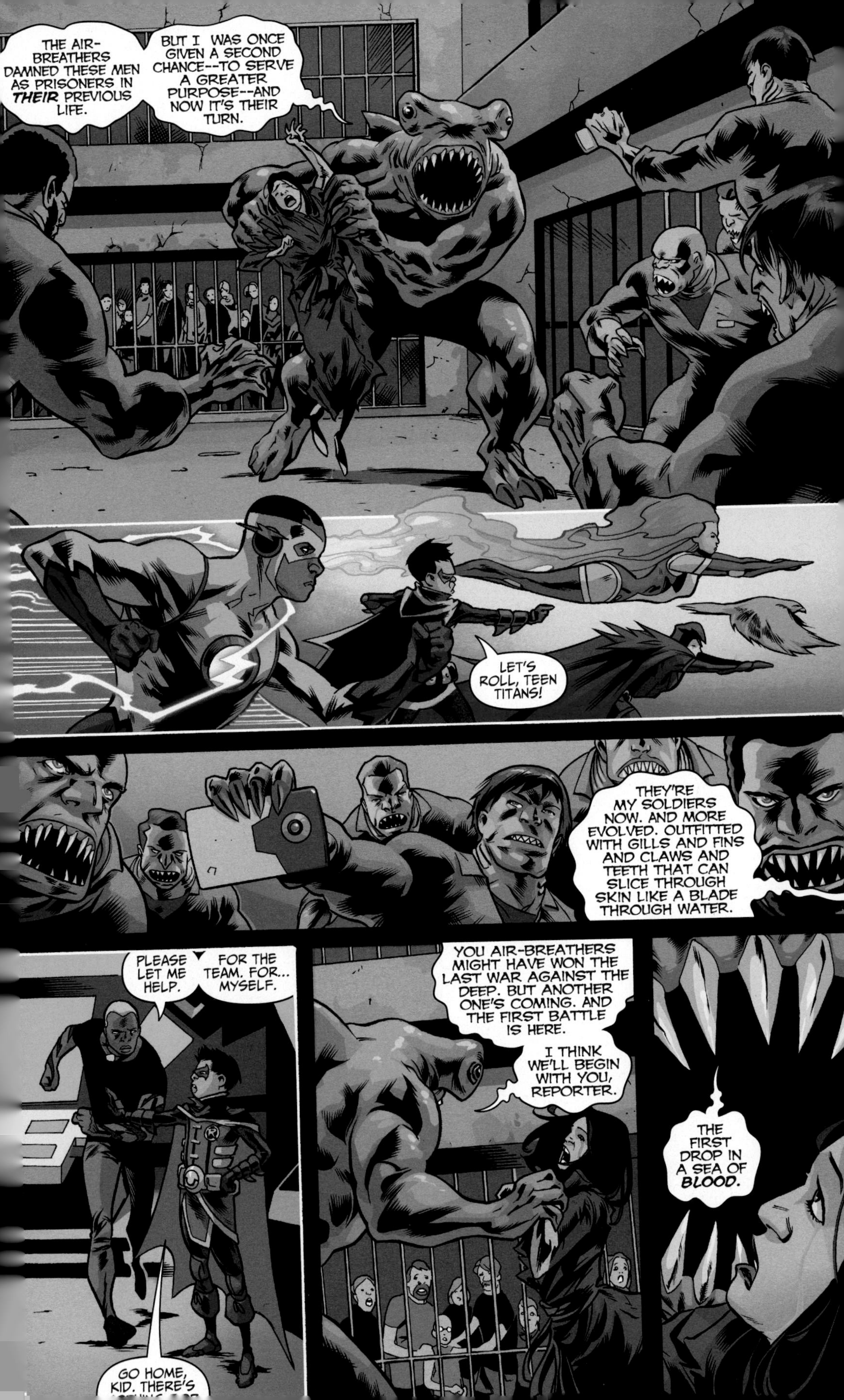

THE AIR-BREATHERS DAMNED THESE MEN AS PRISONERS IN *THEIR* PREVIOUS LIFE.
BUT I WAS ONCE GIVEN A SECOND CHANCE--TO SERVE A GREATER PURPOSE--AND NOW IT'S THEIR TURN.
LET'S ROLL, TEEN TITANS!
THEY'RE MY SOLDIERS NOW. AND MORE EVOLVED. OUTFITTED WITH GILLS AND FINS AND CLAWS AND TEETH THAT CAN SLICE THROUGH SKIN LIKE A BLADE THROUGH WATER.
PLEASE LET ME HELP.
FOR THE TEAM. FOR... MYSELF.
GO HOME, KID. THERE'S
YOU AIR-BREATHERS MIGHT HAVE WON THE LAST WAR AGAINST THE DEEP. BUT ANOTHER ONE'S COMING. AND THE FIRST BATTLE IS HERE.
I THINK WE'LL BEGIN WITH YOU, REPORTER.
THE FIRST DROP IN A SEA OF *BLOOD.*

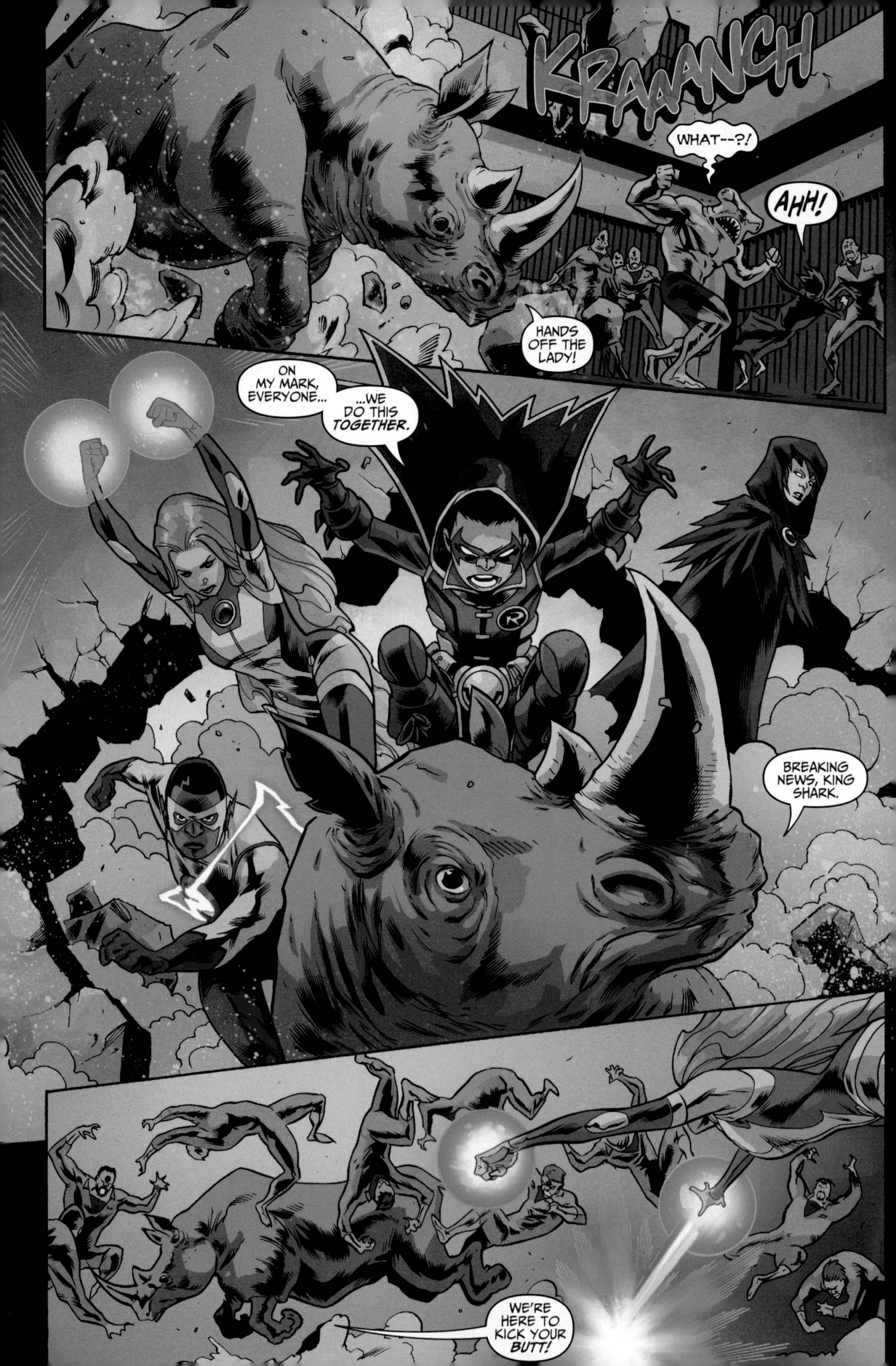
KRAAANCH
WHAT--?!
AHH!
HANDS OFF THE LADY!
ON MY MARK, EVERYONE...
...WE DO THIS TOGETHER.
BREAKING NEWS, KING SHARK.
WE'RE HERE TO KICK YOUR BUTT!

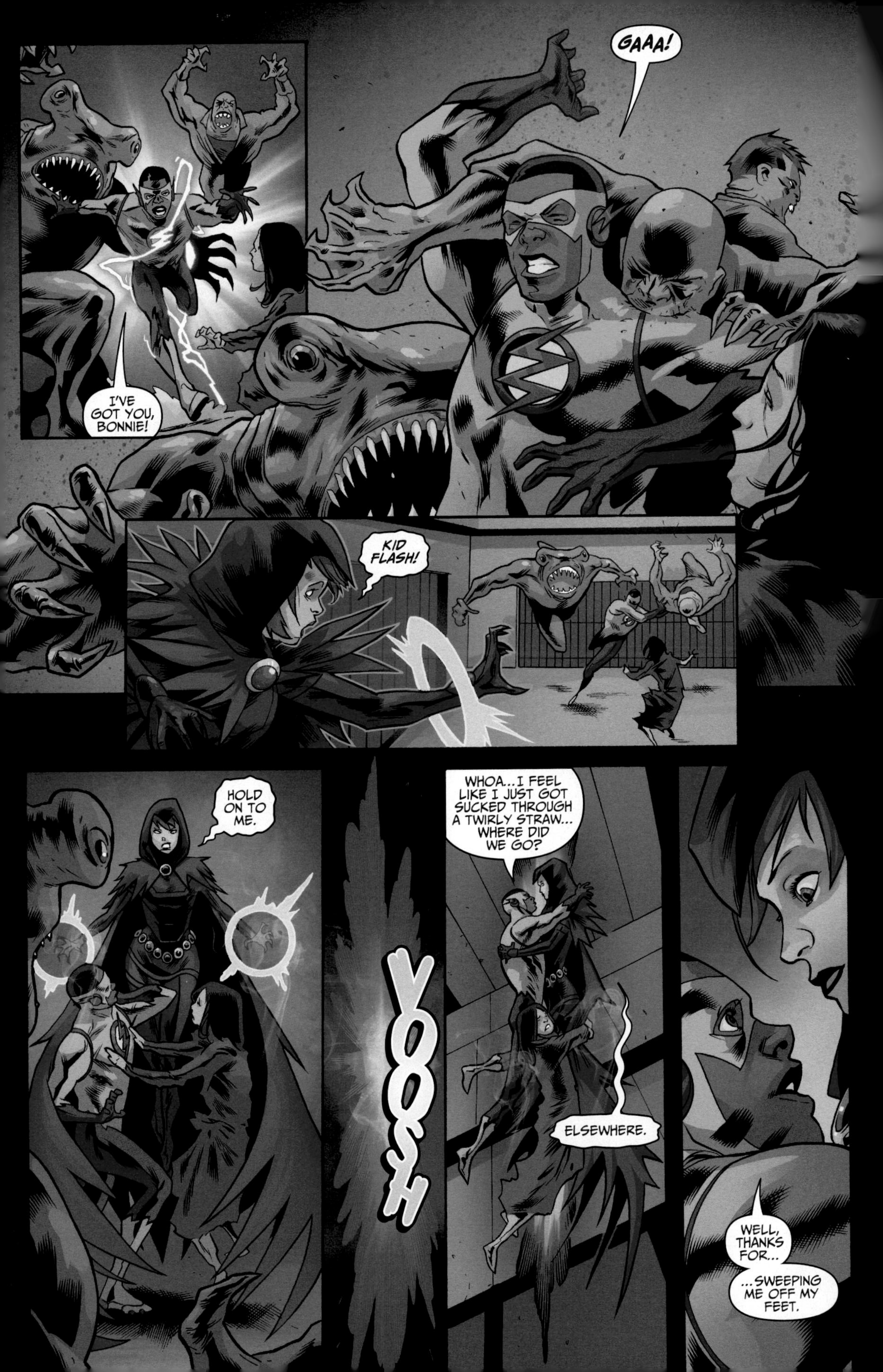
I'VE GOT YOU, BONNIE!
GAAA!
KID FLASH!
HOLD ON TO ME.
VOOSH
WHOA...I FEEL LIKE I JUST GOT SUCKED THROUGH A TWIRLY STRAW... WHERE DID WE GO?
ELSEWHERE.
WELL, THANKS FOR...
...SWEEPING ME OFF MY FEET.

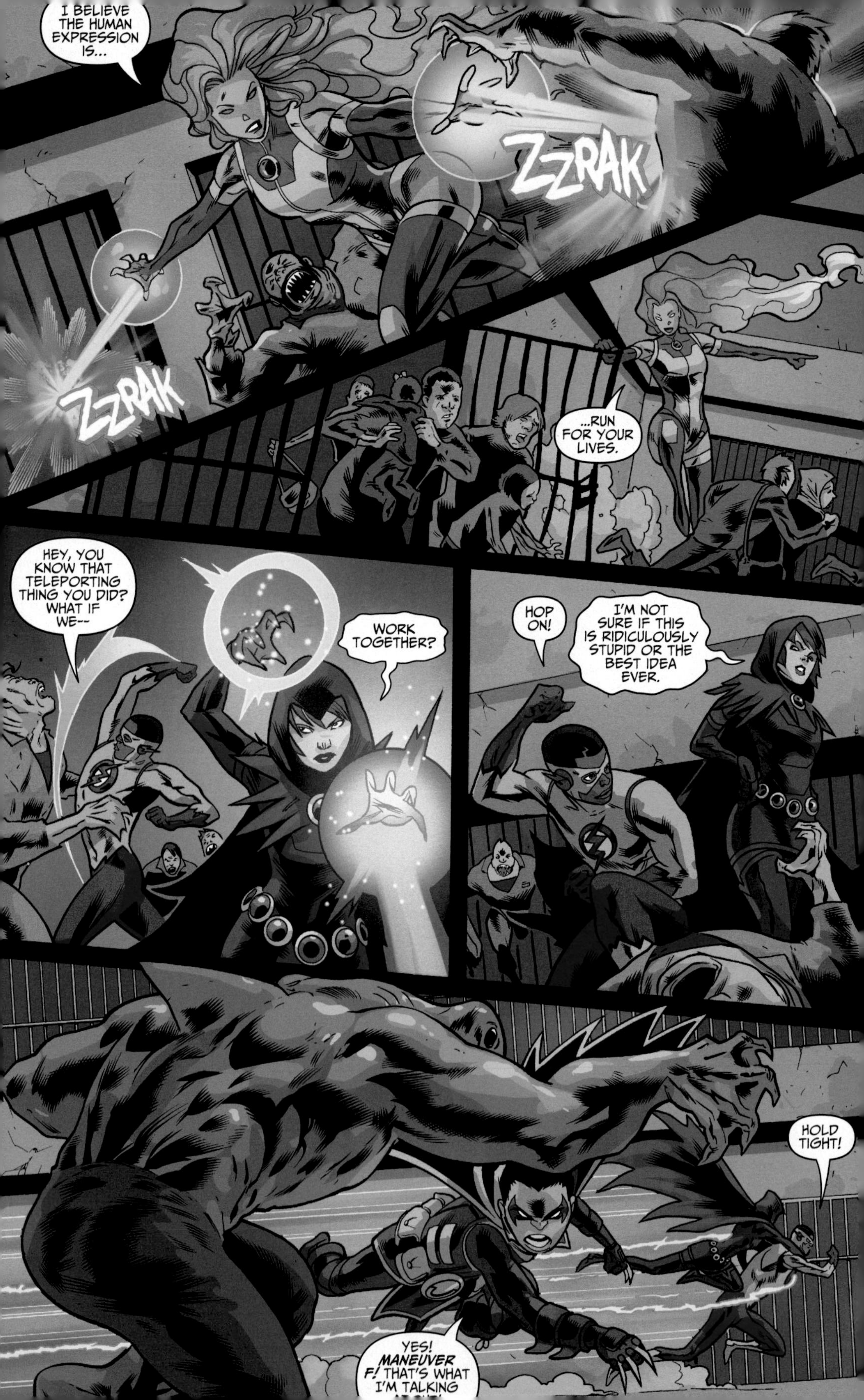
I BELIEVE THE HUMAN EXPRESSION IS...
ZZRAK
ZZRAK
...RUN FOR YOUR LIVES.
HEY, YOU KNOW THAT TELEPORTING THING YOU DID? WHAT IF WE--
WORK TOGETHER?
HOP ON!
I'M NOT SURE IF THIS IS RIDICULOUSLY STUPID OR THE BEST IDEA EVER.
HOLD TIGHT!
YES! MANEUVER F! THAT'S WHAT I'M TALKING

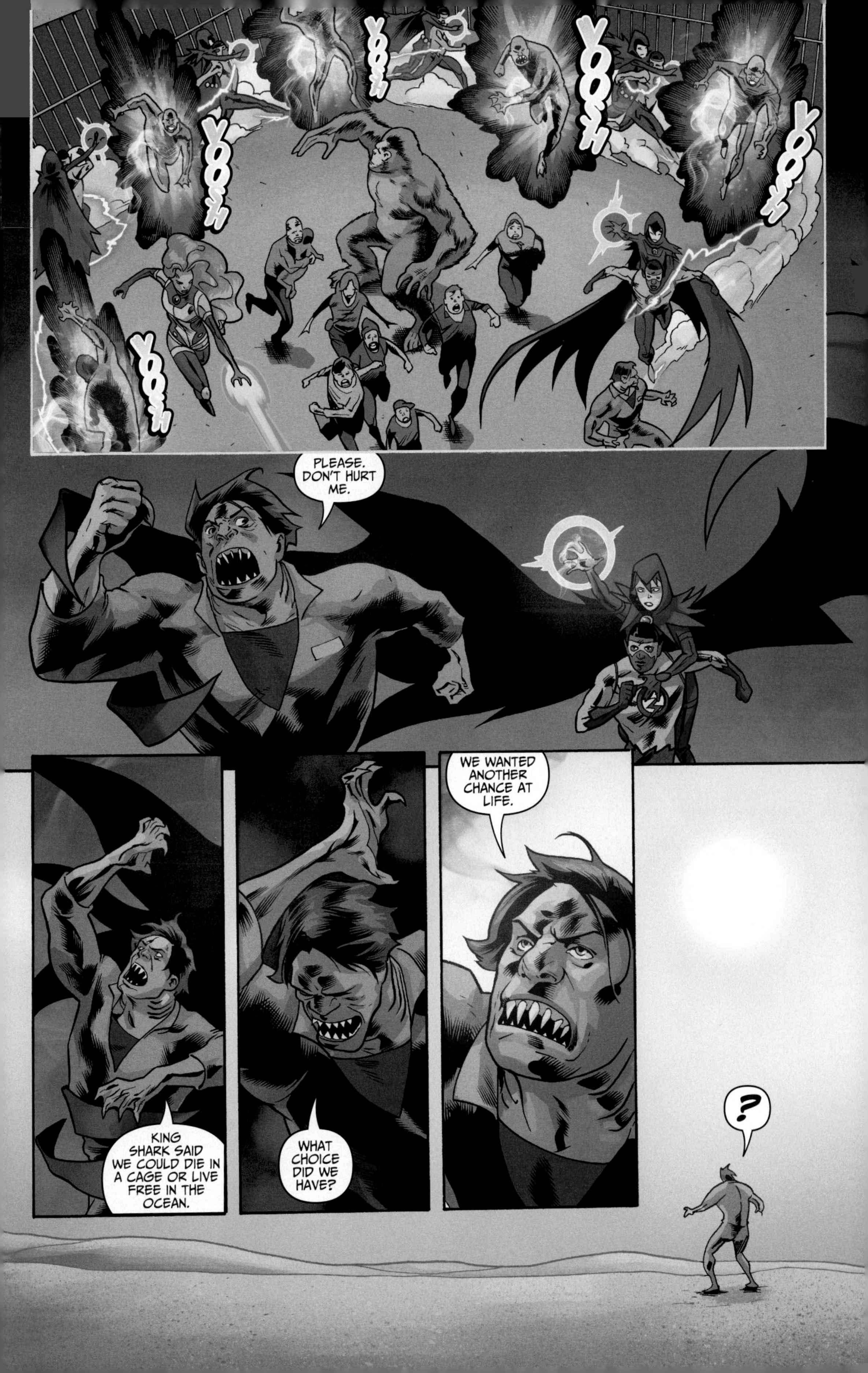
YOOSH
YOOSH
YOOSH
YOOSH
YOOSH
PLEASE. DON'T HURT ME.
KING SHARK SAID WE COULD DIE IN A CAGE OR LIVE FREE IN THE OCEAN.
WHAT CHOICE DID WE HAVE?
WE WANTED ANOTHER CHANCE AT LIFE.
?

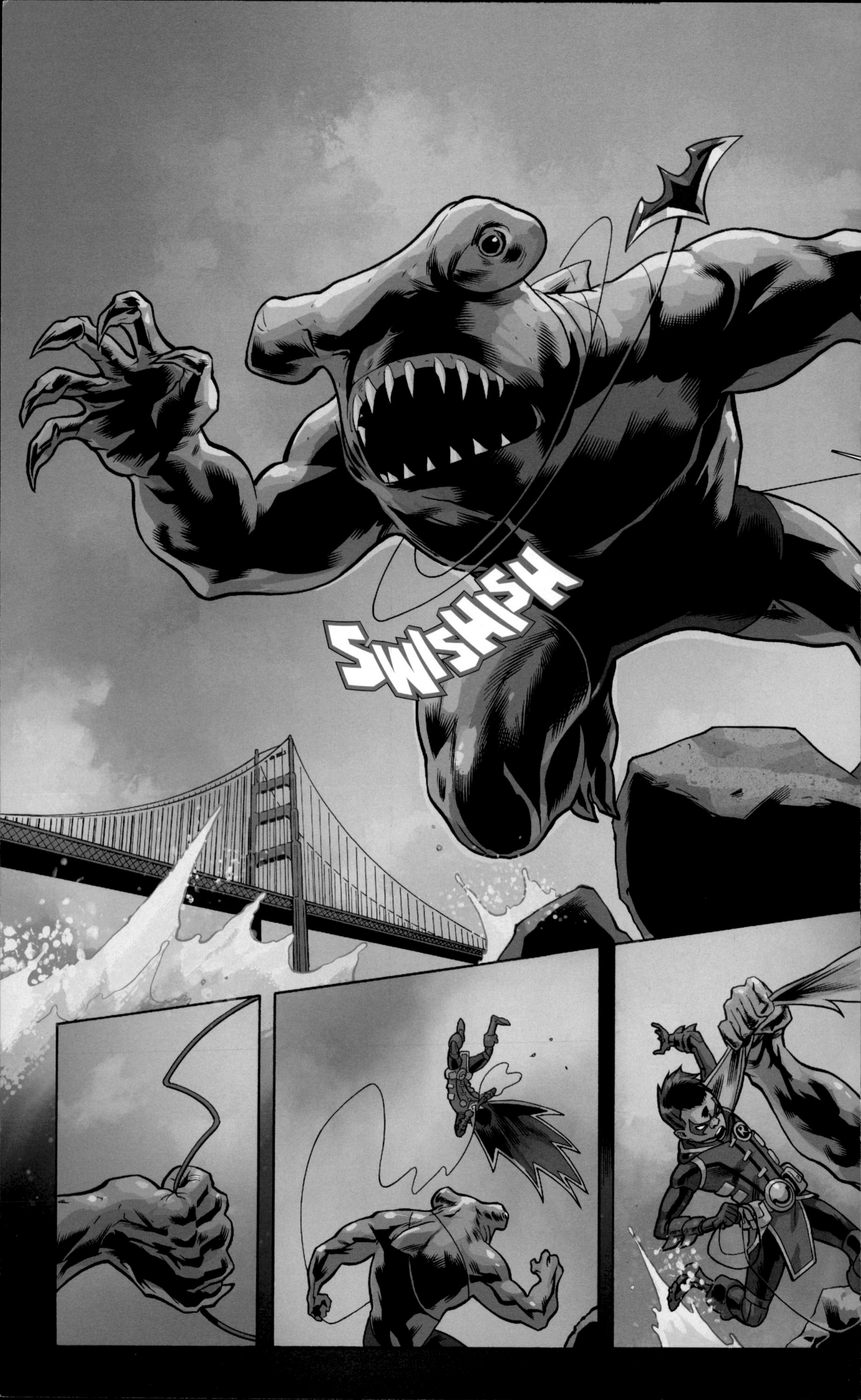
SWISHSH

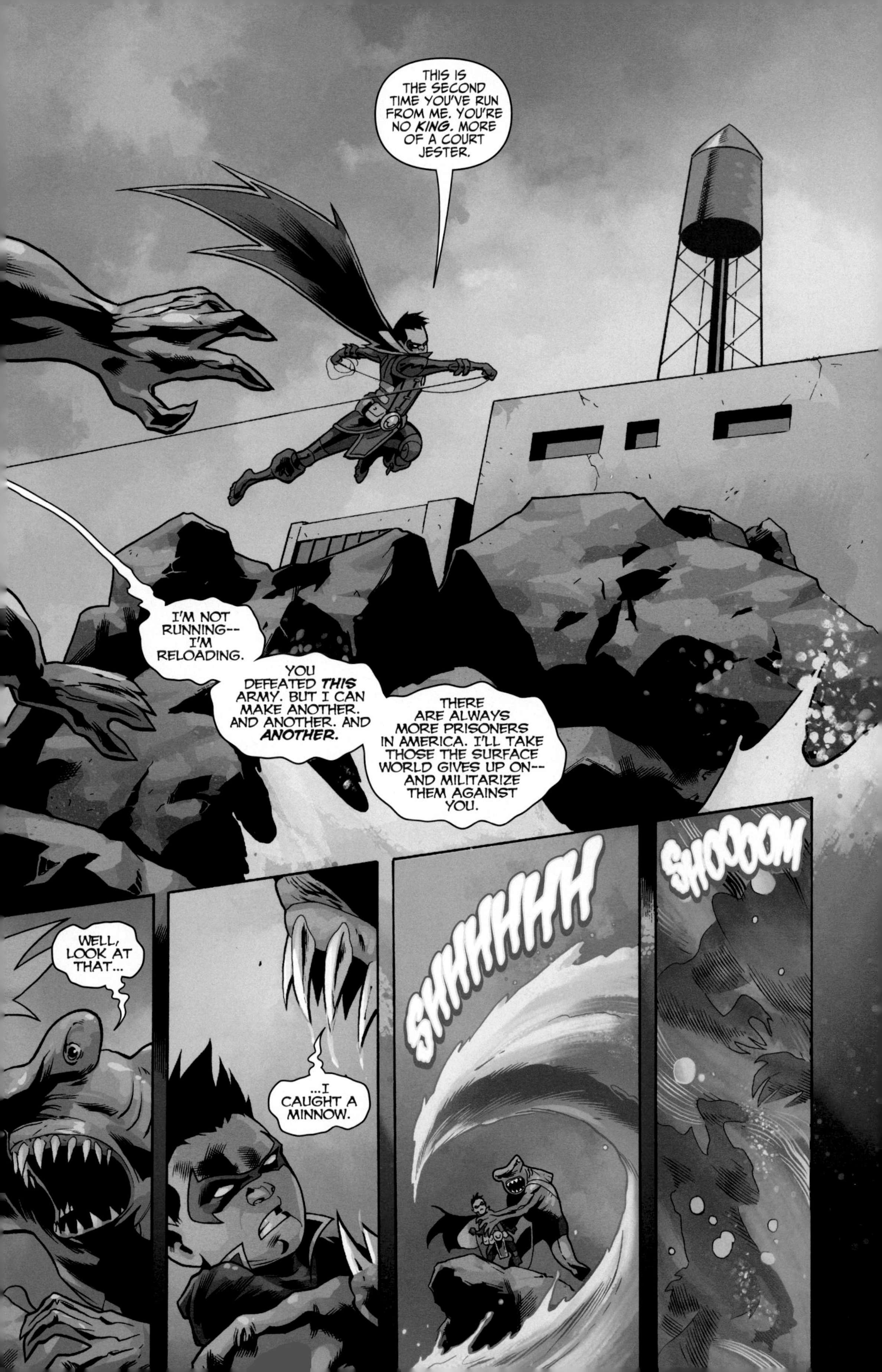
THIS IS THE SECOND TIME YOU'VE RUN FROM ME. YOU'RE NO *KING*. MORE OF A COURT JESTER.
I'M NOT RUNNING-- I'M RELOADING.
YOU DEFEATED *THIS* ARMY. BUT I CAN MAKE ANOTHER. AND ANOTHER. AND *ANOTHER*.
THERE ARE ALWAYS MORE PRISONERS IN AMERICA. I'LL TAKE THOSE THE SURFACE WORLD GIVES UP ON-- AND MILITARIZE THEM AGAINST YOU.
WELL, LOOK AT THAT...
...I CAUGHT A MINNOW.
SHHHHHH
SHOOOOM

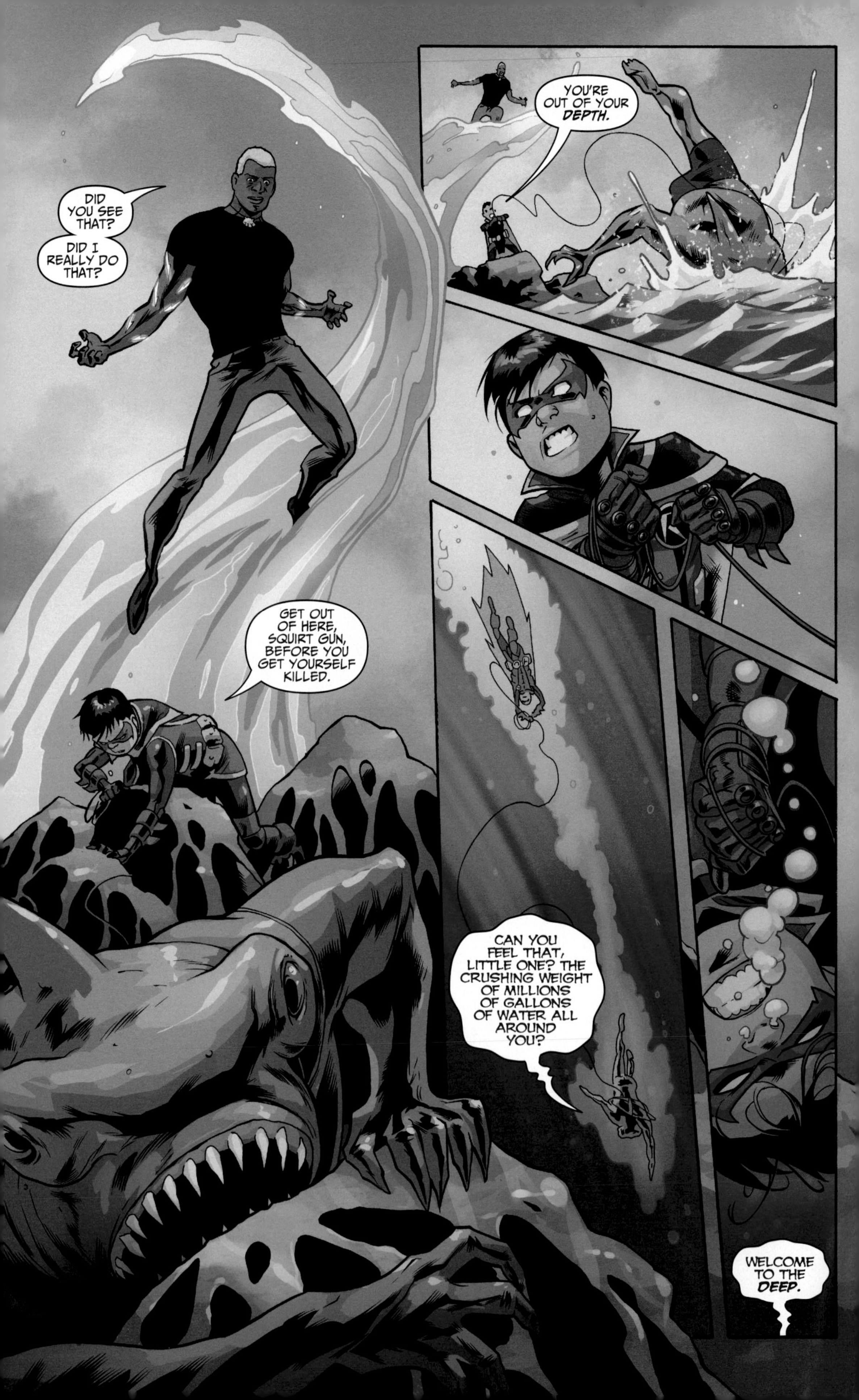
DID YOU SEE THAT?
DID I REALLY DO THAT?
YOU'RE OUT OF YOUR DEPTH.
GET OUT OF HERE, SQUIRT GUN, BEFORE YOU GET YOURSELF KILLED.
CAN YOU FEEL THAT, LITTLE ONE? THE CRUSHING WEIGHT OF MILLIONS OF GALLONS OF WATER ALL AROUND YOU?
WELCOME TO THE DEEP.

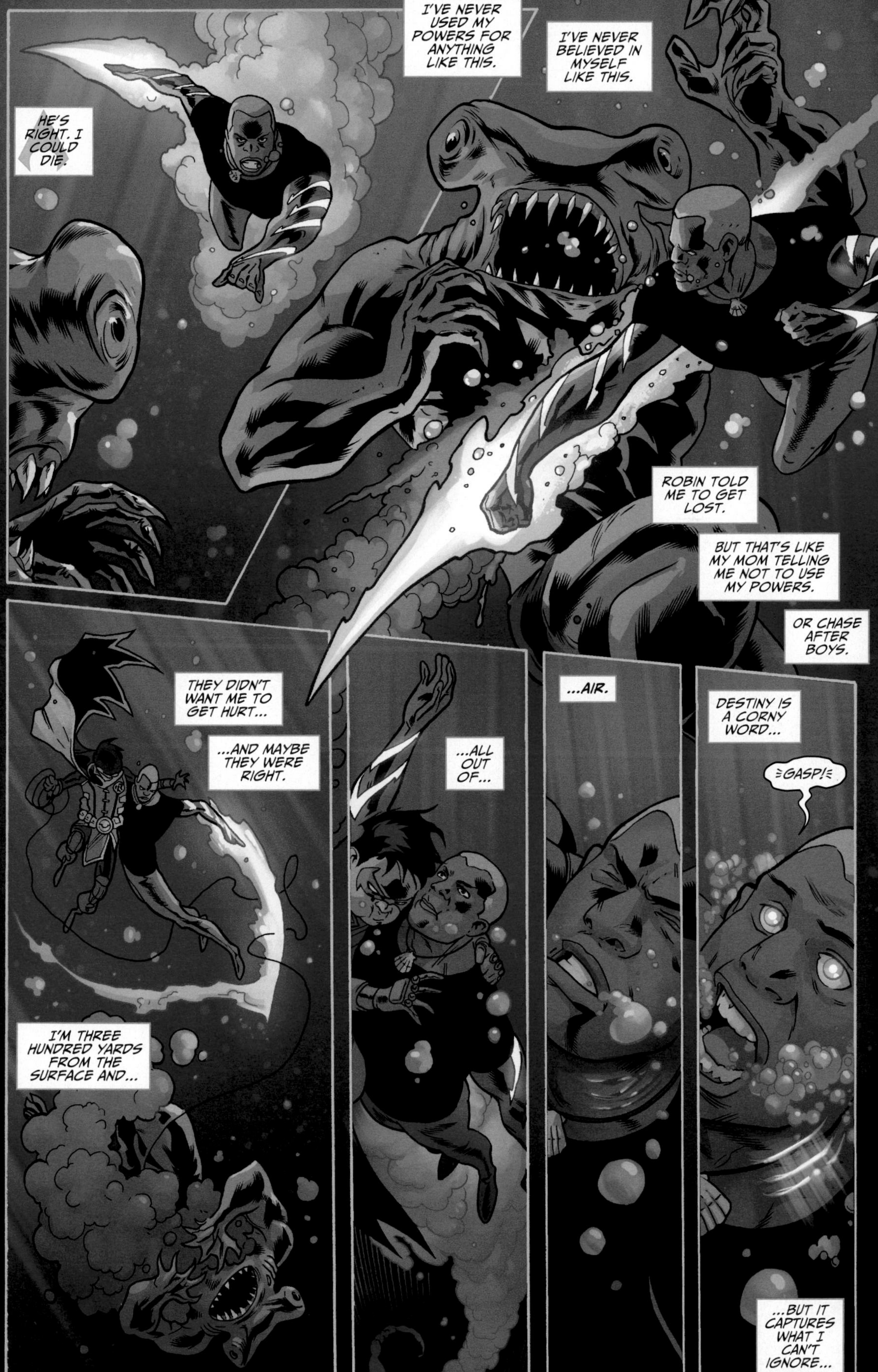
HE'S RIGHT. I COULD DIE.
I'VE NEVER USED MY POWERS FOR ANYTHING LIKE THIS.
I'VE NEVER BELIEVED IN MYSELF LIKE THIS.
ROBIN TOLD ME TO GET LOST.
BUT THAT'S LIKE MY MOM TELLING ME NOT TO USE MY POWERS.
OR CHASE AFTER BOYS.
THEY DIDN'T WANT ME TO GET HURT...
...AND MAYBE THEY WERE RIGHT.
I'M THREE HUNDRED YARDS FROM THE SURFACE AND...
...ALL OUT OF...
...AIR.
DESTINY IS A CORNY WORD...
GASP!
...BUT IT CAPTURES WHAT I CAN'T IGNORE...

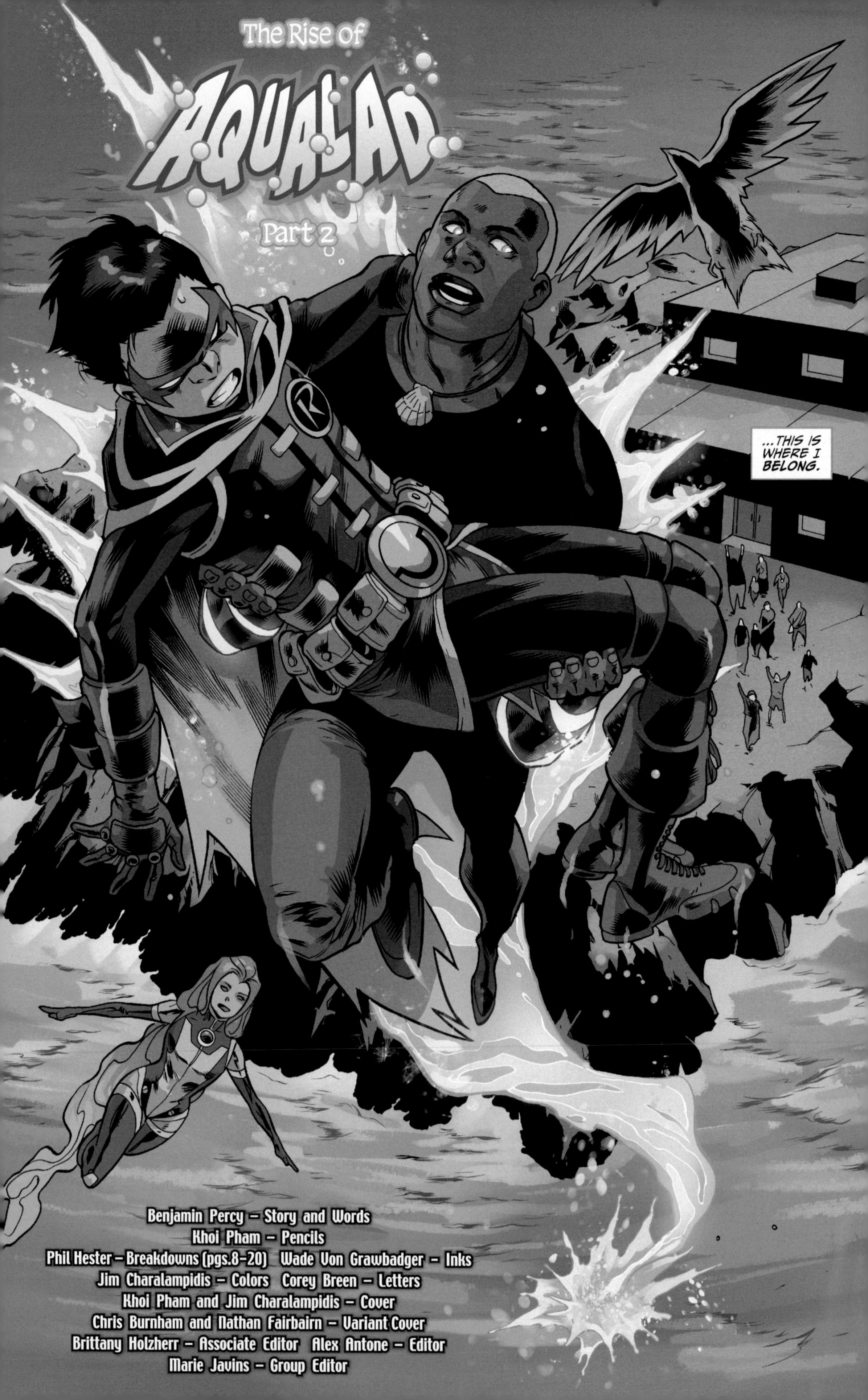
The Rise of
AQUALAD
Part 2
...THIS IS WHERE I BELONG.
Benjamin Percy – Story and Words
Khoi Pham – Pencils
Phil Hester – Breakdowns (pgs.8-20) Wade Von Grawbadger – Inks
Jim Charalampidis – Colors Corey Breen – Letters
Khoi Pham and Jim Charalampidis – Cover
Chris Burnham and Nathan Fairbairn – Variant Cover
Brittany Holzherr – Associate Editor Alex Antone – Editor
Marie Javins – Group Editor

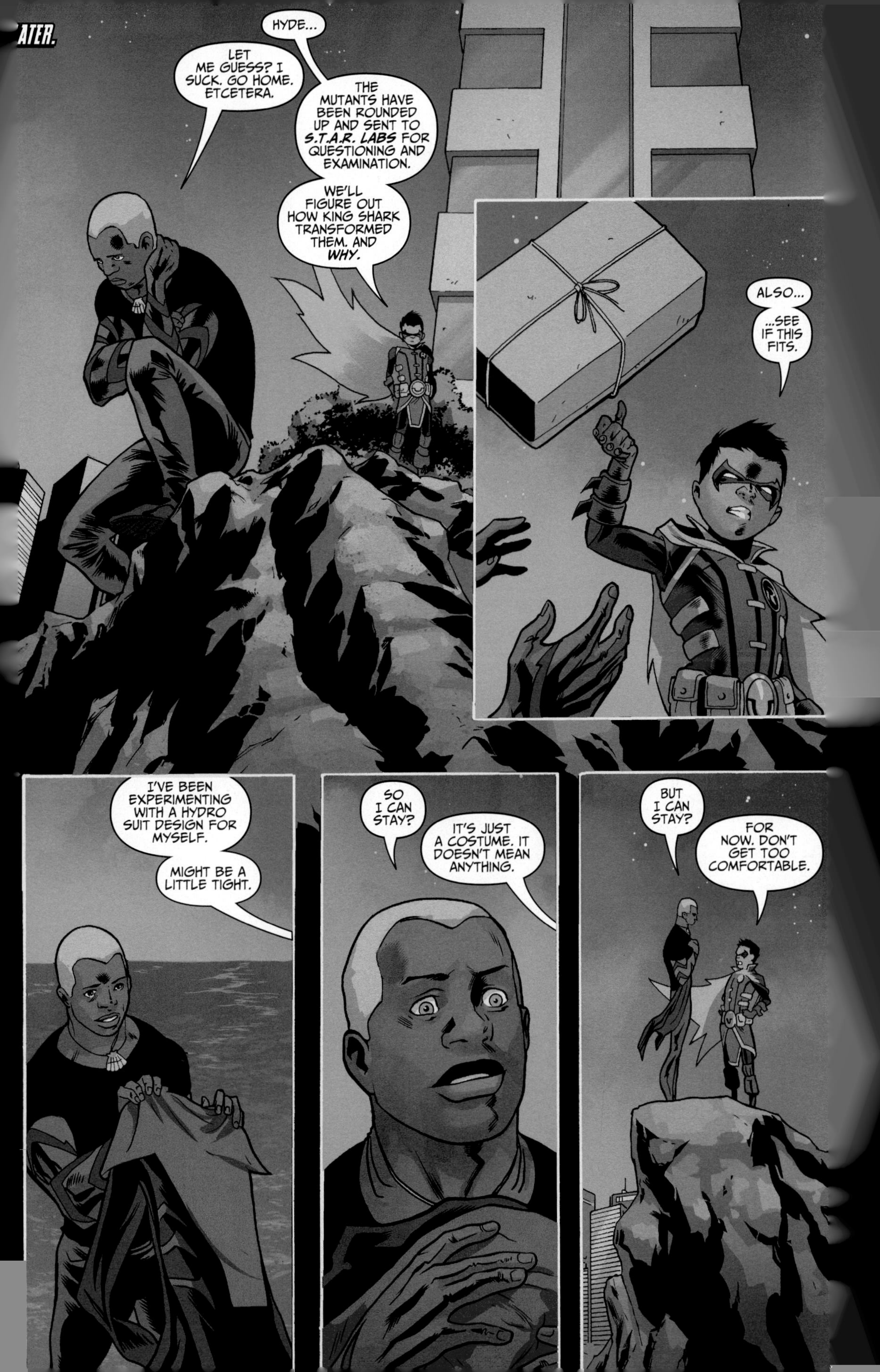
LATER.
LET ME GUESS? I SUCK. GO HOME. ETCETERA.
HYDE...
THE MUTANTS HAVE BEEN ROUNDED UP AND SENT TO S.T.A.R. LABS FOR QUESTIONING AND EXAMINATION.
WE'LL FIGURE OUT HOW KING SHARK TRANSFORMED THEM. AND WHY.
ALSO...
...SEE IF THIS FITS.
I'VE BEEN EXPERIMENTING WITH A HYDRO SUIT DESIGN FOR MYSELF.
MIGHT BE A LITTLE TIGHT.
SO I CAN STAY?
IT'S JUST A COSTUME. IT DOESN'T MEAN ANYTHING.
BUT I CAN STAY?
FOR NOW. DON'T GET TOO COMFORTABLE.

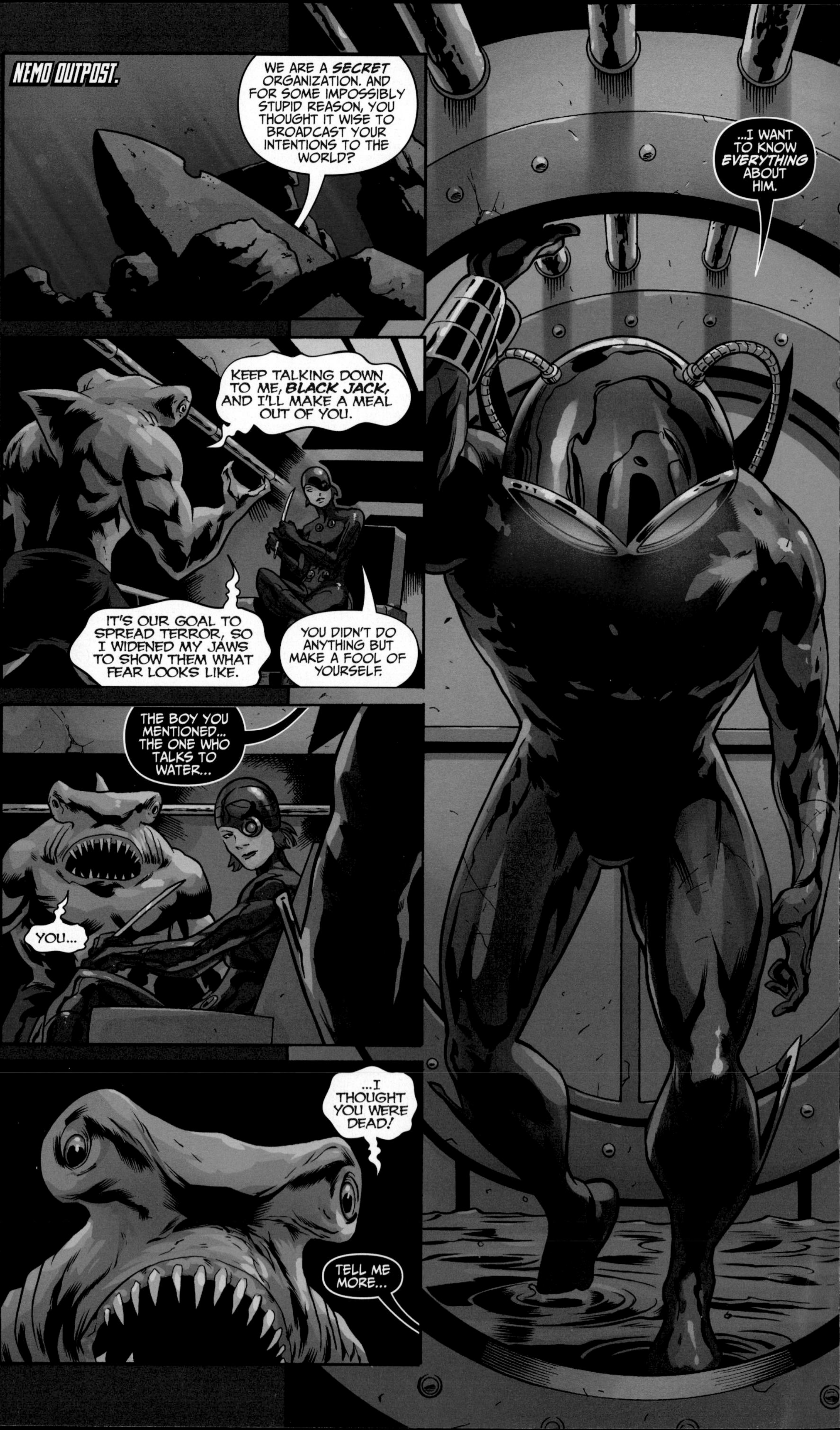
NEMO OUTPOST.
WE ARE A SECRET ORGANIZATION. AND FOR SOME IMPOSSIBLY STUPID REASON, YOU THOUGHT IT WISE TO BROADCAST YOUR INTENTIONS TO THE WORLD?
KEEP TALKING DOWN TO ME, BLACK JACK, AND I'LL MAKE A MEAL OUT OF YOU.
IT'S OUR GOAL TO SPREAD TERROR, SO I WIDENED MY JAWS TO SHOW THEM WHAT FEAR LOOKS LIKE.
YOU DIDN'T DO ANYTHING BUT MAKE A FOOL OF YOURSELF.
THE BOY YOU MENTIONED... THE ONE WHO TALKS TO WATER...
YOU...
...I THOUGHT YOU WERE DEAD!
TELL ME MORE...
...I WANT TO KNOW EVERYTHING ABOUT HIM.

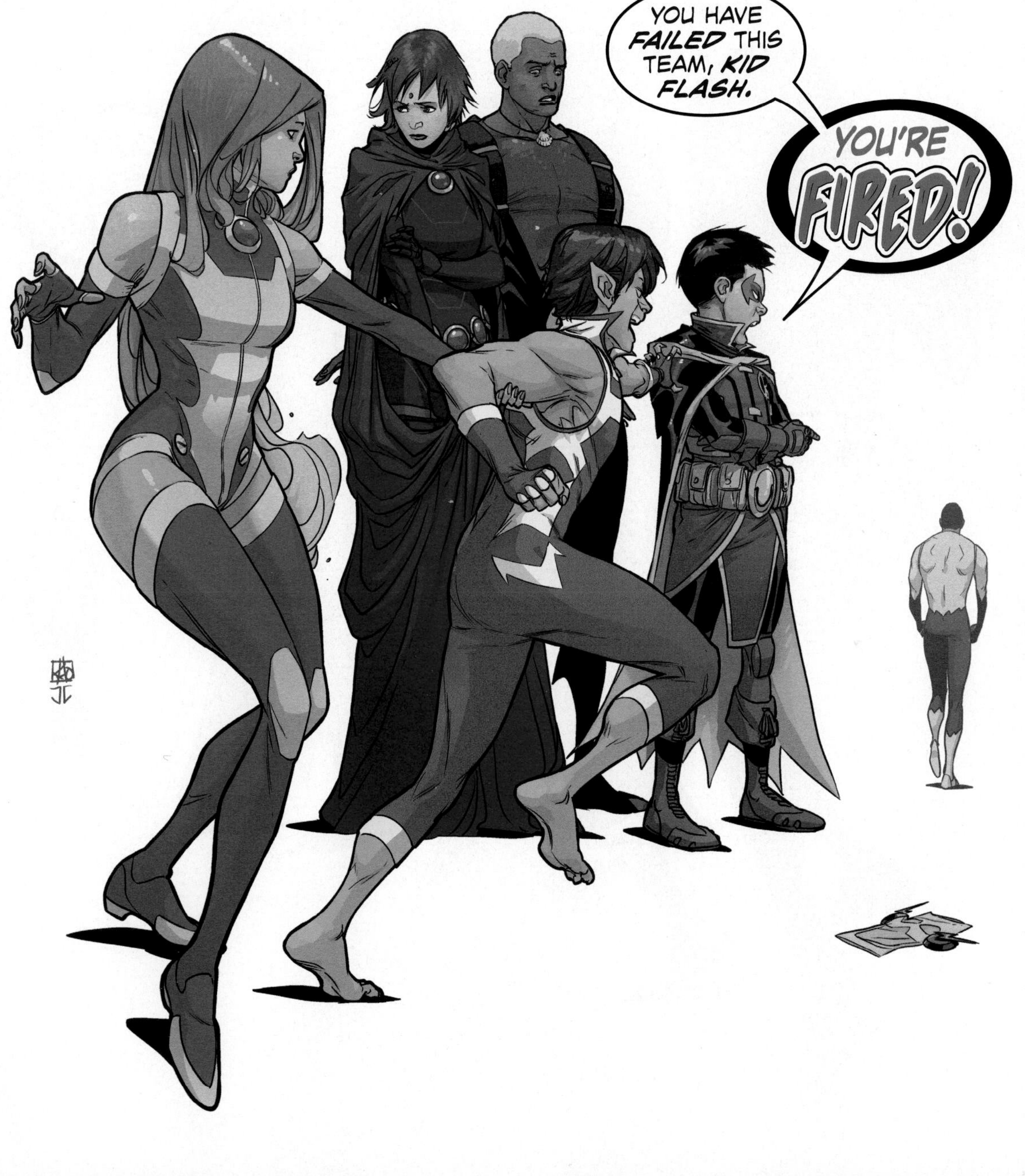
YOU HAVE FAILED THIS TEAM, KID FLASH.
YOU'RE FIRED!

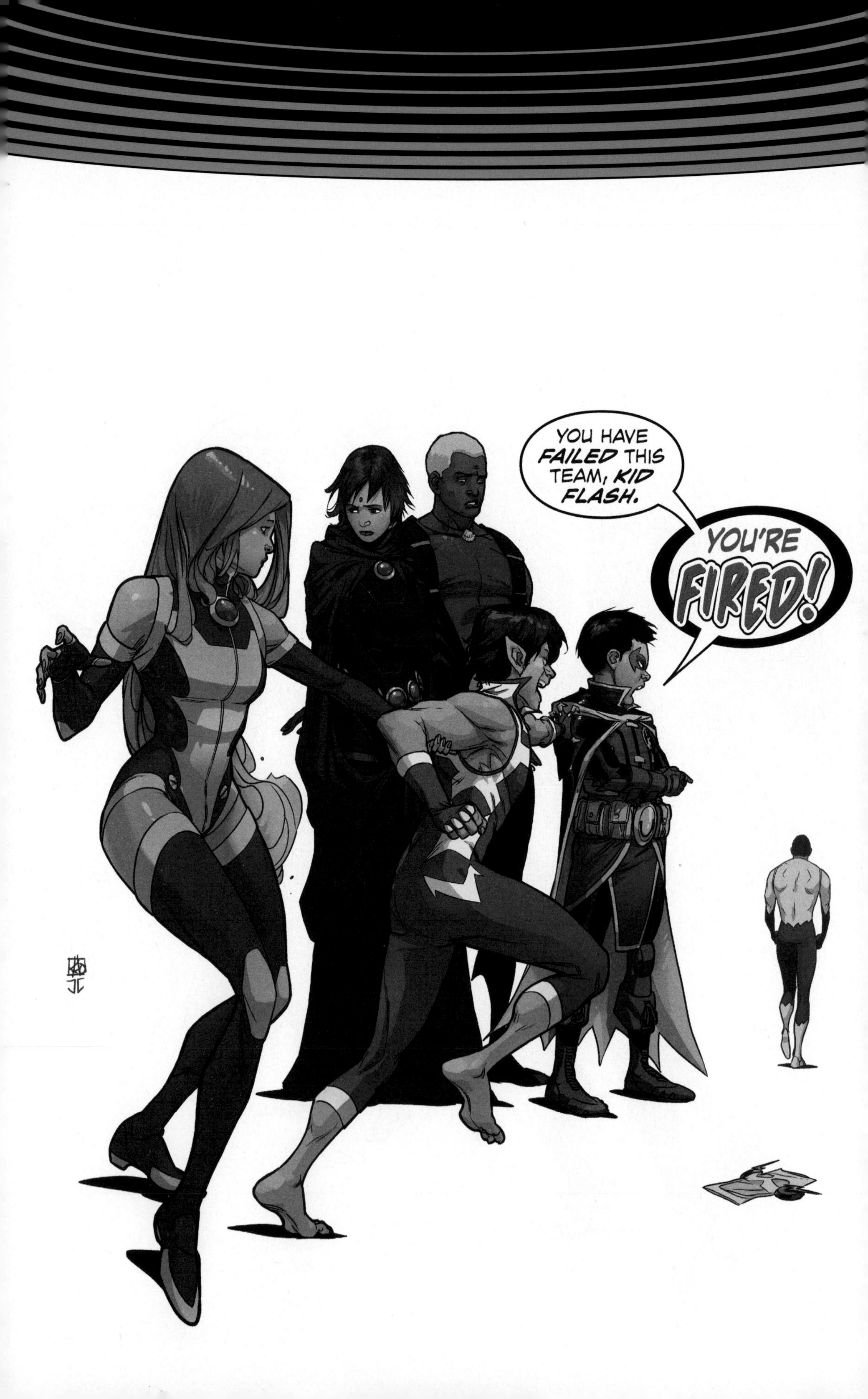
YOU HAVE FAILED THIS TEAM, KID FLASH.
YOU'RE FIRED!

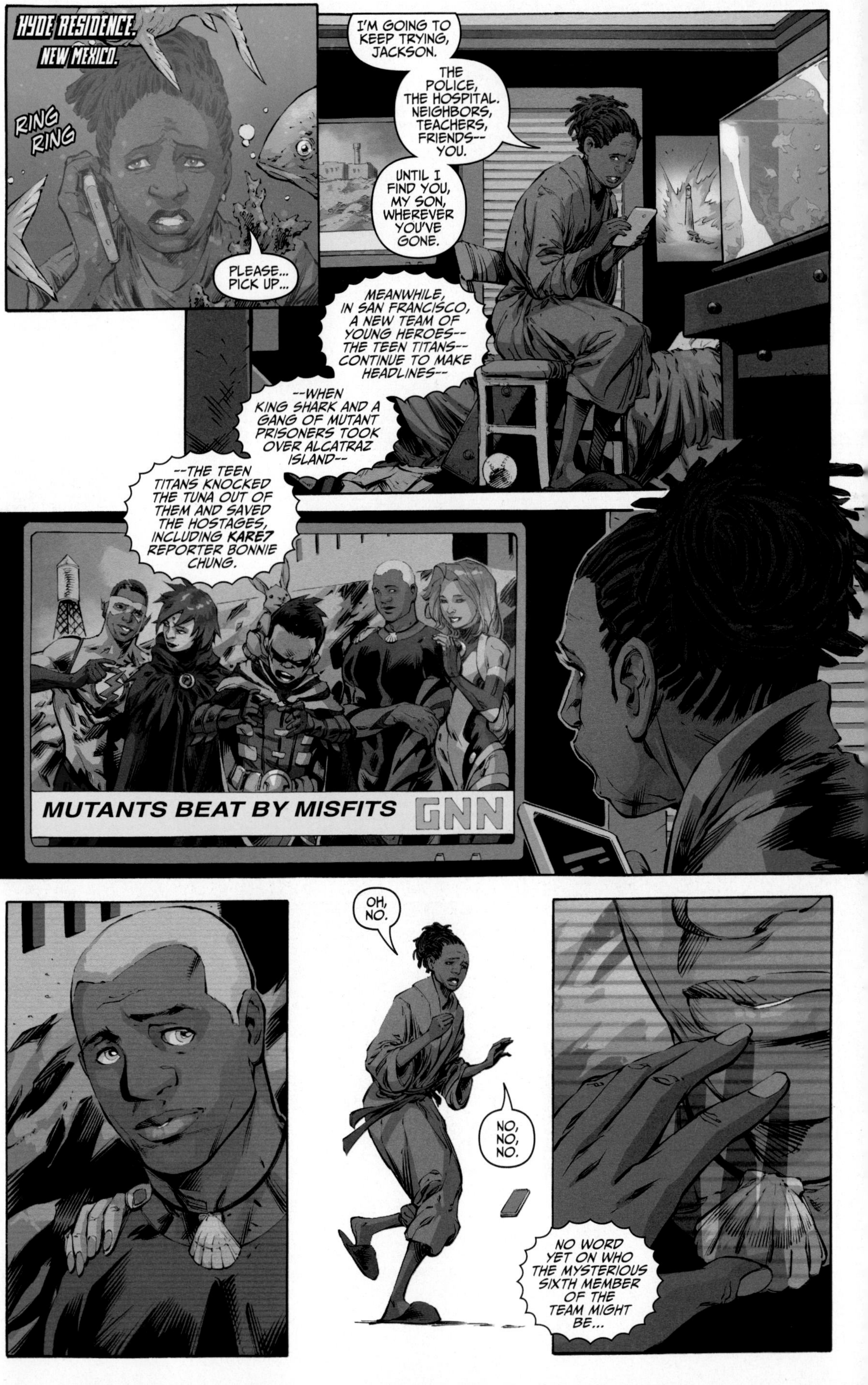
HYDE RESIDENCE. NEW MEXICO.
RING RING
PLEASE... PICK UP...
I'M GOING TO KEEP TRYING, JACKSON.
THE POLICE, THE HOSPITAL. NEIGHBORS, TEACHERS, FRIENDS-- YOU.
UNTIL I FIND YOU, MY SON, WHEREVER YOU'VE GONE.
MEANWHILE, IN SAN FRANCISCO, A NEW TEAM OF YOUNG HEROES-- THE TEEN TITANS-- CONTINUE TO MAKE HEADLINES--
--WHEN KING SHARK AND A GANG OF MUTANT PRISONERS TOOK OVER ALCATRAZ ISLAND--
--THE TEEN TITANS KNOCKED THE TUNA OUT OF THEM AND SAVED THE HOSTAGES, INCLUDING KARE7 REPORTER BONNIE CHUNG.
MUTANTS BEAT BY MISFITS
GNN
OH, NO.
NO, NO, NO.
NO WORD YET ON WHO THE MYSTERIOUS SIXTH MEMBER OF THE TEAM MIGHT BE...

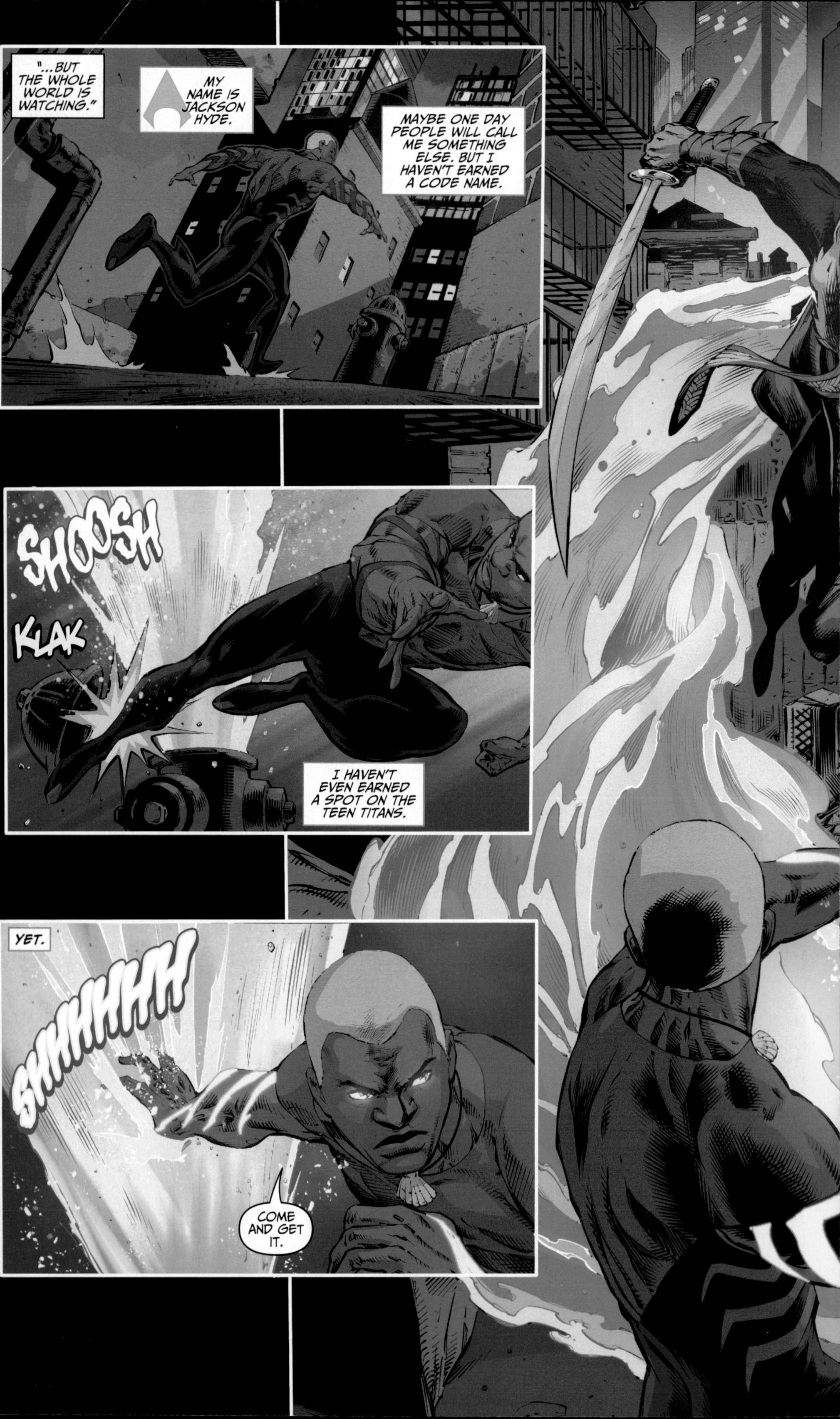
"...BUT THE WHOLE WORLD IS WATCHING."
MY NAME IS JACKSON HYDE.
MAYBE ONE DAY PEOPLE WILL CALL ME SOMETHING ELSE. BUT I HAVEN'T EARNED A CODE NAME.
SHOOSH
KLAK
I HAVEN'T EVEN EARNED A SPOT ON THE TEEN TITANS.
YET.
SHHHHHH
COME AND GET IT.

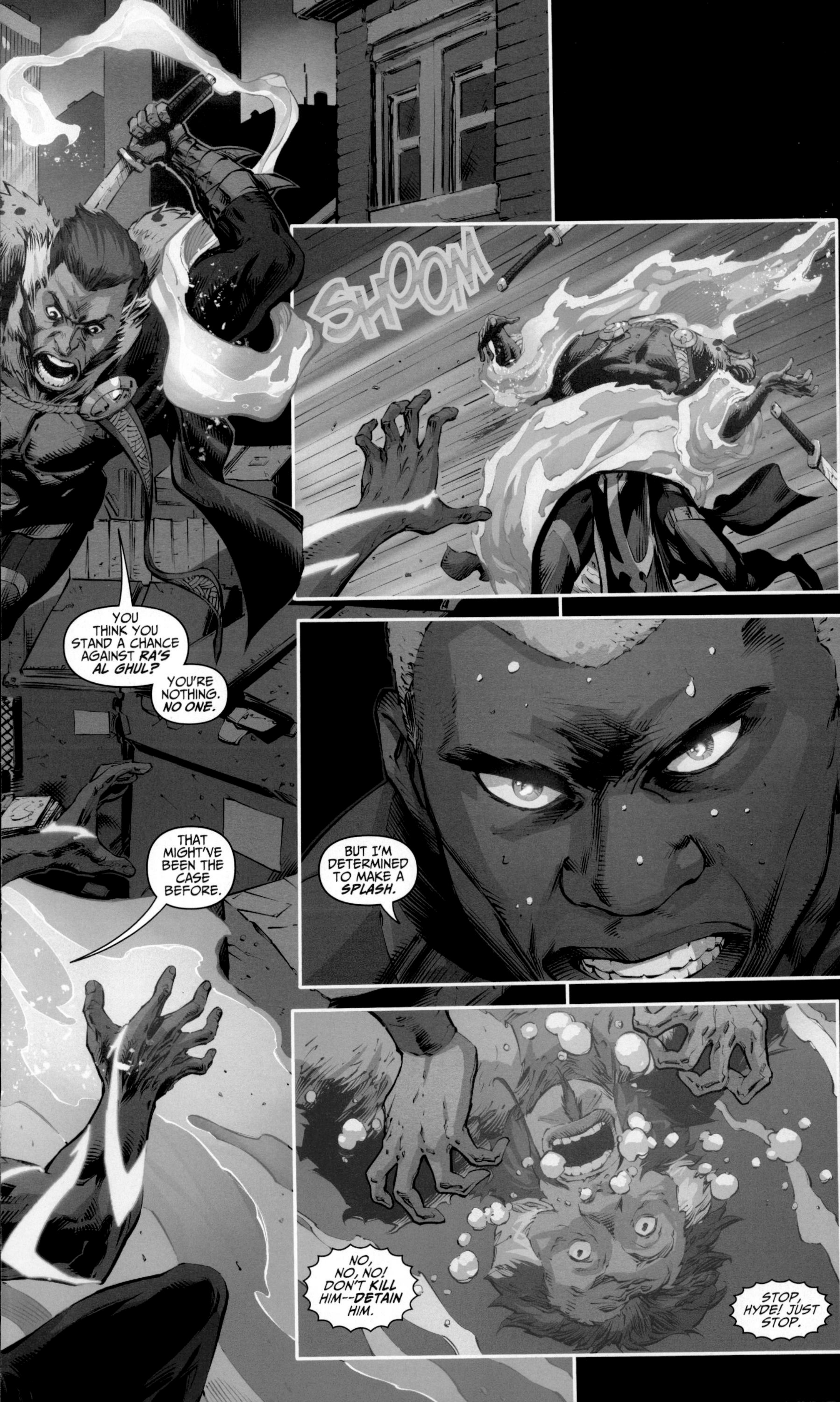
SHOOM
YOU THINK YOU STAND A CHANCE AGAINST RA'S AL GHUL?
YOU'RE NOTHING. NO ONE.
THAT MIGHT'VE BEEN THE CASE BEFORE.
BUT I'M DETERMINED TO MAKE A SPLASH.
NO, NO, NO! DON'T KILL HIM--DETAIN HIM.
STOP, HYDE! JUST STOP.

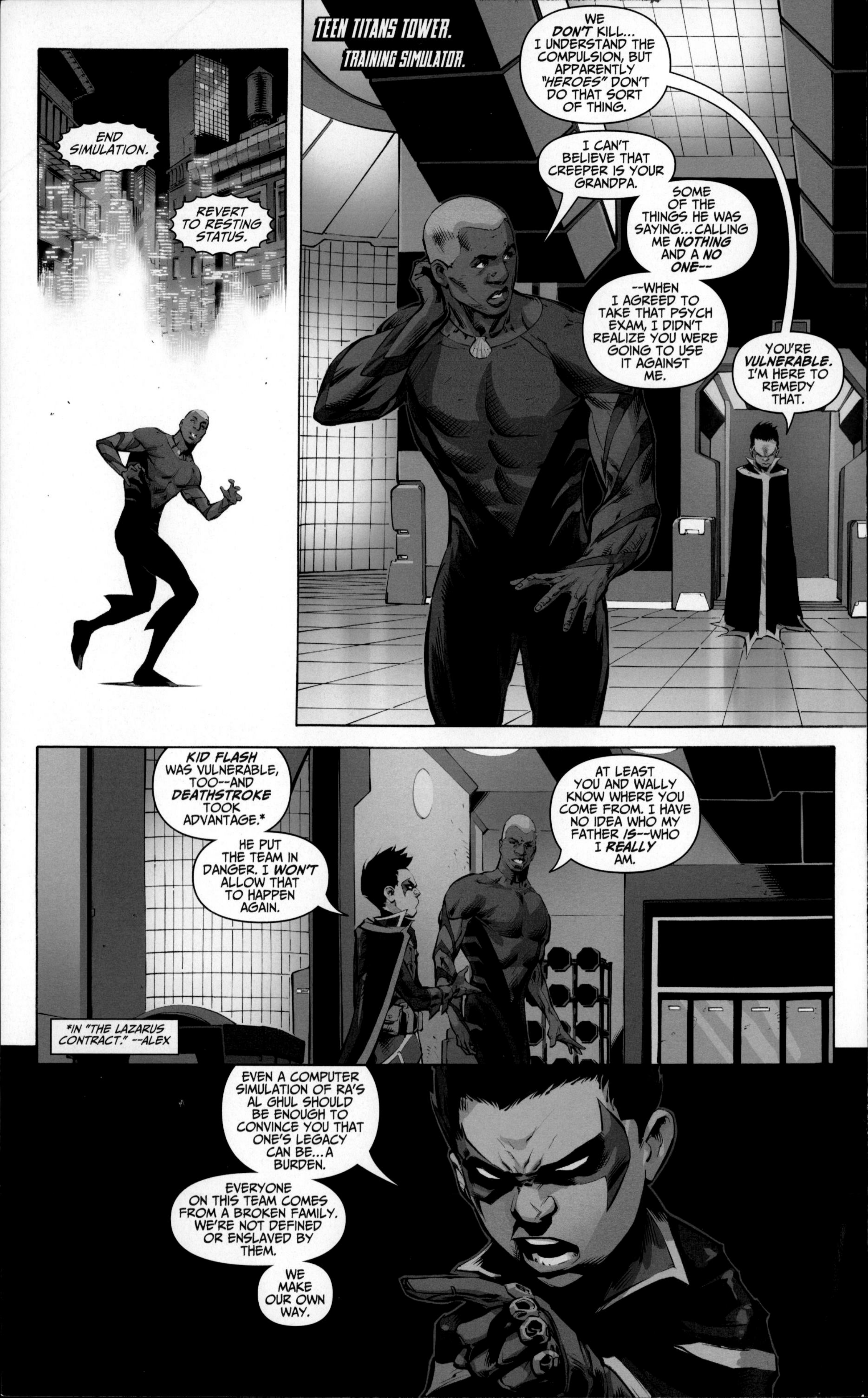
TEEN TITANS TOWER.
TRAINING SIMULATOR.
END SIMULATION.
REVERT TO RESTING STATUS.
WE DON'T KILL... I UNDERSTAND THE COMPULSION, BUT APPARENTLY "HEROES" DON'T DO THAT SORT OF THING.
I CAN'T BELIEVE THAT CREEPER IS YOUR GRANDPA.
SOME OF THE THINGS HE WAS SAYING...CALLING ME NOTHING AND A NO ONE--
--WHEN I AGREED TO TAKE THAT PSYCH EXAM, I DIDN'T REALIZE YOU WERE GOING TO USE IT AGAINST ME.
YOU'RE VULNERABLE. I'M HERE TO REMEDY THAT.
KID FLASH WAS VULNERABLE, TOO--AND DEATHSTROKE TOOK ADVANTAGE.*
HE PUT THE TEAM IN DANGER. I WON'T ALLOW THAT TO HAPPEN AGAIN.
AT LEAST YOU AND WALLY KNOW WHERE YOU COME FROM. I HAVE NO IDEA WHO MY FATHER IS--WHO I REALLY AM.
*IN "THE LAZARUS CONTRACT." --ALEX
EVEN A COMPUTER SIMULATION OF RA'S AL GHUL SHOULD BE ENOUGH TO CONVINCE YOU THAT ONE'S LEGACY CAN BE...A BURDEN.
EVERYONE ON THIS TEAM COMES FROM A BROKEN FAMILY. WE'RE NOT DEFINED OR ENSLAVED BY THEM.
WE MAKE OUR OWN WAY.

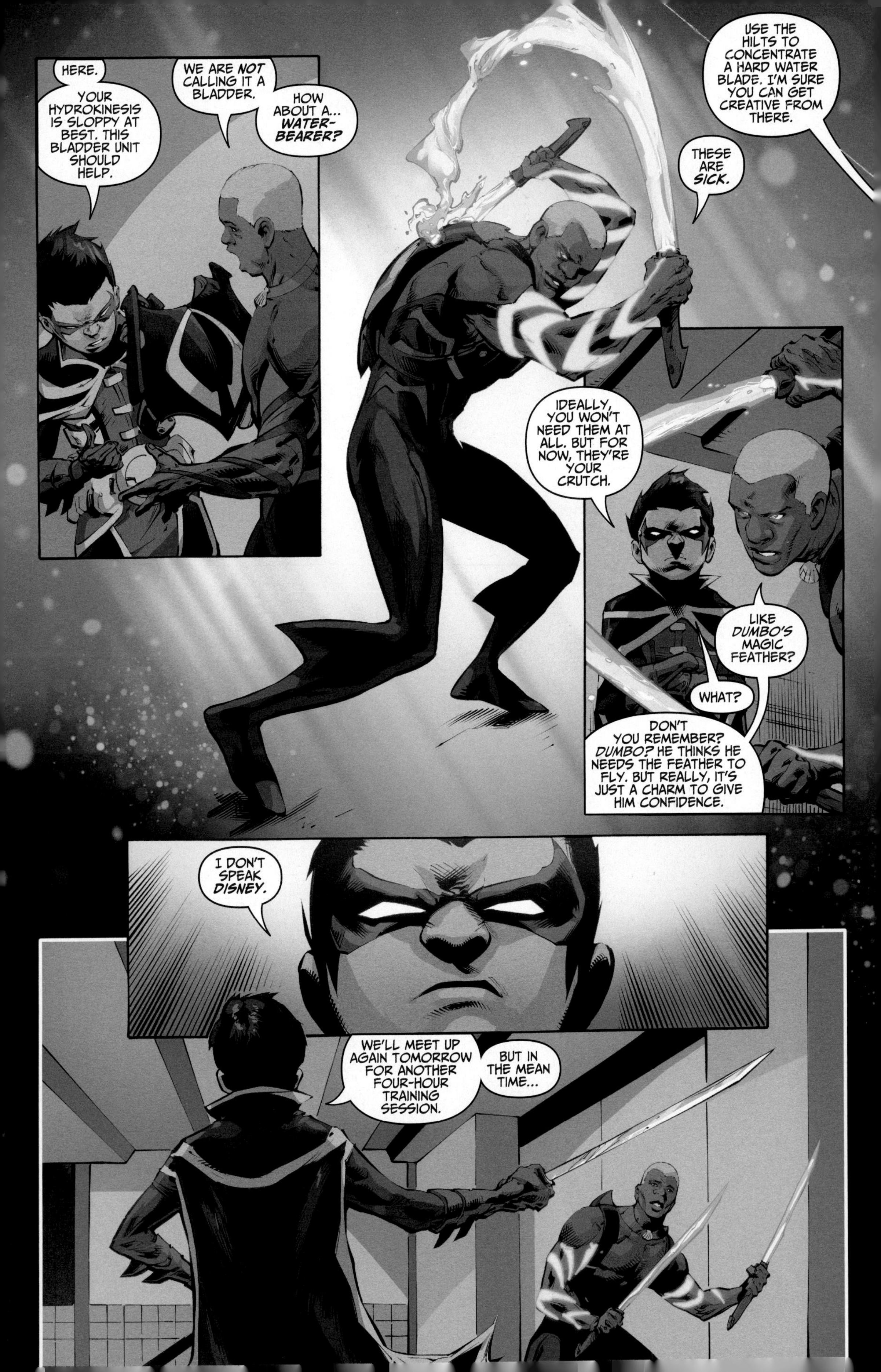
HERE.
YOUR HYDROKINESIS IS SLOPPY AT BEST. THIS BLADDER UNIT SHOULD HELP.
WE ARE NOT CALLING IT A BLADDER.
HOW ABOUT A... WATER-BEARER?
USE THE HILTS TO CONCENTRATE A HARD WATER BLADE. I'M SURE YOU CAN GET CREATIVE FROM THERE.
THESE ARE SICK.
IDEALLY, YOU WON'T NEED THEM AT ALL. BUT FOR NOW, THEY'RE YOUR CRUTCH.
LIKE DUMBO'S MAGIC FEATHER?
WHAT?
DON'T YOU REMEMBER? DUMBO? HE THINKS HE NEEDS THE FEATHER TO FLY. BUT REALLY, IT'S JUST A CHARM TO GIVE HIM CONFIDENCE.
I DON'T SPEAK DISNEY.
WE'LL MEET UP AGAIN TOMORROW FOR ANOTHER FOUR-HOUR TRAINING SESSION.
BUT IN THE MEAN TIME...

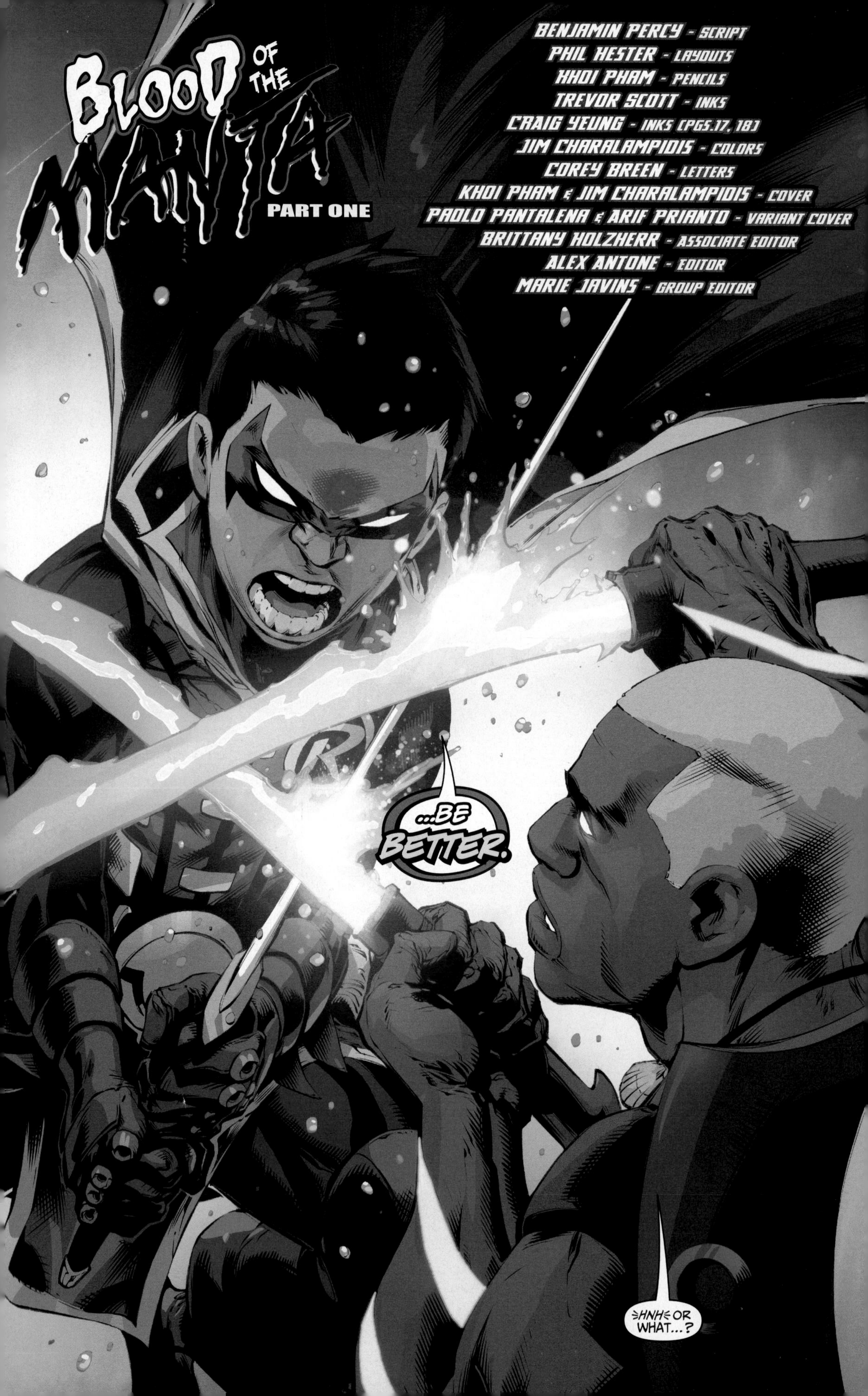
BLOOD OF THE MANTA
PART ONE
BENJAMIN PERCY - SCRIPT
PHIL HESTER - LAYOUTS
KHOI PHAM - PENCILS
TREVOR SCOTT - INKS
CRAIG YEUNG - INKS [PGS.17, 18]
JIM CHARALAMPIDIS - COLORS
COREY BREEN - LETTERS
KHOI PHAM & JIM CHARALAMPIDIS - COVER
PAOLO PANTALENA & ARIF PRIANTO - VARIANT COVER
BRITTANY HOLZHERR - ASSOCIATE EDITOR
ALEX ANTONE - EDITOR
MARIE JAVINS - GROUP EDITOR
...BE BETTER.
HNH OR WHAT...?

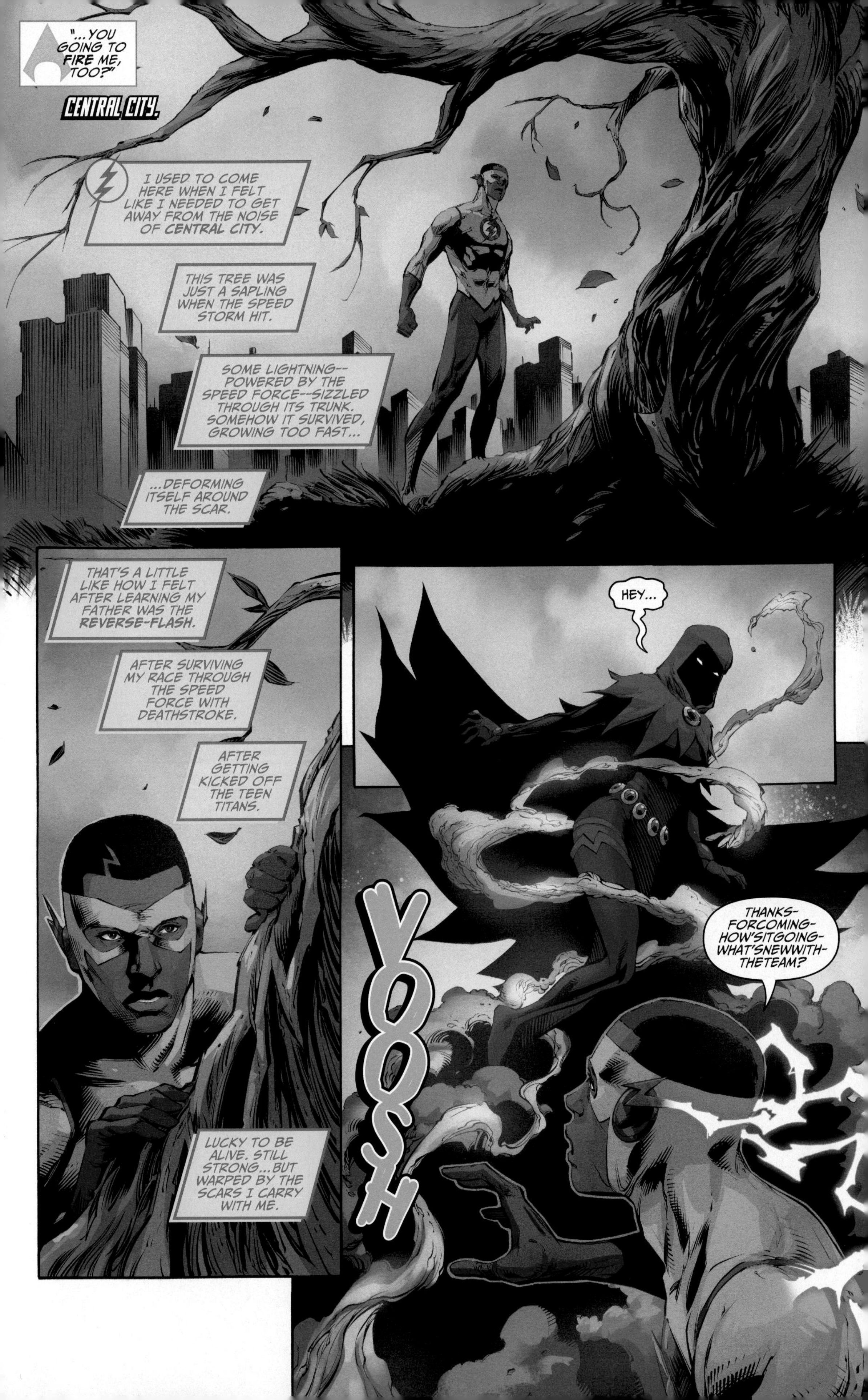
"...YOU GOING TO FIRE ME, TOO?"
CENTRAL CITY.
I USED TO COME HERE WHEN I FELT LIKE I NEEDED TO GET AWAY FROM THE NOISE OF CENTRAL CITY.
THIS TREE WAS JUST A SAPLING WHEN THE SPEED STORM HIT.
SOME LIGHTNING--POWERED BY THE SPEED FORCE--SIZZLED THROUGH ITS TRUNK. SOMEHOW IT SURVIVED, GROWING TOO FAST...
...DEFORMING ITSELF AROUND THE SCAR.
THAT'S A LITTLE LIKE HOW I FELT AFTER LEARNING MY FATHER WAS THE REVERSE-FLASH.
AFTER SURVIVING MY RACE THROUGH THE SPEED FORCE WITH DEATHSTROKE.
AFTER GETTING KICKED OFF THE TEEN TITANS.
LUCKY TO BE ALIVE. STILL STRONG...BUT WARPED BY THE SCARS I CARRY WITH ME.
HEY...
VOOSH
THANKS-FORCOMING-HOW'SITGOING-WHAT'SNEWWITH-THETEAM?

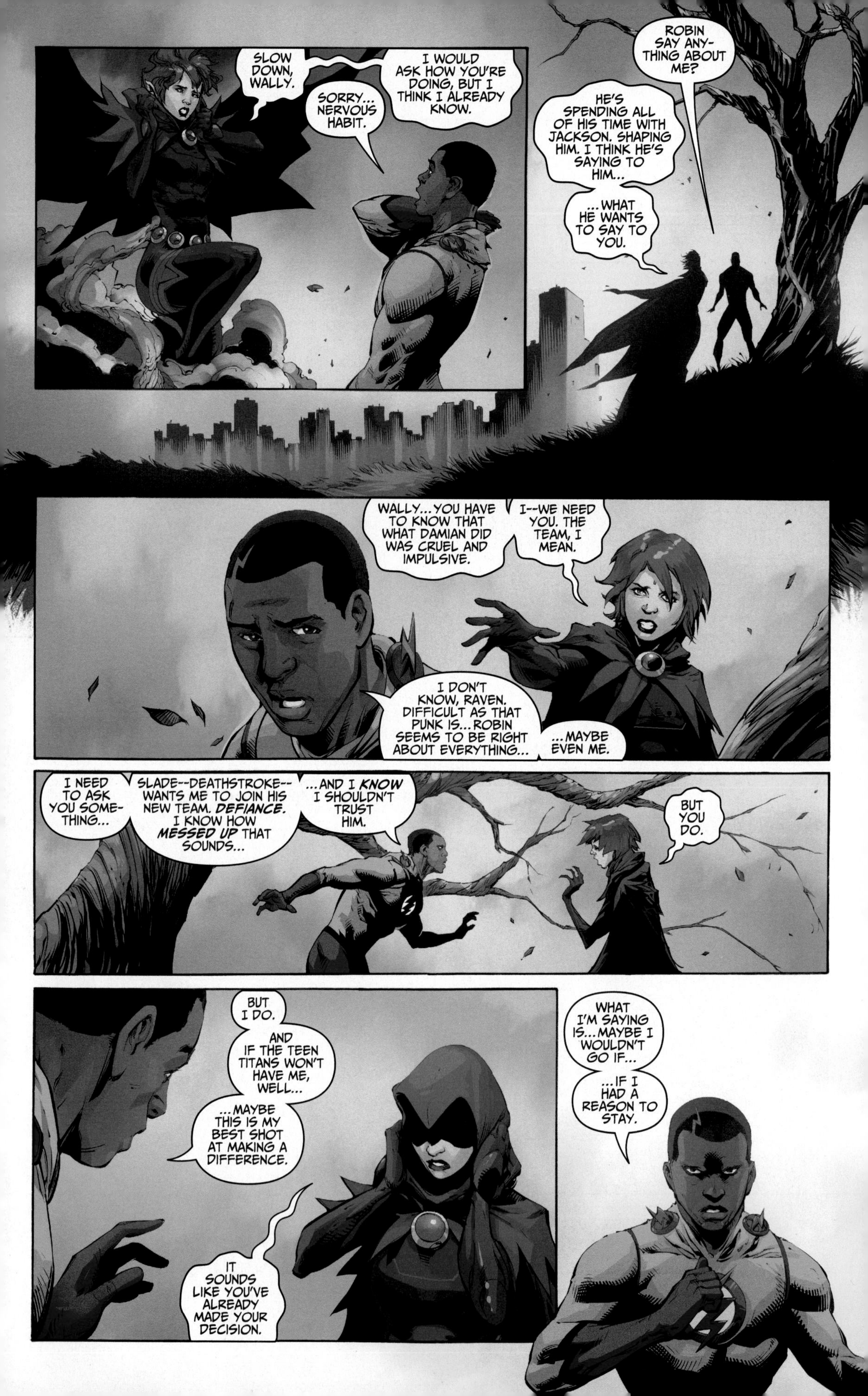
SLOW DOWN, WALLY.
SORRY... NERVOUS HABIT.
I WOULD ASK HOW YOU'RE DOING, BUT I THINK I ALREADY KNOW.
ROBIN SAY ANYTHING ABOUT ME?
HE'S SPENDING ALL OF HIS TIME WITH JACKSON. SHAPING HIM. I THINK HE'S SAYING TO HIM...
...WHAT HE WANTS TO SAY TO YOU.
WALLY...YOU HAVE TO KNOW THAT WHAT DAMIAN DID WAS CRUEL AND IMPULSIVE.
I--WE NEED YOU. THE TEAM, I MEAN.
I DON'T KNOW, RAVEN. DIFFICULT AS THAT PUNK IS...ROBIN SEEMS TO BE RIGHT ABOUT EVERYTHING...
...MAYBE EVEN ME.
I NEED TO ASK YOU SOMETHING...
SLADE--DEATHSTROKE--WANTS ME TO JOIN HIS NEW TEAM. DEFIANCE. I KNOW HOW MESSED UP THAT SOUNDS...
...AND I KNOW I SHOULDN'T TRUST HIM.
BUT YOU DO.
BUT I DO.
AND IF THE TEEN TITANS WON'T HAVE ME, WELL...
...MAYBE THIS IS MY BEST SHOT AT MAKING A DIFFERENCE.
IT SOUNDS LIKE YOU'VE ALREADY MADE YOUR DECISION.
WHAT I'M SAYING IS...MAYBE I WOULDN'T GO IF...
...IF I HAD A REASON TO STAY.

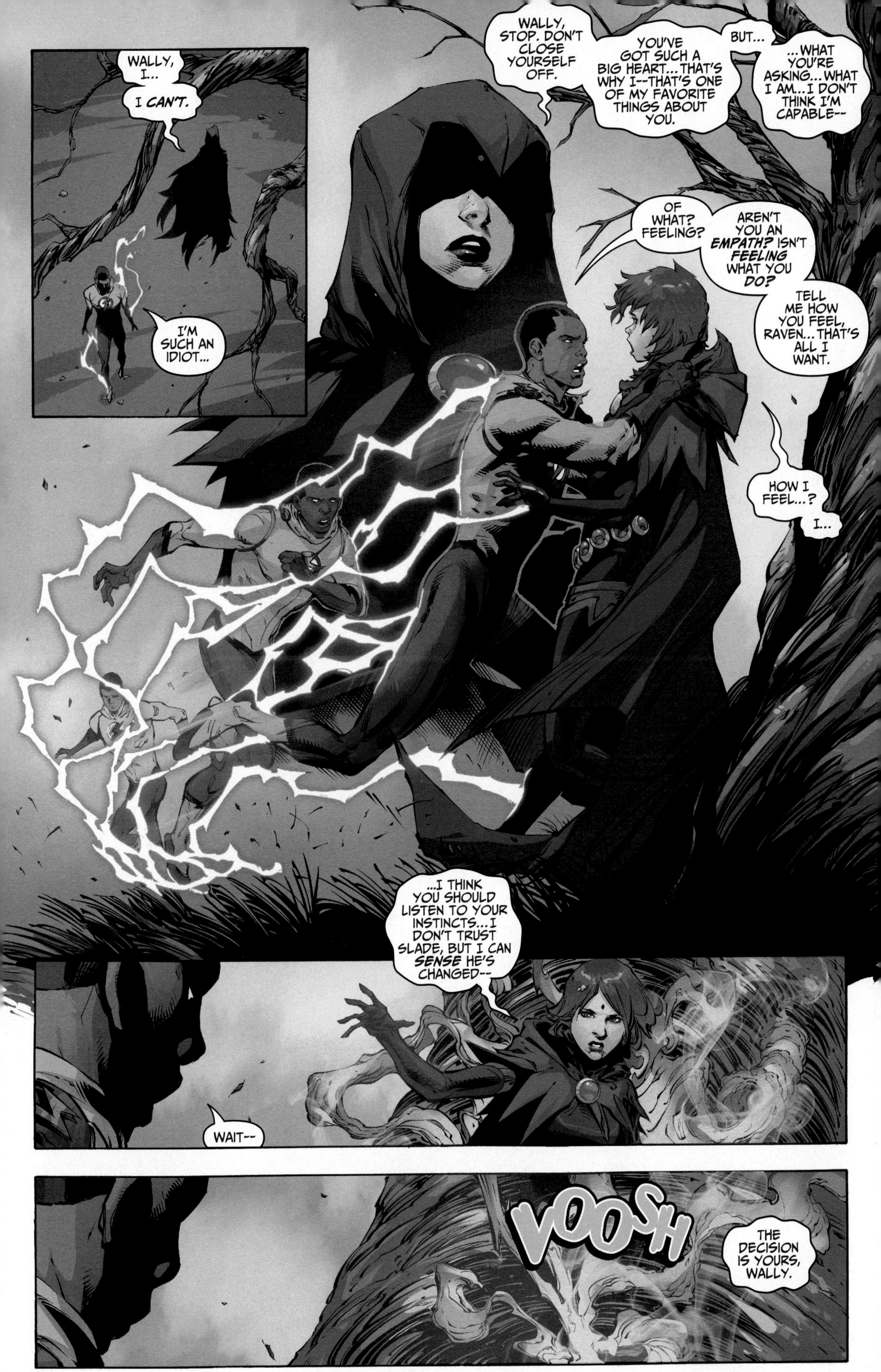
WALLY, I...
I *CAN'T.*
I'M SUCH AN IDIOT...
WALLY, STOP. DON'T CLOSE YOURSELF OFF.
YOU'VE GOT SUCH A BIG HEART...THAT'S WHY I--THAT'S ONE OF MY FAVORITE THINGS ABOUT YOU.
BUT...
...WHAT YOU'RE ASKING...WHAT I AM...I DON'T THINK I'M CAPABLE--
OF WHAT? FEELING?
AREN'T YOU AN *EMPATH?* ISN'T *FEELING* WHAT YOU *DO?*
TELL ME HOW YOU FEEL, RAVEN...THAT'S ALL I WANT.
HOW I FEEL...?
I...
...I THINK YOU SHOULD LISTEN TO YOUR INSTINCTS...I DON'T TRUST SLADE, BUT I CAN *SENSE* HE'S CHANGED--
WAIT--
VOOSH
THE DECISION IS YOURS, WALLY.

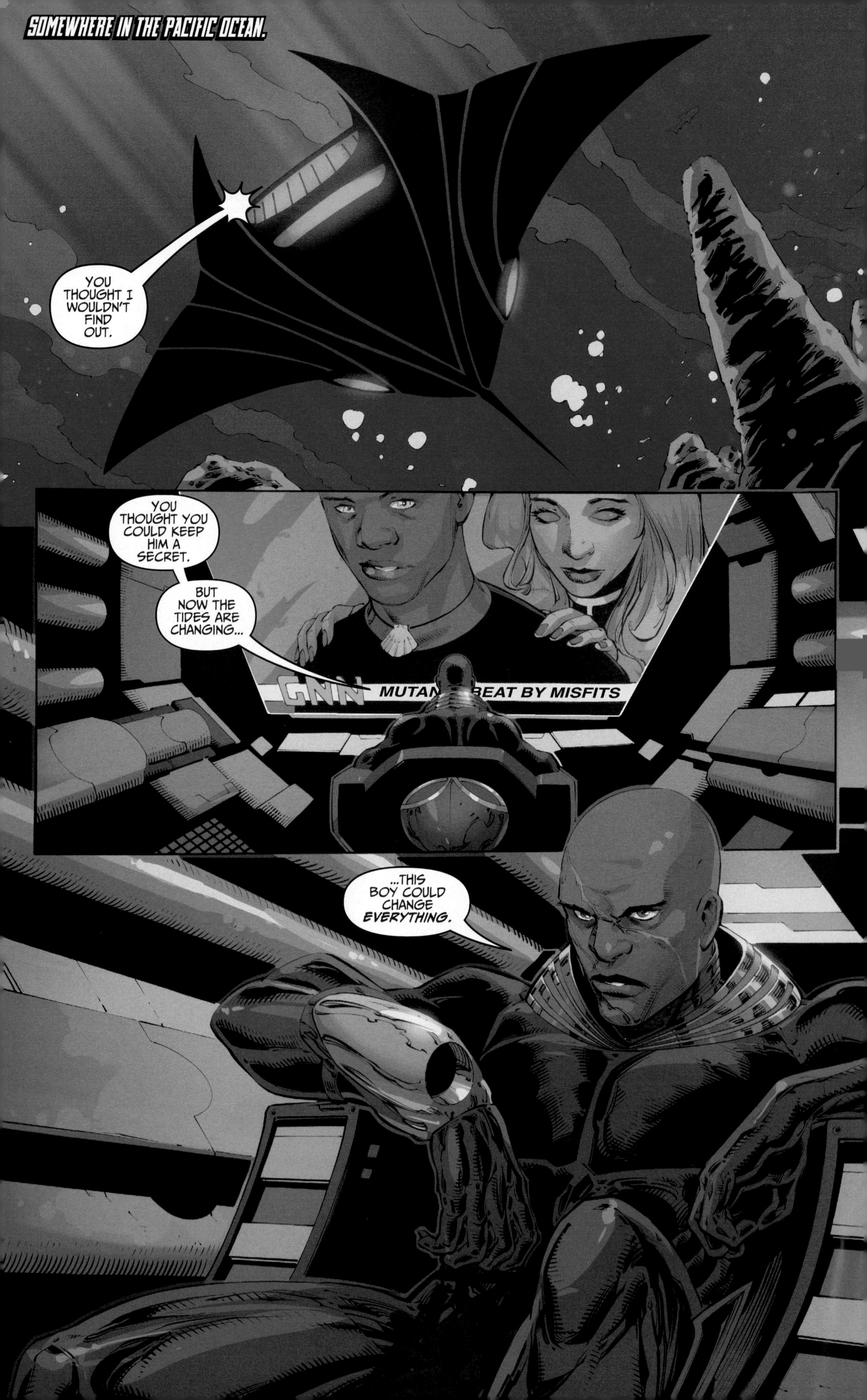
SOMEWHERE IN THE PACIFIC OCEAN.
YOU THOUGHT I WOULDN'T FIND OUT.
YOU THOUGHT YOU COULD KEEP HIM A SECRET.
BUT NOW THE TIDES ARE CHANGING...
GNN
MUTAN BEAT BY MISFITS
...THIS BOY COULD CHANGE EVERYTHING.

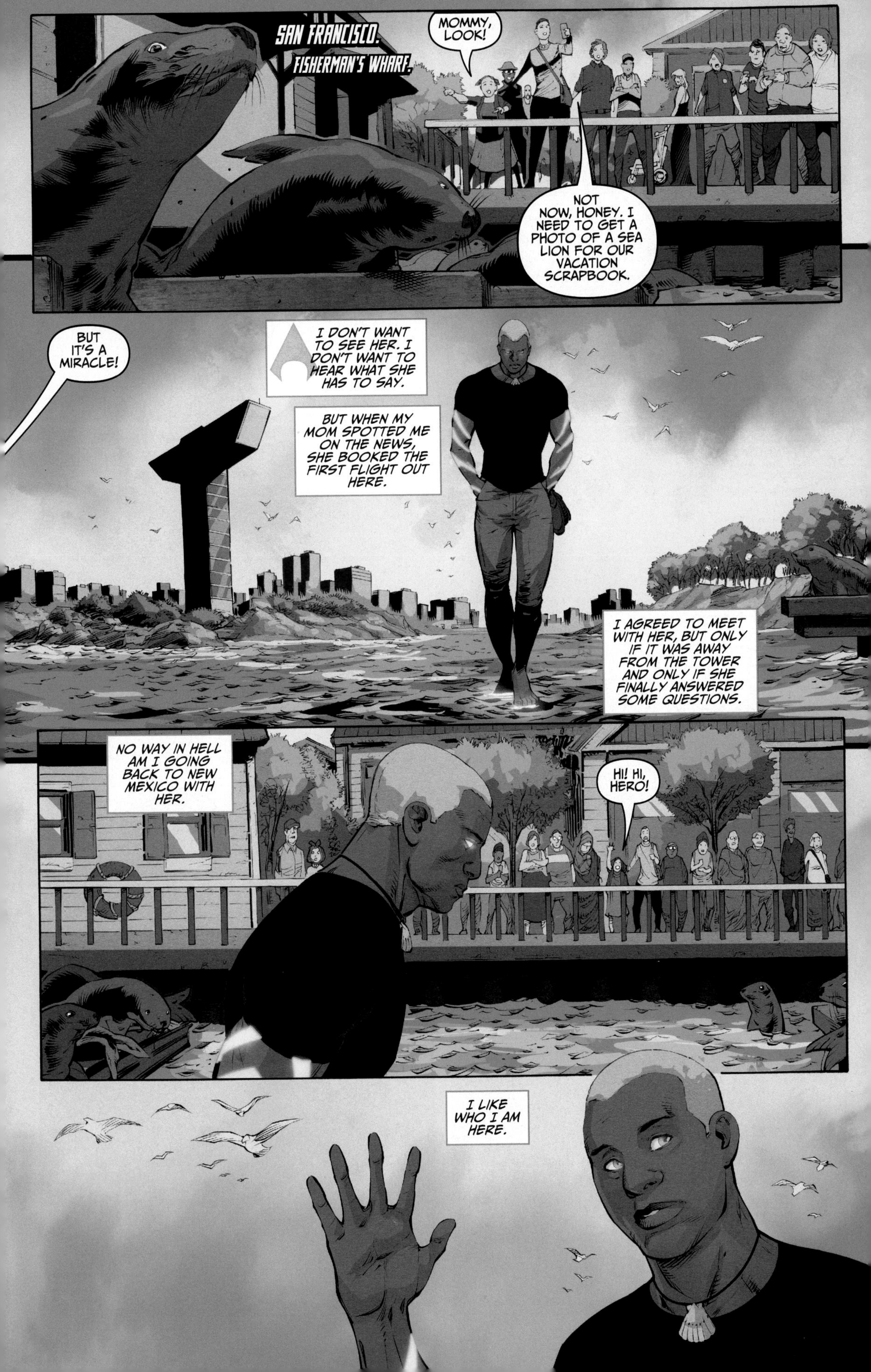
SAN FRANCISCO.
FISHERMAN'S WHARF.
MOMMY, LOOK!
NOT NOW, HONEY. I NEED TO GET A PHOTO OF A SEA LION FOR OUR VACATION SCRAPBOOK.
BUT IT'S A MIRACLE!
I DON'T WANT TO SEE HER. I DON'T WANT TO HEAR WHAT SHE HAS TO SAY.
BUT WHEN MY MOM SPOTTED ME ON THE NEWS, SHE BOOKED THE FIRST FLIGHT OUT HERE.
I AGREED TO MEET WITH HER, BUT ONLY IF IT WAS AWAY FROM THE TOWER AND ONLY IF SHE FINALLY ANSWERED SOME QUESTIONS.
NO WAY IN HELL AM I GOING BACK TO NEW MEXICO WITH HER.
HI! HI, HERO!
I LIKE WHO I AM HERE.

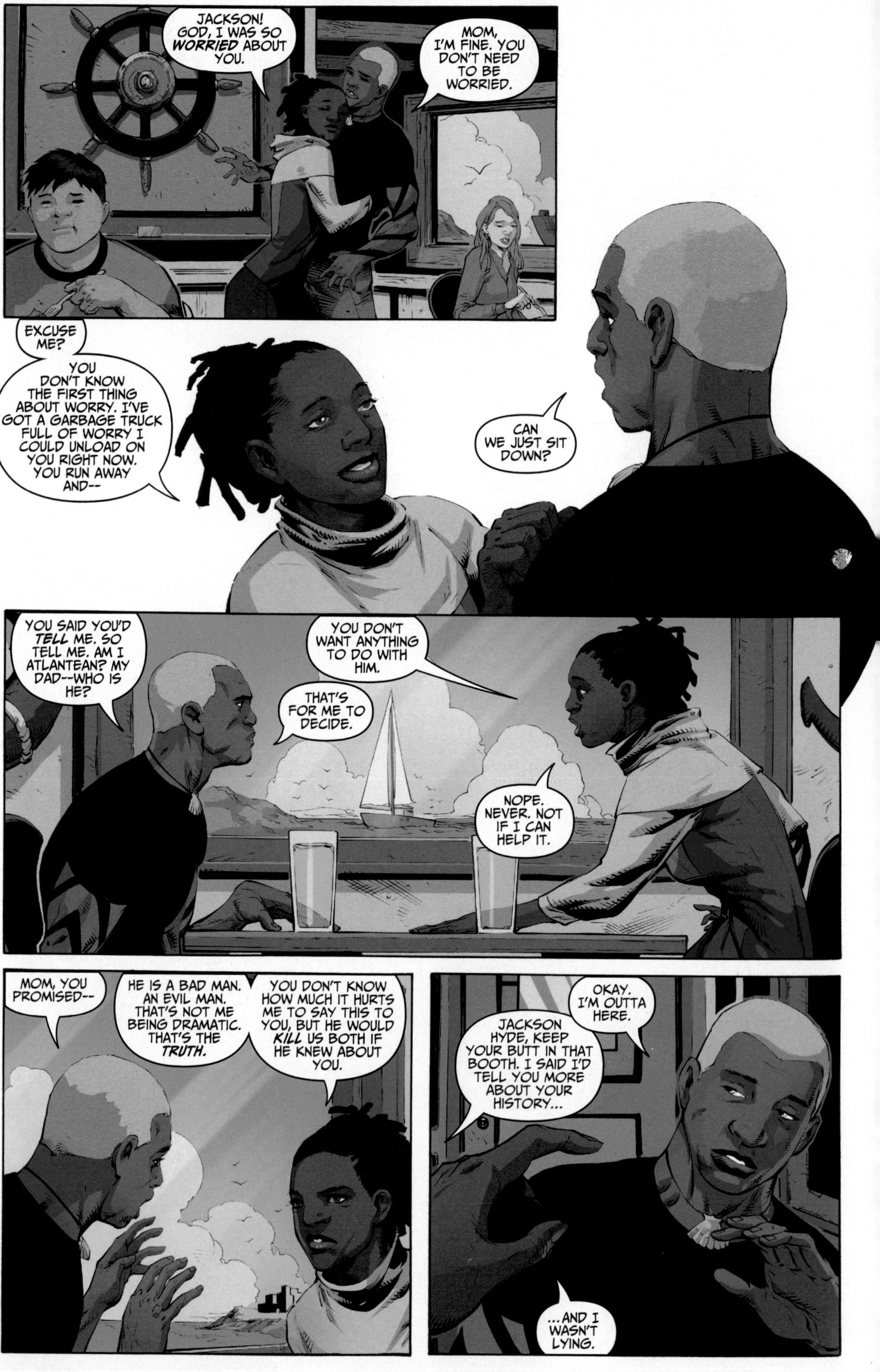
JACKSON! GOD, I WAS SO WORRIED ABOUT YOU.
MOM, I'M FINE. YOU DON'T NEED TO BE WORRIED.
EXCUSE ME?
YOU DON'T KNOW THE FIRST THING ABOUT WORRY. I'VE GOT A GARBAGE TRUCK FULL OF WORRY I COULD UNLOAD ON YOU RIGHT NOW. YOU RUN AWAY AND--
CAN WE JUST SIT DOWN?
YOU SAID YOU'D TELL ME. SO TELL ME. AM I ATLANTEAN? MY DAD--WHO IS HE?
YOU DON'T WANT ANYTHING TO DO WITH HIM.
THAT'S FOR ME TO DECIDE.
NOPE. NEVER. NOT IF I CAN HELP IT.
MOM, YOU PROMISED--
HE IS A BAD MAN. AN EVIL MAN. THAT'S NOT ME BEING DRAMATIC. THAT'S THE TRUTH.
YOU DON'T KNOW HOW MUCH IT HURTS ME TO SAY THIS TO YOU, BUT HE WOULD KILL US BOTH IF HE KNEW ABOUT YOU.
OKAY. I'M OUTTA HERE.
JACKSON HYDE, KEEP YOUR BUTT IN THAT BOOTH. I SAID I'D TELL YOU MORE ABOUT YOUR HISTORY...
...AND I WASN'T LYING.

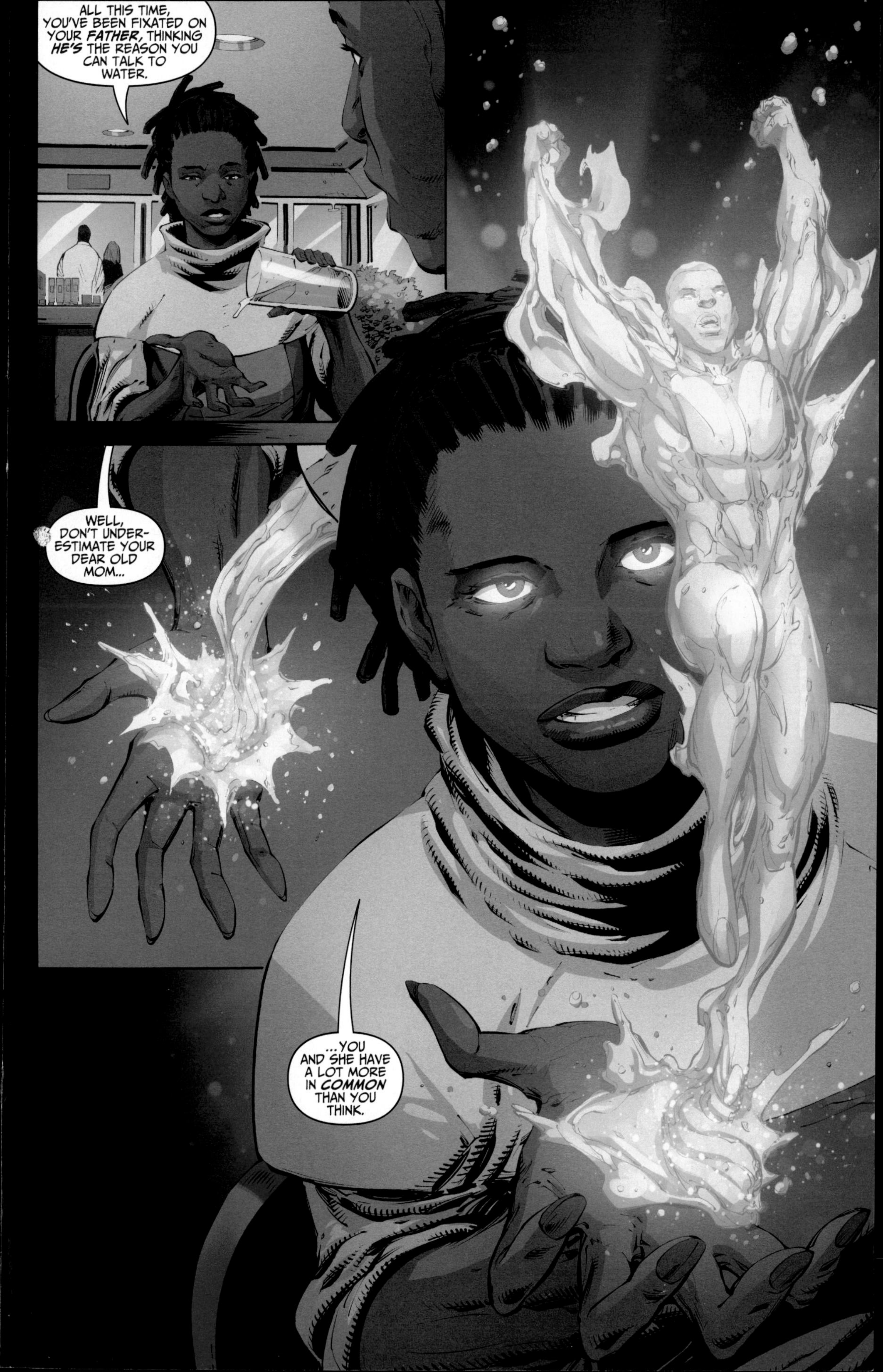
ALL THIS TIME, YOU'VE BEEN FIXATED ON YOUR ***FATHER,*** THINKING ***HE'S*** THE REASON YOU CAN TALK TO WATER.
WELL, DON'T UNDER-ESTIMATE YOUR DEAR OLD MOM...
...YOU AND SHE HAVE A LOT MORE IN ***COMMON*** THAN YOU THINK.

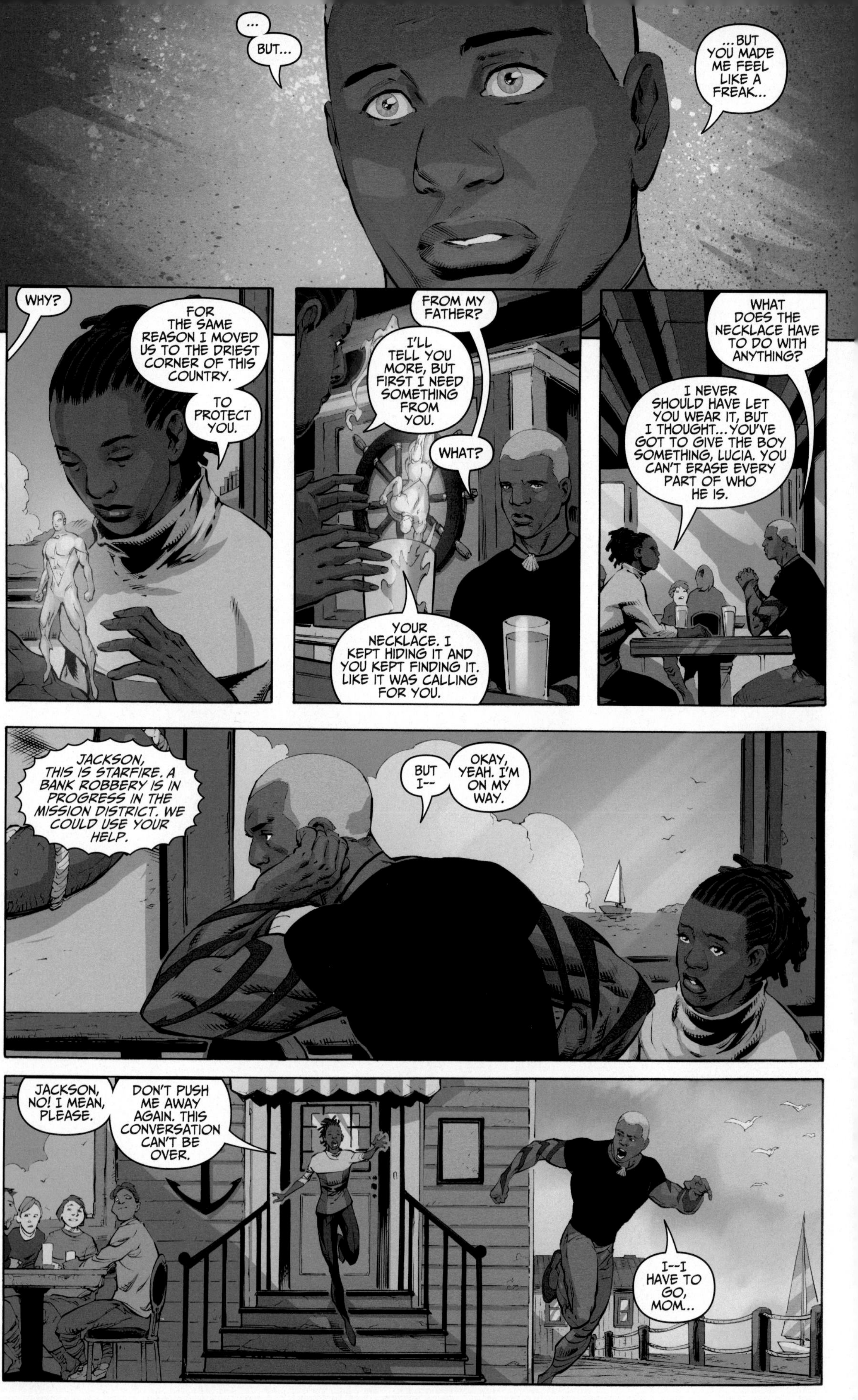
...
BUT...
...BUT YOU MADE ME FEEL LIKE A FREAK...
WHY?
FOR THE SAME REASON I MOVED US TO THE DRIEST CORNER OF THIS COUNTRY.
TO PROTECT YOU.
FROM MY FATHER?
I'LL TELL YOU MORE, BUT FIRST I NEED SOMETHING FROM YOU.
WHAT?
YOUR NECKLACE. I KEPT HIDING IT AND YOU KEPT FINDING IT. LIKE IT WAS CALLING FOR YOU.
WHAT DOES THE NECKLACE HAVE TO DO WITH ANYTHING?
I NEVER SHOULD HAVE LET YOU WEAR IT, BUT I THOUGHT...YOU'VE GOT TO GIVE THE BOY SOMETHING, LUCIA. YOU CAN'T ERASE EVERY PART OF WHO HE IS.
JACKSON, THIS IS STARFIRE. A BANK ROBBERY IS IN PROGRESS IN THE MISSION DISTRICT. WE COULD USE YOUR HELP.
BUT I--
OKAY, YEAH. I'M ON MY WAY.
JACKSON, NO! I MEAN, PLEASE.
DON'T PUSH ME AWAY AGAIN. THIS CONVERSATION CAN'T BE OVER.
I--I HAVE TO GO, MOM...

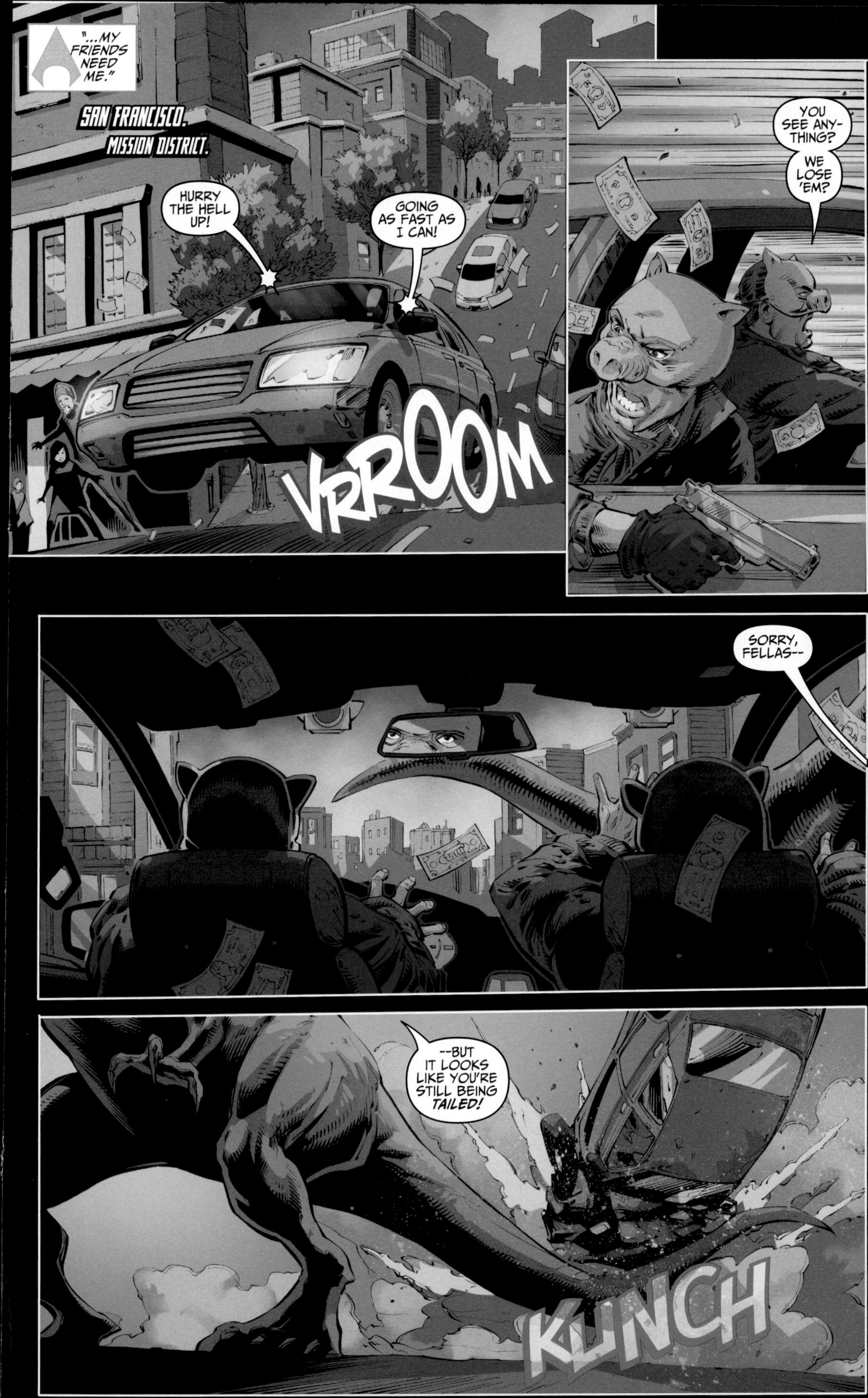
"...MY FRIENDS NEED ME."
SAN FRANCISCO. MISSION DISTRICT.
HURRY THE HELL UP!
GOING AS FAST AS I CAN!
VRROOM
YOU SEE ANY-THING?
WE LOSE 'EM?
SORRY, FELLAS--
--BUT IT LOOKS LIKE YOU'RE STILL BEING TAILED!
KLUNCH

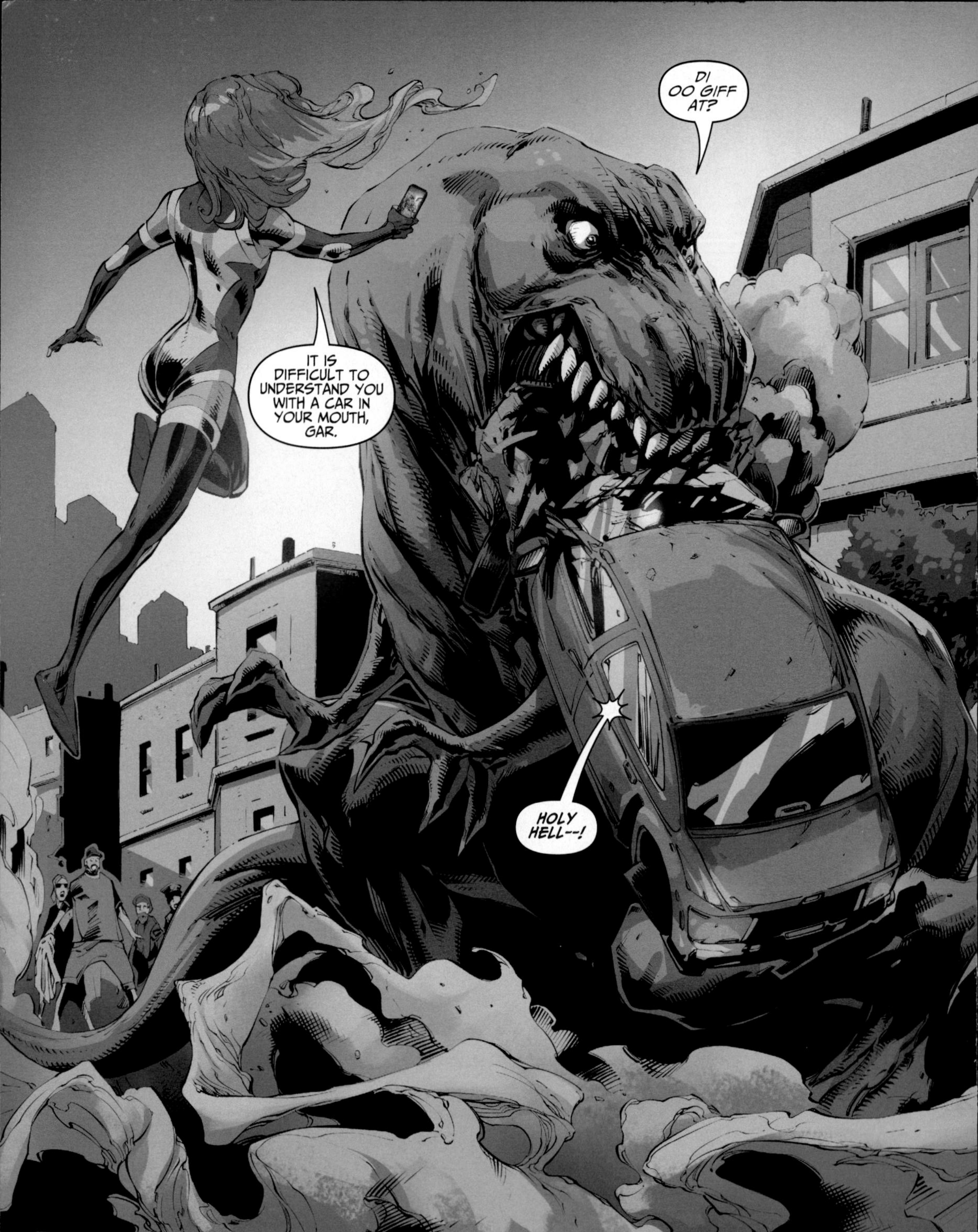
DI OO GIFF AT?
IT IS DIFFICULT TO UNDERSTAND YOU WITH A CAR IN YOUR MOUTH, GAR.
HOLY HELL--!

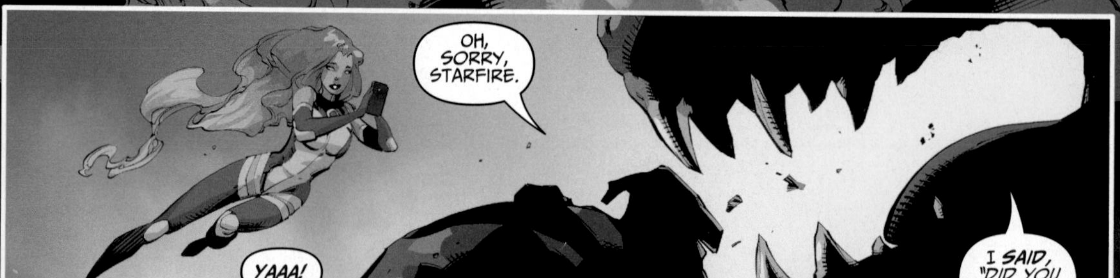
OH, SORRY, STARFIRE.
YAAA!
I SAID, "DID YOU GET THAT?"

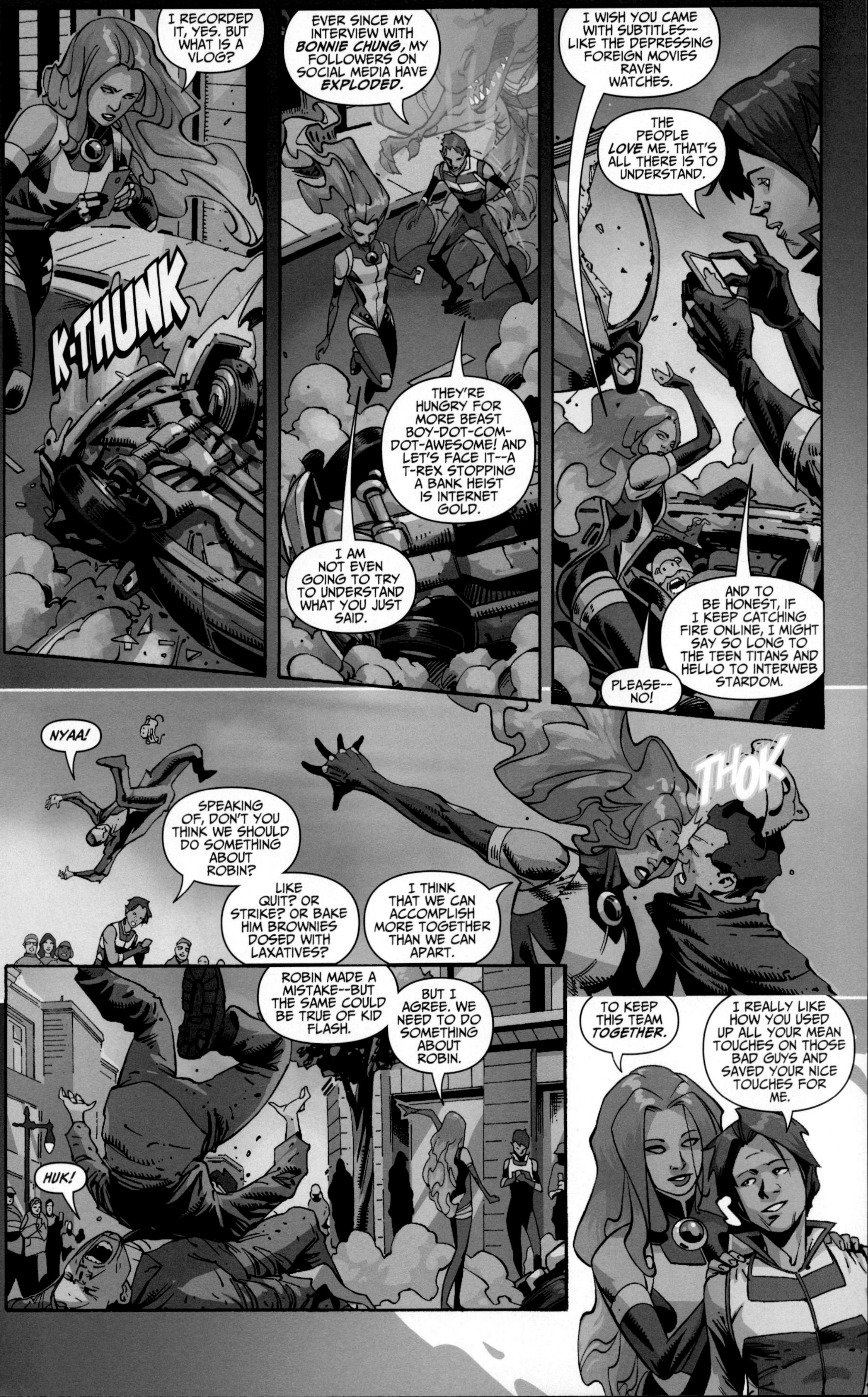
I RECORDED IT, YES. BUT WHAT IS A VLOG?
K-THUNK
EVER SINCE MY INTERVIEW WITH BONNIE CHUNG, MY FOLLOWERS ON SOCIAL MEDIA HAVE EXPLODED.
THEY'RE HUNGRY FOR MORE BEAST BOY-DOT-COM-DOT-AWESOME! AND LET'S FACE IT--A T-REX STOPPING A BANK HEIST IS INTERNET GOLD.
I AM NOT EVEN GOING TO TRY TO UNDERSTAND WHAT YOU JUST SAID.
I WISH YOU CAME WITH SUBTITLES--LIKE THE DEPRESSING FOREIGN MOVIES RAVEN WATCHES.
THE PEOPLE LOVE ME. THAT'S ALL THERE IS TO UNDERSTAND.
AND TO BE HONEST, IF I KEEP CATCHING FIRE ONLINE, I MIGHT SAY SO LONG TO THE TEEN TITANS AND HELLO TO INTERWEB STARDOM.
PLEASE--NO!
NYAA!
THOK
SPEAKING OF, DON'T YOU THINK WE SHOULD DO SOMETHING ABOUT ROBIN?
LIKE QUIT? OR STRIKE? OR BAKE HIM BROWNIES DOSED WITH LAXATIVES?
I THINK THAT WE CAN ACCOMPLISH MORE TOGETHER THAN WE CAN APART.
ROBIN MADE A MISTAKE--BUT THE SAME COULD BE TRUE OF KID FLASH.
BUT I AGREE. WE NEED TO DO SOMETHING ABOUT ROBIN.
HUK!
TO KEEP THIS TEAM TOGETHER.
I REALLY LIKE HOW YOU USED UP ALL YOUR MEAN TOUCHES ON THOSE BAD GUYS AND SAVED YOUR NICE TOUCHES FOR ME.

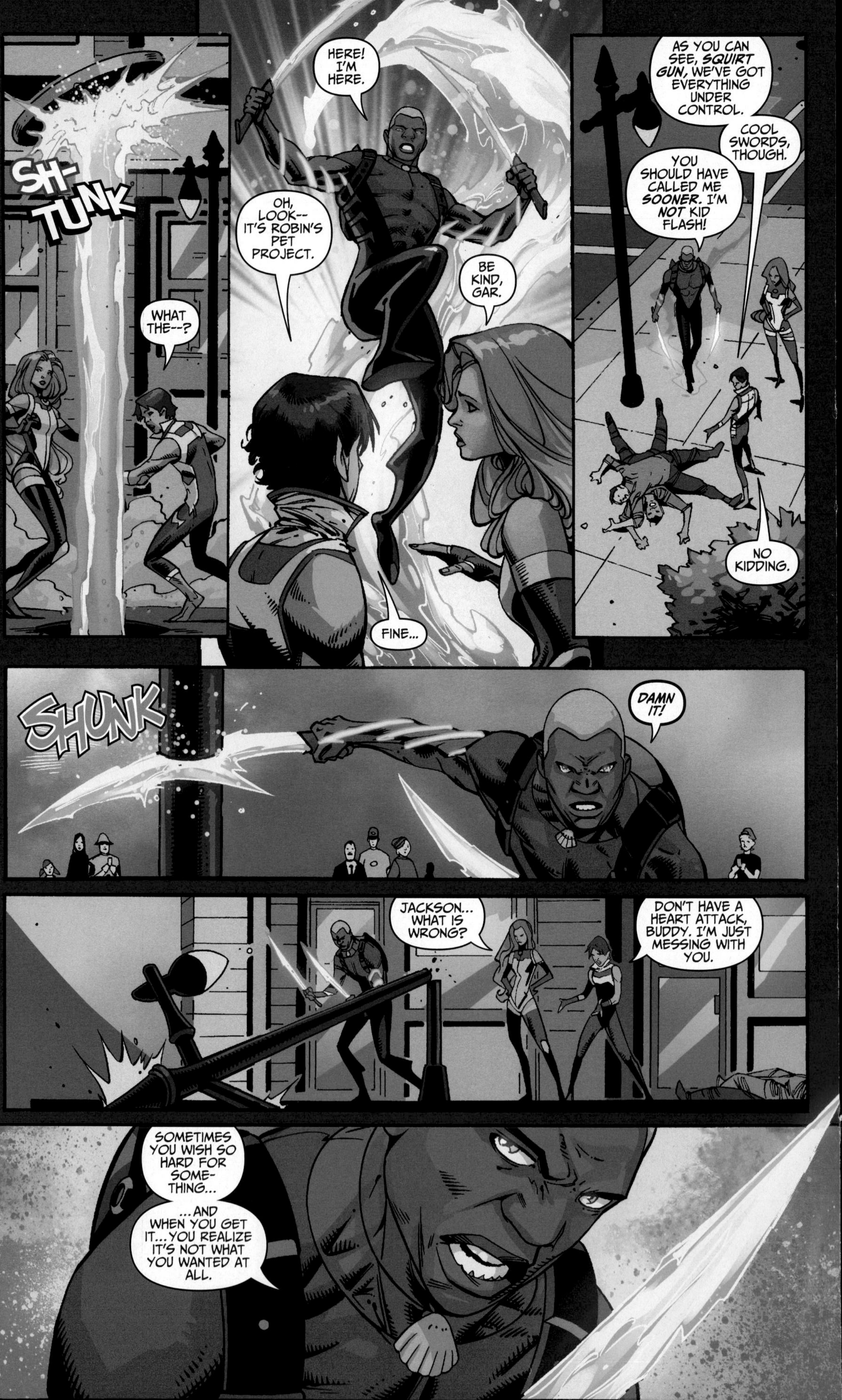
SH-TUNK
WHAT THE--?
HERE! I'M HERE.
OH, LOOK-- IT'S ROBIN'S PET PROJECT.
BE KIND, GAR.
FINE...
AS YOU CAN SEE, SQUIRT GUN, WE'VE GOT EVERYTHING UNDER CONTROL.
COOL SWORDS, THOUGH.
YOU SHOULD HAVE CALLED ME SOONER. I'M NOT KID FLASH!
NO KIDDING.
SHUNK
DAMN IT!
JACKSON... WHAT IS WRONG?
DON'T HAVE A HEART ATTACK, BUDDY. I'M JUST MESSING WITH YOU.
SOMETIMES YOU WISH SO HARD FOR SOMETHING...
...AND WHEN YOU GET IT...YOU REALIZE IT'S NOT WHAT YOU WANTED AT ALL.

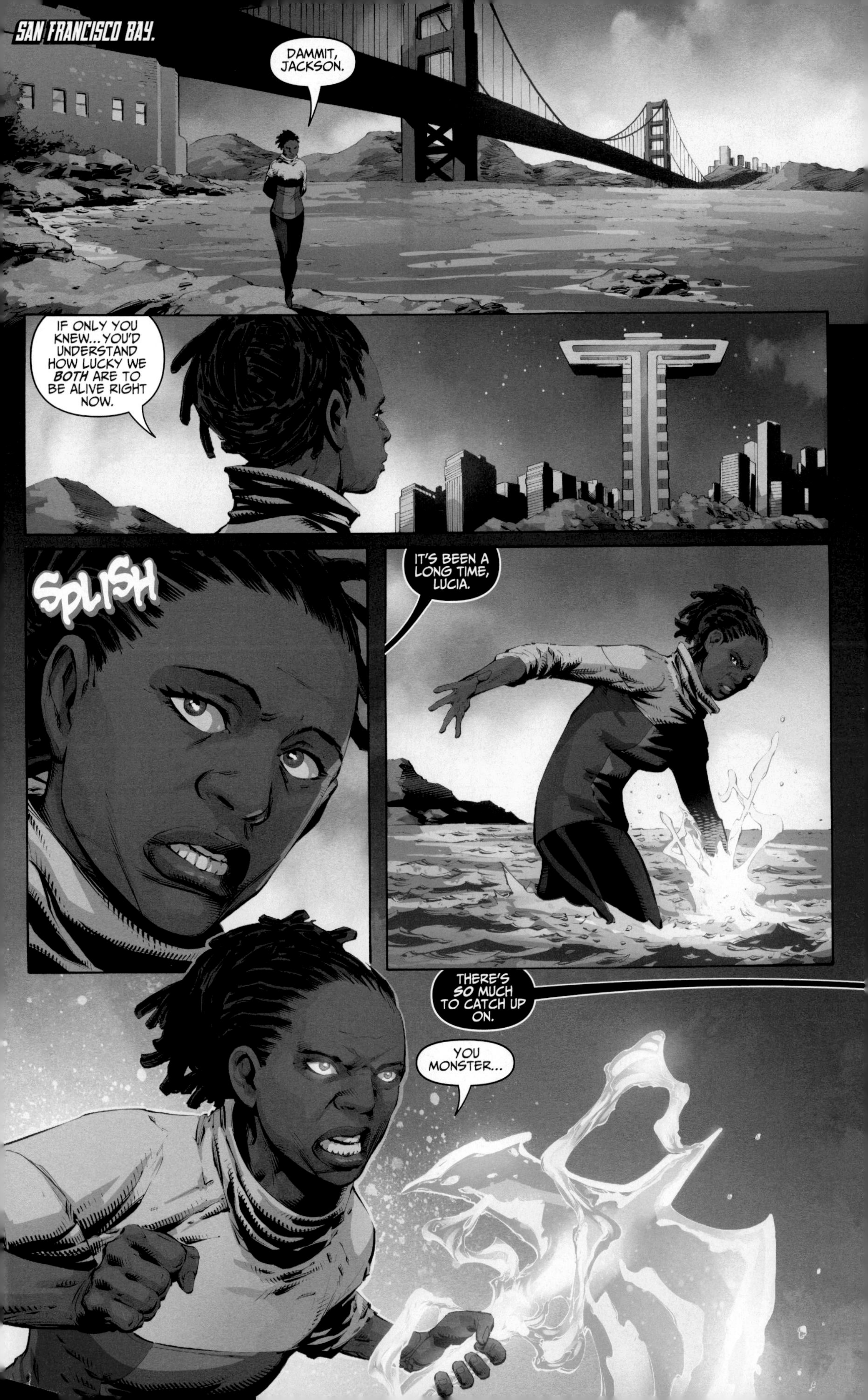
SAN FRANCISCO BAY.
DAMMIT, JACKSON.
IF ONLY YOU KNEW...YOU'D UNDERSTAND HOW LUCKY WE BOTH ARE TO BE ALIVE RIGHT NOW.
SPLISH
IT'S BEEN A LONG TIME, LUCIA.
THERE'S SO MUCH TO CATCH UP ON.
YOU MONSTER...

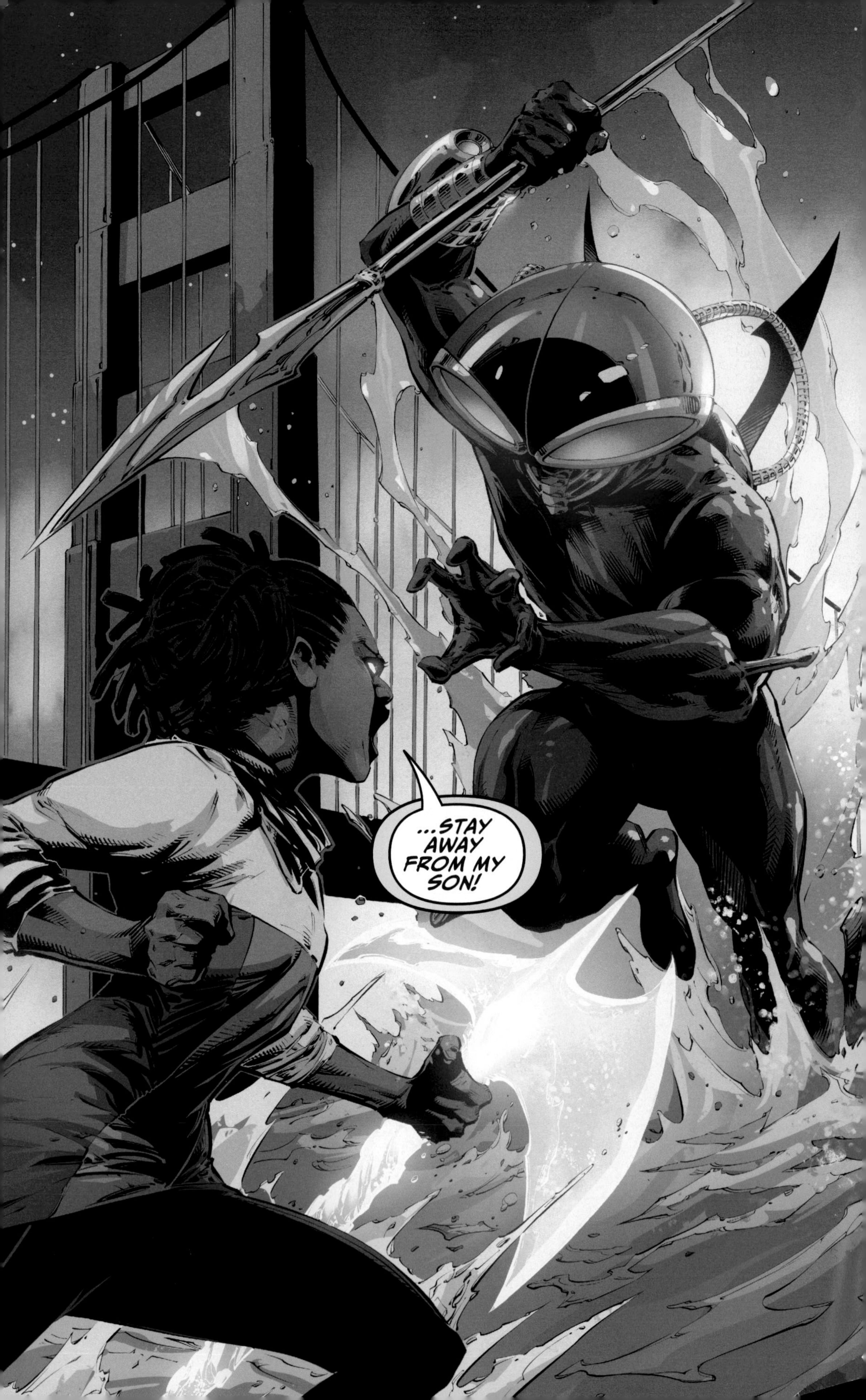
...STAY AWAY FROM MY SON!

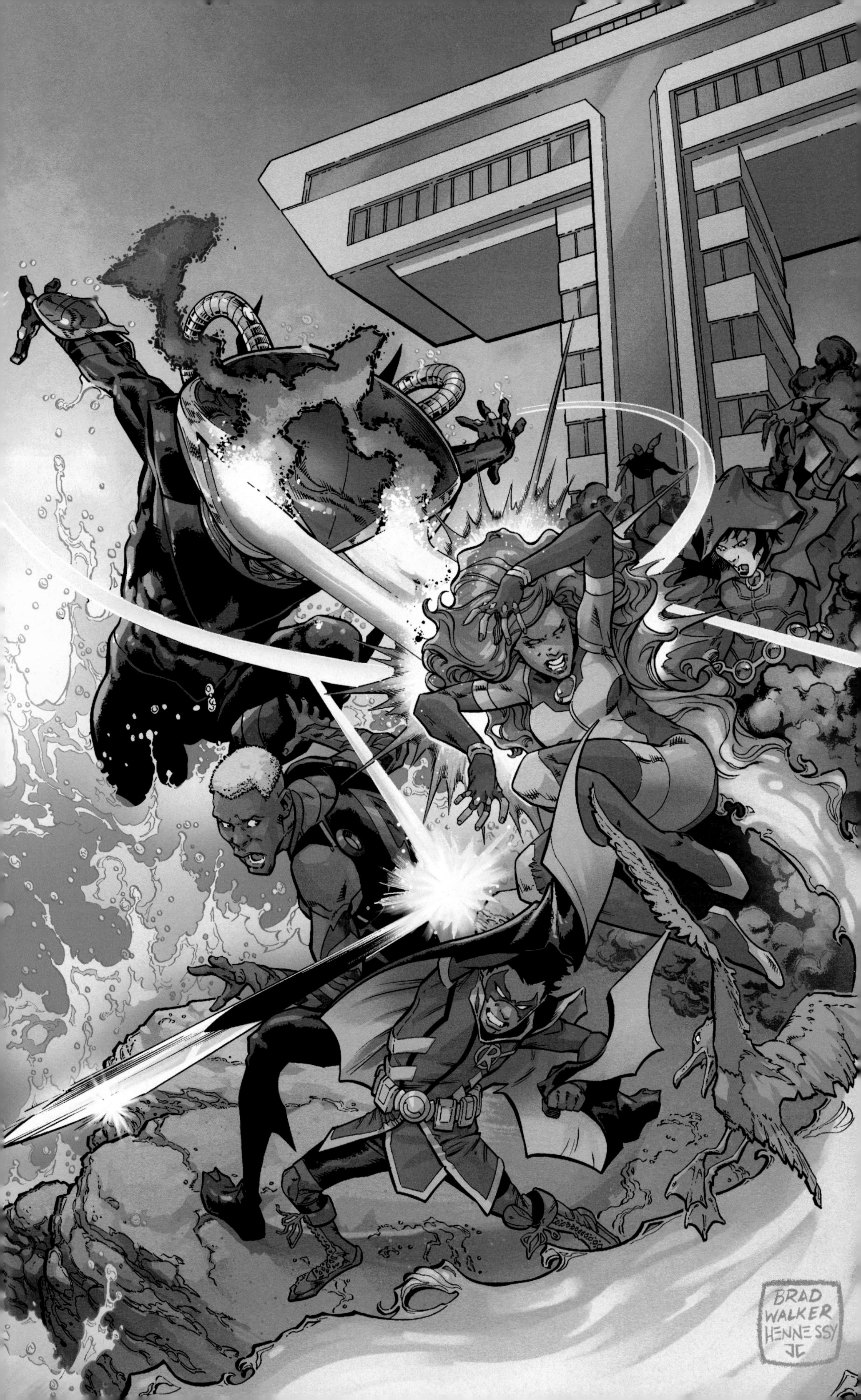
BRAD
WALKER
HENNESSY
JC

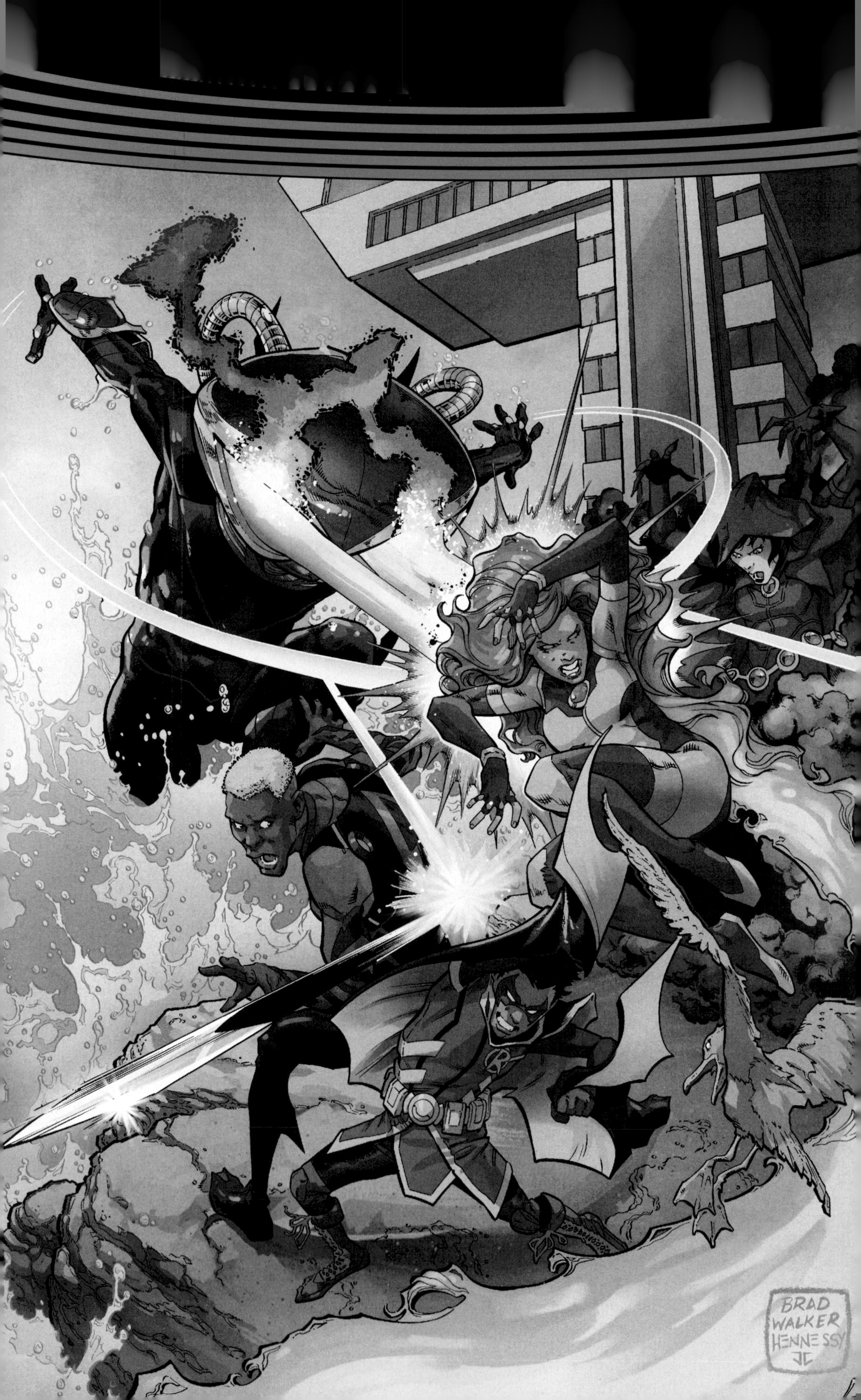
BRAD
WALKER
HENNESSY
JC

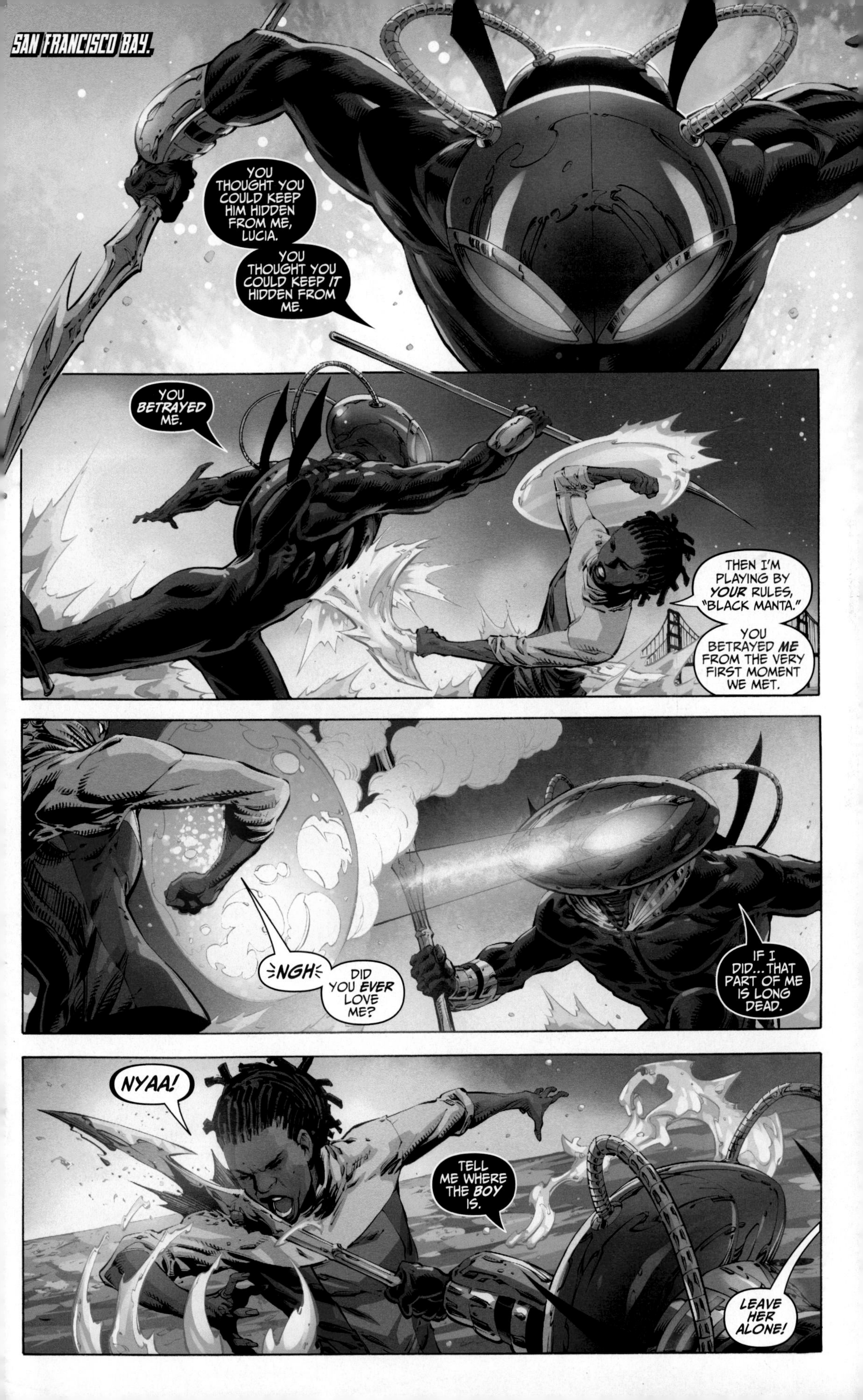
SAN FRANCISCO BAY.
YOU THOUGHT YOU COULD KEEP HIM HIDDEN FROM ME, LUCIA.
YOU THOUGHT YOU COULD KEEP IT HIDDEN FROM ME.
YOU BETRAYED ME.
THEN I'M PLAYING BY YOUR RULES, "BLACK MANTA."
YOU BETRAYED ME FROM THE VERY FIRST MOMENT WE MET.
NGH
DID YOU EVER LOVE ME?
IF I DID... THAT PART OF ME IS LONG DEAD.
NYAA!
TELL ME WHERE THE BOY IS.
LEAVE HER ALONE!

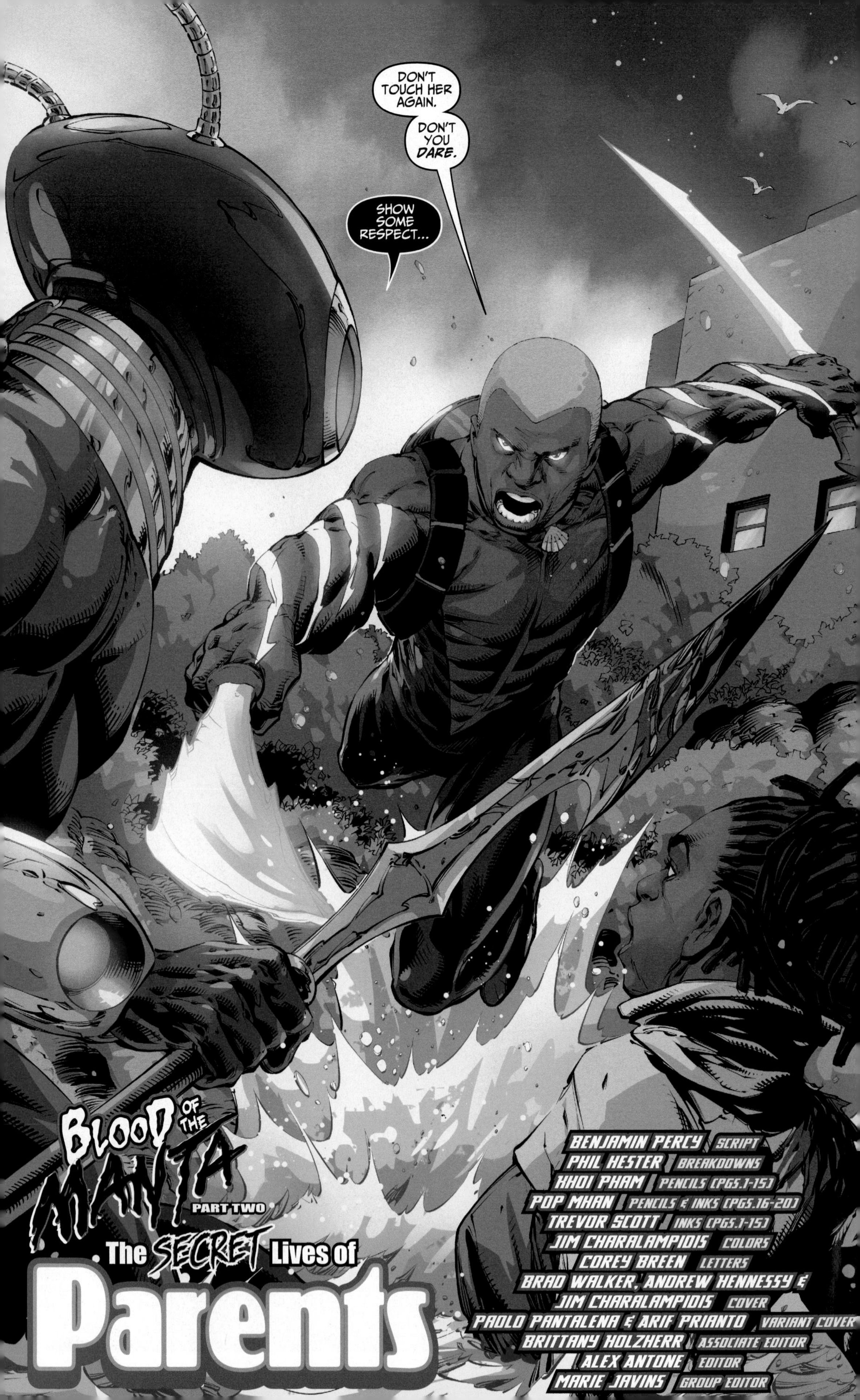
DON'T TOUCH HER AGAIN.
DON'T YOU DARE.
SHOW SOME RESPECT...
BLOOD OF THE MANTA PART TWO
The SECRET Lives of Parents
BENJAMIN PERCY SCRIPT
PHIL HESTER BREAKDOWNS
KHOI PHAM PENCILS (PGS.1-15)
POP MHAN PENCILS & INKS (PGS.16-20)
TREVOR SCOTT INKS (PGS.1-15)
JIM CHARALAMPIDIS COLORS
COREY BREEN LETTERS
BRAD WALKER, ANDREW HENNESSY & JIM CHARALAMPIDIS COVER
PAOLO PANTALENA & ARIF PRIANTO VARIANT COVER
BRITTANY HOLZHERR ASSOCIATE EDITOR
ALEX ANTONE EDITOR
MARIE JAVINS GROUP EDITOR

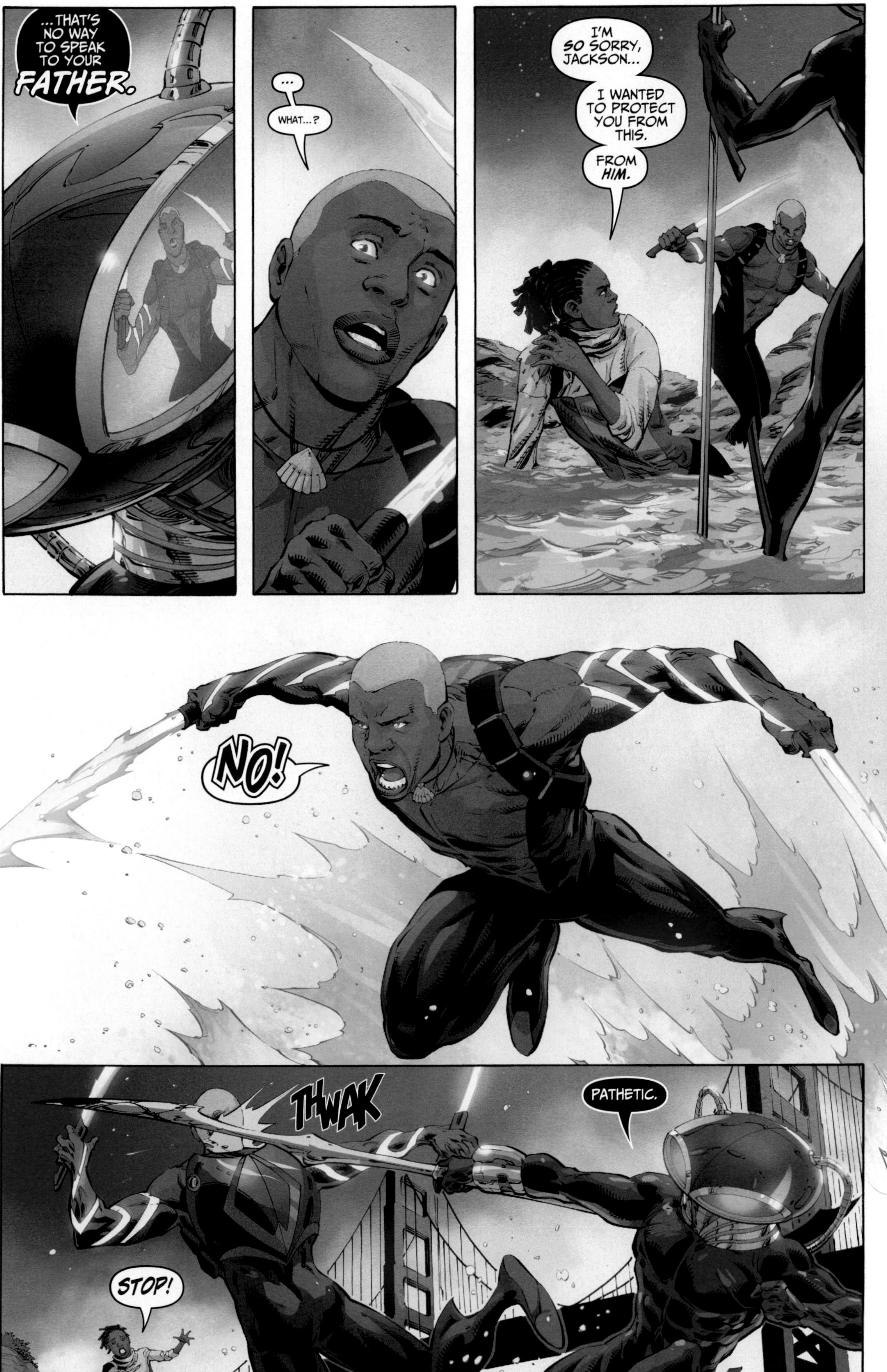
...THAT'S NO WAY TO SPEAK TO YOUR FATHER.
...
WHAT...?
I'M SO SORRY, JACKSON...
I WANTED TO PROTECT YOU FROM THIS.
FROM HIM.
NO!
THWAK
PATHETIC.
STOP!

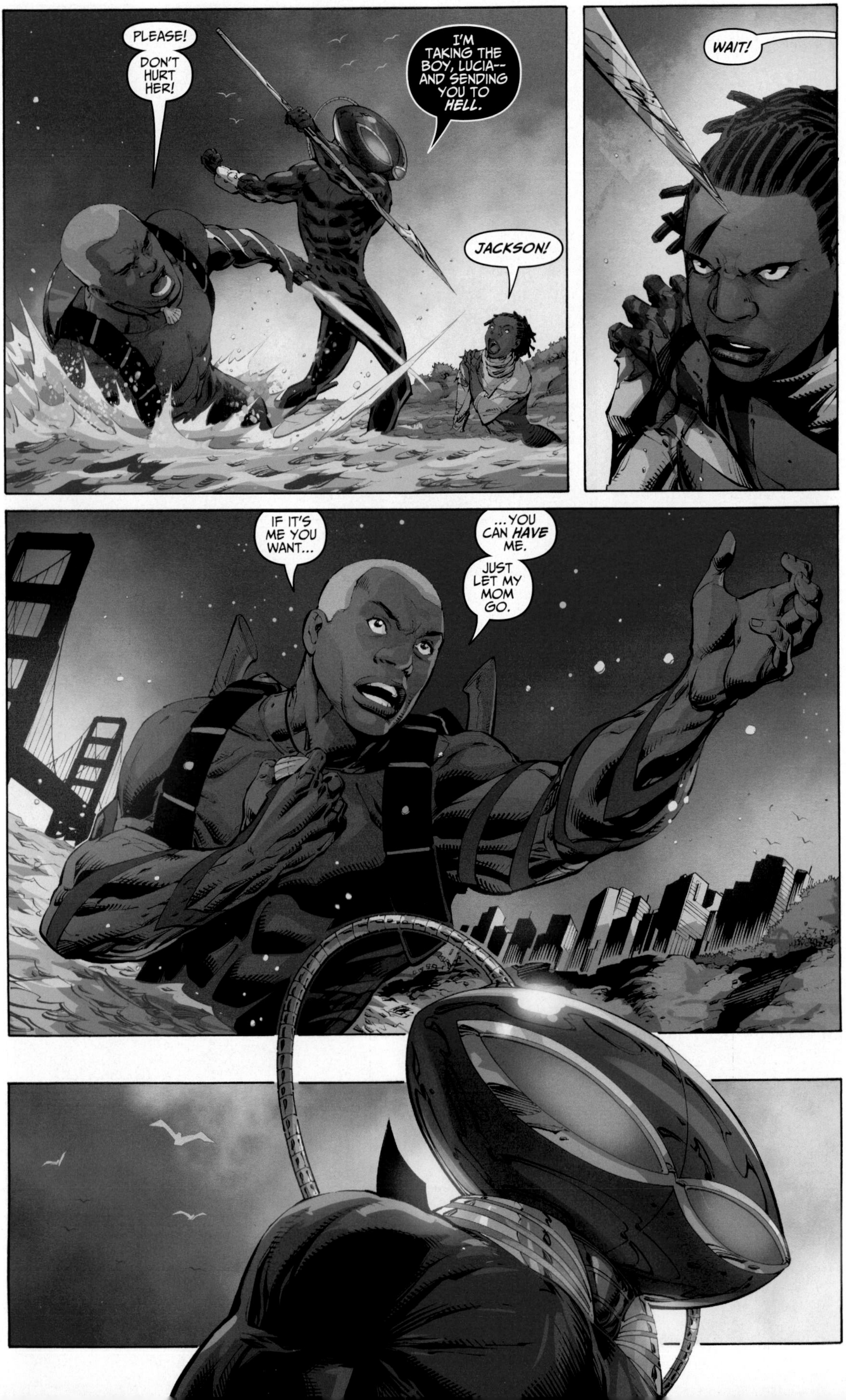
PLEASE!
DON'T HURT HER!
I'M TAKING THE BOY, LUCIA-- AND SENDING YOU TO HELL.
JACKSON!
WAIT!
IF IT'S ME YOU WANT...
...YOU CAN HAVE ME.
JUST LET MY MOM GO.

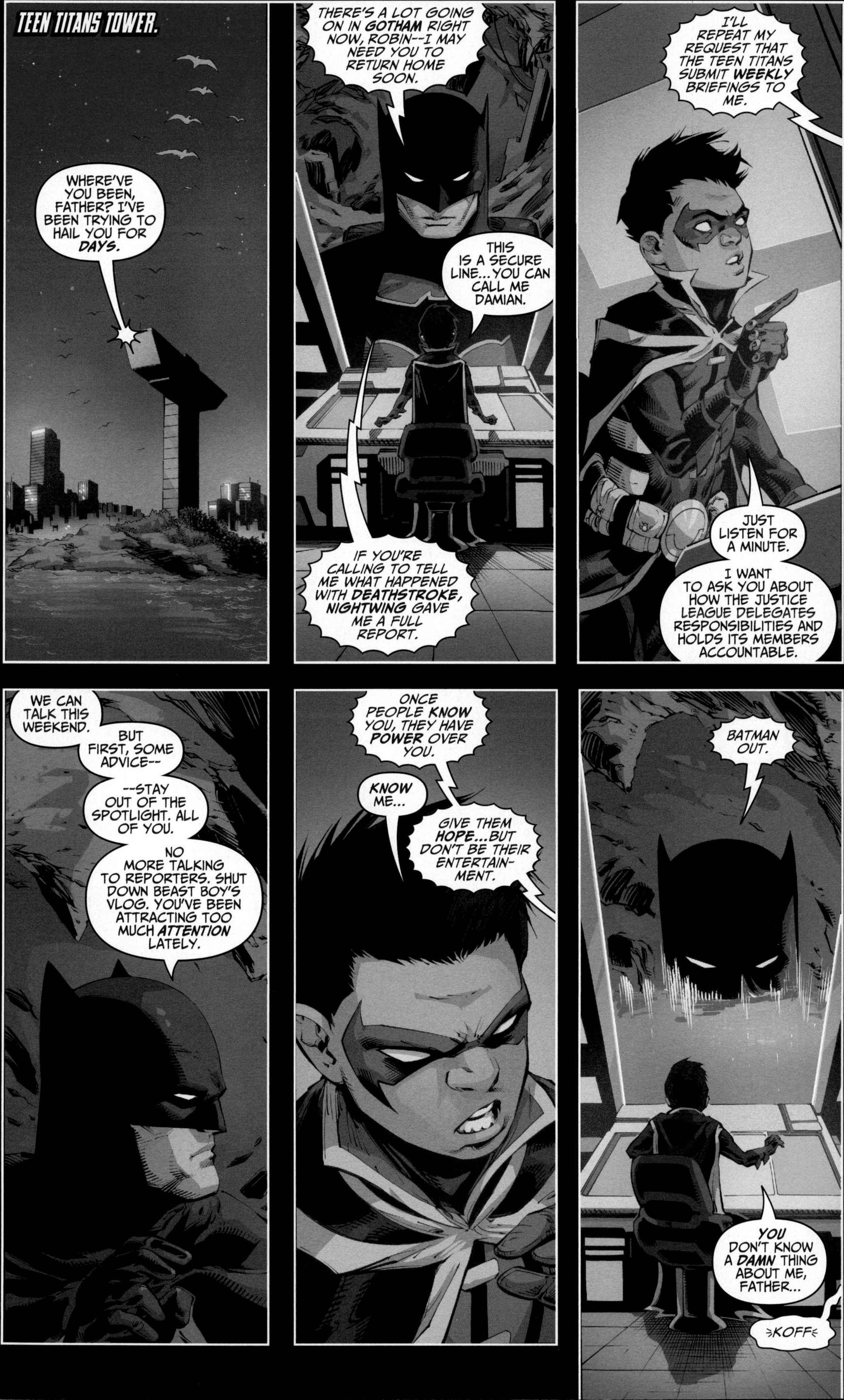

TEEN TITANS TOWER.
WHERE'VE YOU BEEN, FATHER? I'VE BEEN TRYING TO HAIL YOU FOR DAYS.
THERE'S A LOT GOING ON IN GOTHAM RIGHT NOW, ROBIN--I MAY NEED YOU TO RETURN HOME SOON.
THIS IS A SECURE LINE...YOU CAN CALL ME DAMIAN.
IF YOU'RE CALLING TO TELL ME WHAT HAPPENED WITH DEATHSTROKE, NIGHTWING GAVE ME A FULL REPORT.
I'LL REPEAT MY REQUEST THAT THE TEEN TITANS SUBMIT WEEKLY BRIEFINGS TO ME.
JUST LISTEN FOR A MINUTE.
I WANT TO ASK YOU ABOUT HOW THE JUSTICE LEAGUE DELEGATES RESPONSIBILITIES AND HOLDS ITS MEMBERS ACCOUNTABLE.
WE CAN TALK THIS WEEKEND.
BUT FIRST, SOME ADVICE--
--STAY OUT OF THE SPOTLIGHT. ALL OF YOU.
NO MORE TALKING TO REPORTERS. SHUT DOWN BEAST BOY'S VLOG. YOU'VE BEEN ATTRACTING TOO MUCH ATTENTION LATELY.
ONCE PEOPLE KNOW YOU, THEY HAVE POWER OVER YOU.
KNOW ME...
GIVE THEM HOPE...BUT DON'T BE THEIR ENTERTAIN-MENT.
BATMAN OUT.
YOU DON'T KNOW A DAMN THING ABOUT ME, FATHER...
KOFF

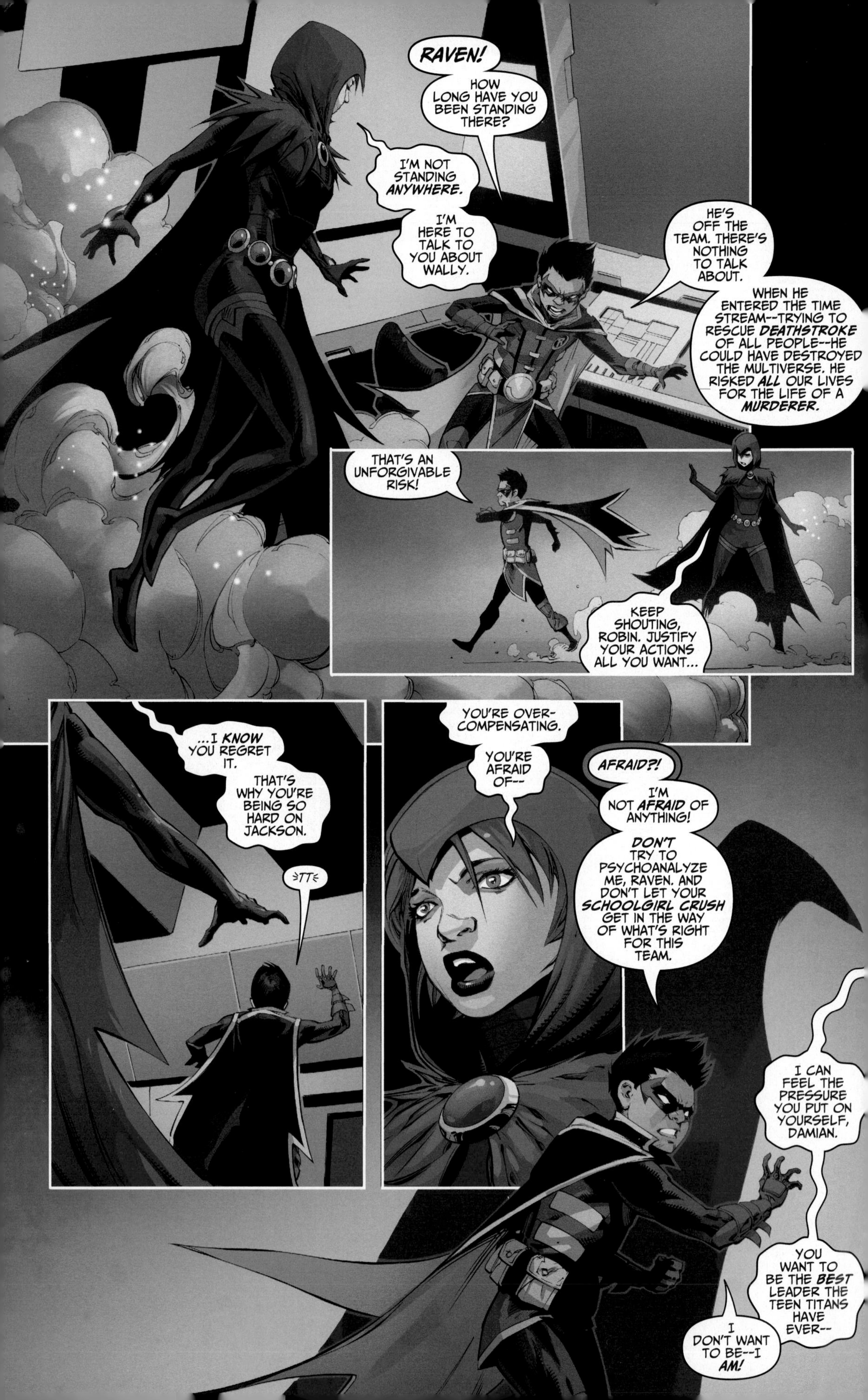
RAVEN!
HOW LONG HAVE YOU BEEN STANDING THERE?
I'M NOT STANDING ANYWHERE.
I'M HERE TO TALK TO YOU ABOUT WALLY.
HE'S OFF THE TEAM. THERE'S NOTHING TO TALK ABOUT.
WHEN HE ENTERED THE TIME STREAM--TRYING TO RESCUE DEATHSTROKE OF ALL PEOPLE--HE COULD HAVE DESTROYED THE MULTIVERSE. HE RISKED ALL OUR LIVES FOR THE LIFE OF A MURDERER.
THAT'S AN UNFORGIVABLE RISK!
KEEP SHOUTING, ROBIN. JUSTIFY YOUR ACTIONS ALL YOU WANT...
...I KNOW YOU REGRET IT.
THAT'S WHY YOU'RE BEING SO HARD ON JACKSON.
TT
YOU'RE OVER-COMPENSATING.
YOU'RE AFRAID OF--
AFRAID?!
I'M NOT AFRAID OF ANYTHING!
DON'T TRY TO PSYCHOANALYZE ME, RAVEN. AND DON'T LET YOUR SCHOOLGIRL CRUSH GET IN THE WAY OF WHAT'S RIGHT FOR THIS TEAM.
I CAN FEEL THE PRESSURE YOU PUT ON YOURSELF, DAMIAN.
YOU WANT TO BE THE BEST LEADER THE TEEN TITANS HAVE EVER--
I DON'T WANT TO BE--I AM!

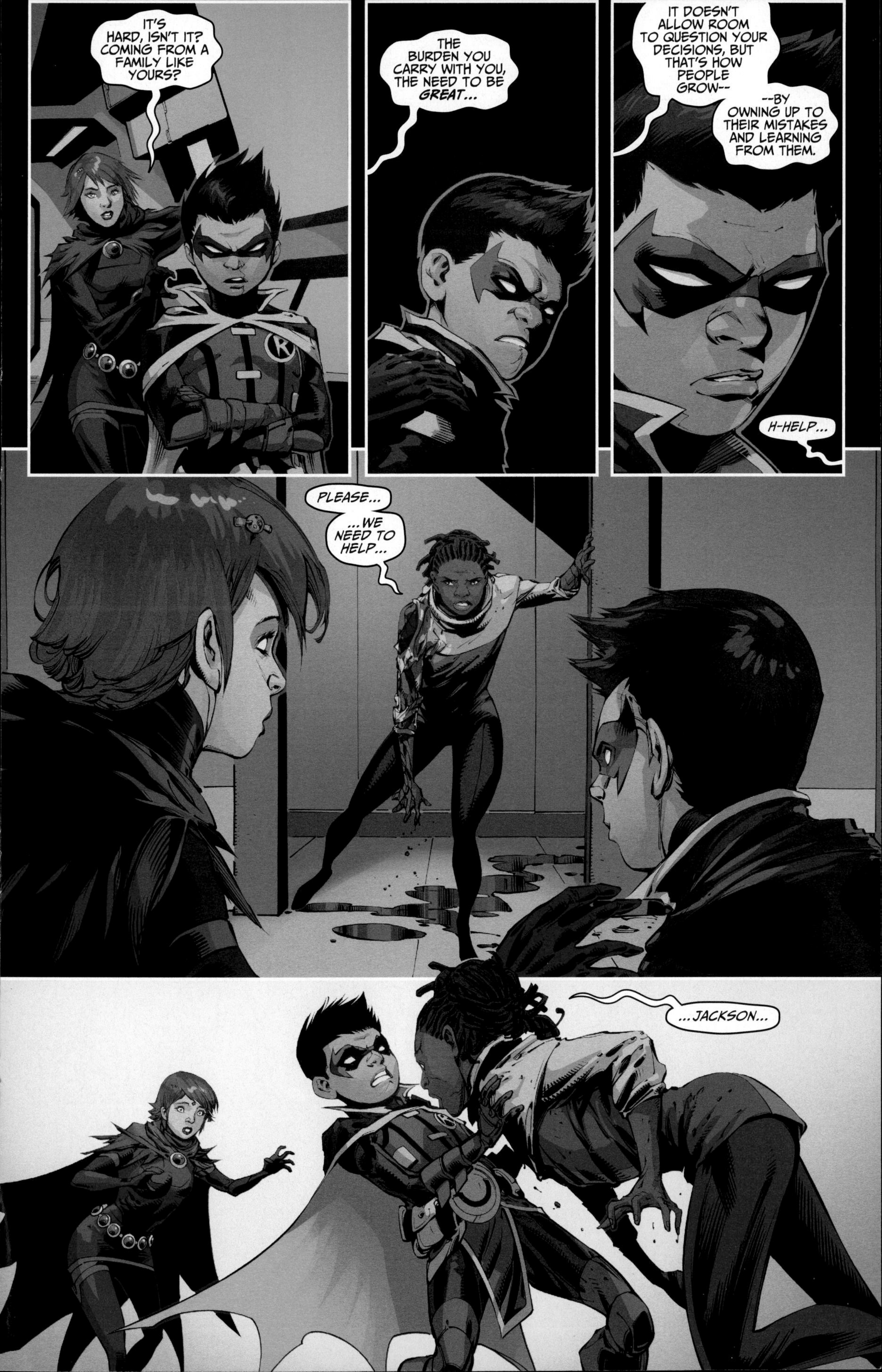
IT'S HARD, ISN'T IT? COMING FROM A FAMILY LIKE YOURS?
THE BURDEN YOU CARRY WITH YOU, THE NEED TO BE GREAT...
IT DOESN'T ALLOW ROOM TO QUESTION YOUR DECISIONS, BUT THAT'S HOW PEOPLE GROW--
--BY OWNING UP TO THEIR MISTAKES AND LEARNING FROM THEM.
H-HELP...
PLEASE...
...WE NEED TO HELP...
...JACKSON...

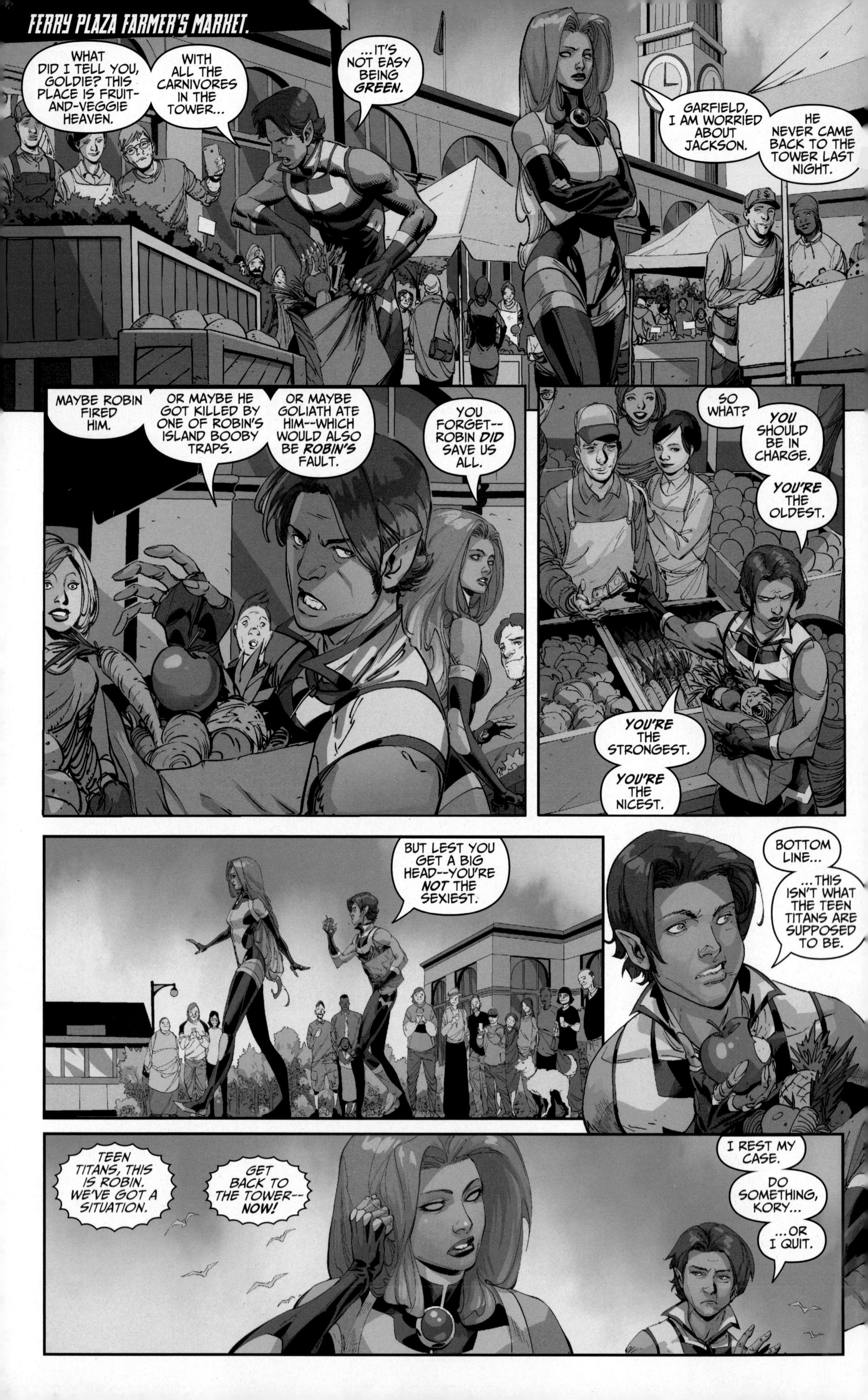
FERRY PLAZA FARMER'S MARKET.
WHAT DID I TELL YOU, GOLDIE? THIS PLACE IS FRUIT-AND-VEGGIE HEAVEN.
WITH ALL THE CARNIVORES IN THE TOWER...
...IT'S NOT EASY BEING GREEN.
GARFIELD, I AM WORRIED ABOUT JACKSON.
HE NEVER CAME BACK TO THE TOWER LAST NIGHT.
MAYBE ROBIN FIRED HIM.
OR MAYBE HE GOT KILLED BY ONE OF ROBIN'S ISLAND BOOBY TRAPS.
OR MAYBE GOLIATH ATE HIM--WHICH WOULD ALSO BE ROBIN'S FAULT.
YOU FORGET--ROBIN DID SAVE US ALL.
SO WHAT?
YOU SHOULD BE IN CHARGE.
YOU'RE THE OLDEST.
YOU'RE THE STRONGEST.
YOU'RE THE NICEST.
BUT LEST YOU GET A BIG HEAD--YOU'RE NOT THE SEXIEST.
BOTTOM LINE...
...THIS ISN'T WHAT THE TEEN TITANS ARE SUPPOSED TO BE.
TEEN TITANS, THIS IS ROBIN. WE'VE GOT A SITUATION.
GET BACK TO THE TOWER--NOW!
I REST MY CASE.
DO SOMETHING, KORY...
...OR I QUIT.

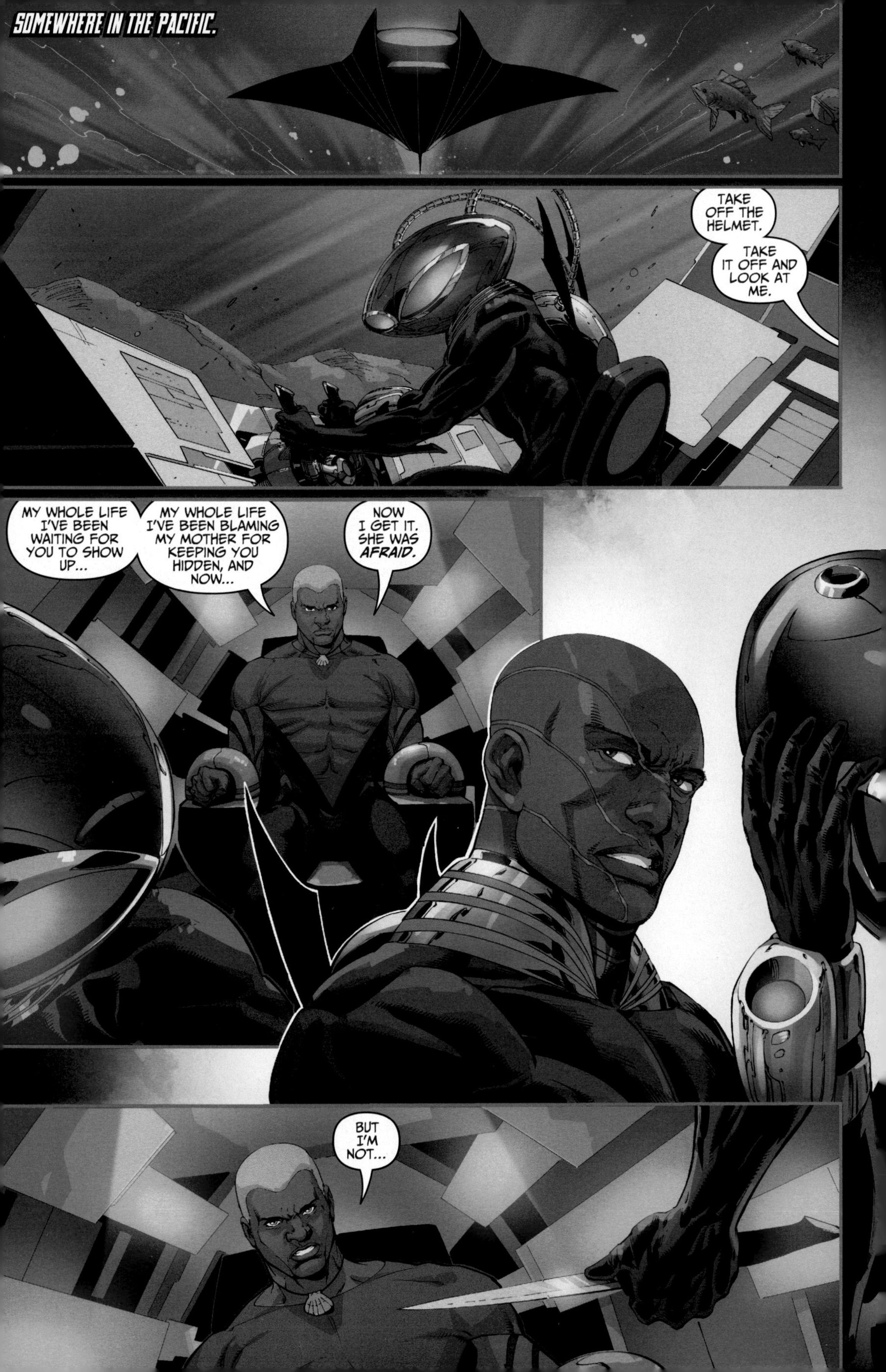
SOMEWHERE IN THE PACIFIC.
TAKE OFF THE HELMET.
TAKE IT OFF AND LOOK AT ME.
MY WHOLE LIFE I'VE BEEN WAITING FOR YOU TO SHOW UP...
MY WHOLE LIFE I'VE BEEN BLAMING MY MOTHER FOR KEEPING YOU HIDDEN, AND NOW...
NOW I GET IT. SHE WAS *AFRAID.*
BUT I'M NOT...

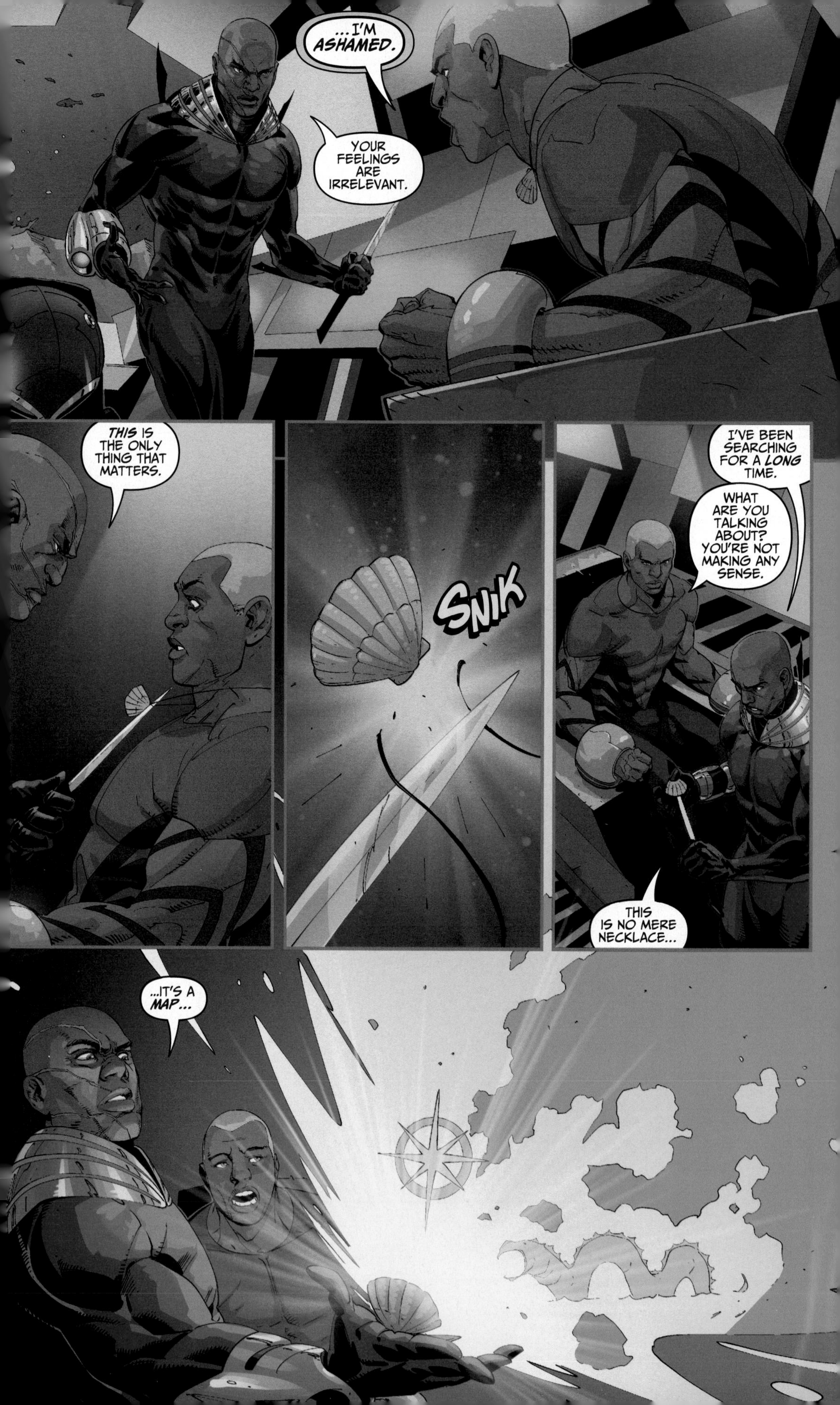
...I'M ASHAMED.
YOUR FEELINGS ARE IRRELEVANT.
THIS IS THE ONLY THING THAT MATTERS.
SNIK
I'VE BEEN SEARCHING FOR A LONG TIME.
WHAT ARE YOU TALKING ABOUT? YOU'RE NOT MAKING ANY SENSE.
THIS IS NO MERE NECKLACE...
...IT'S A MAP...

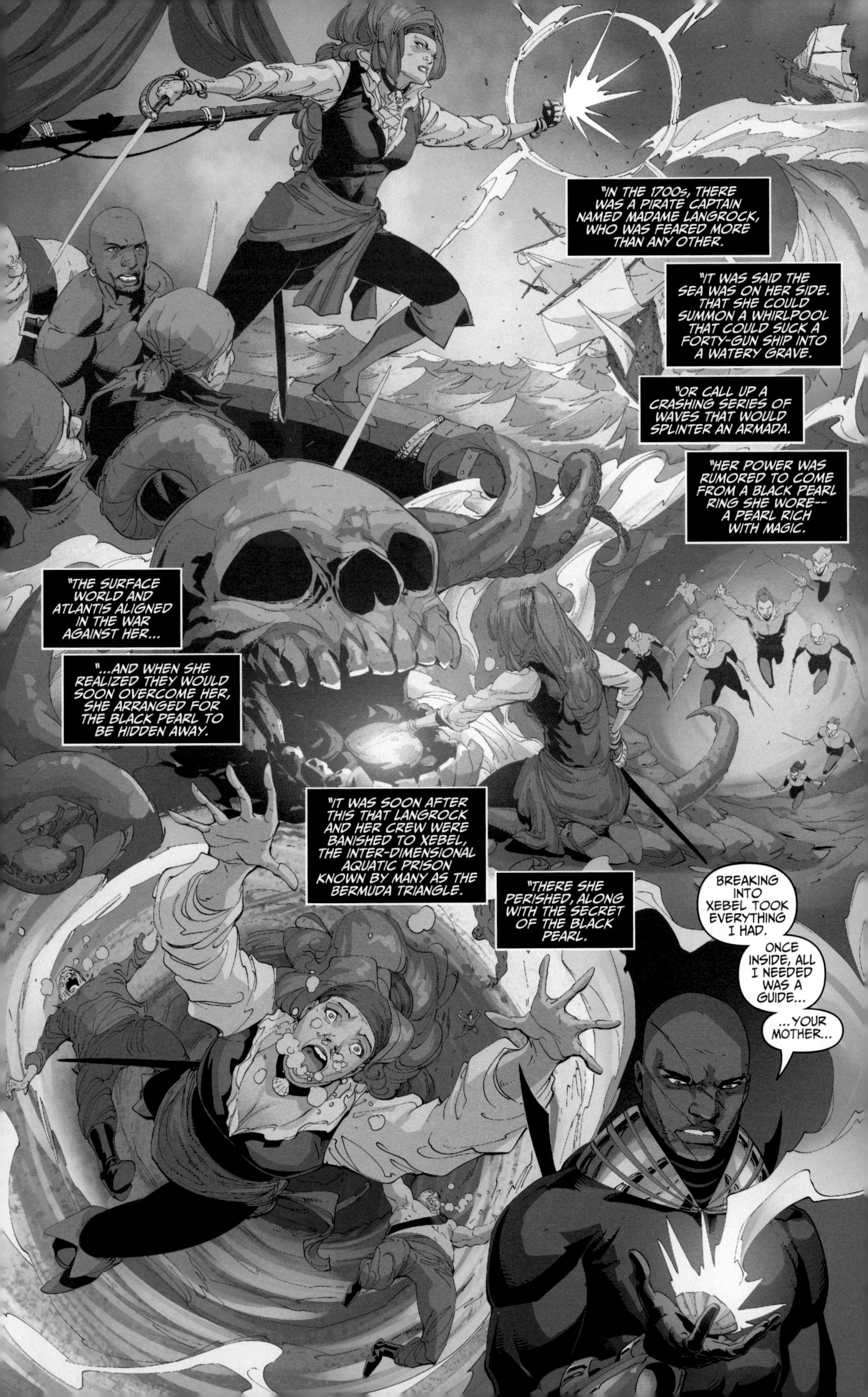
"IN THE 1700s, THERE WAS A PIRATE CAPTAIN NAMED MADAME LANGROCK, WHO WAS FEARED MORE THAN ANY OTHER.
"IT WAS SAID THE SEA WAS ON HER SIDE. THAT SHE COULD SUMMON A WHIRLPOOL THAT COULD SUCK A FORTY-GUN SHIP INTO A WATERY GRAVE.
"OR CALL UP A CRASHING SERIES OF WAVES THAT WOULD SPLINTER AN ARMADA.
"HER POWER WAS RUMORED TO COME FROM A BLACK PEARL RING SHE WORE-- A PEARL RICH WITH MAGIC.
"THE SURFACE WORLD AND ATLANTIS ALIGNED IN THE WAR AGAINST HER...
"...AND WHEN SHE REALIZED THEY WOULD SOON OVERCOME HER, SHE ARRANGED FOR THE BLACK PEARL TO BE HIDDEN AWAY.
"IT WAS SOON AFTER THIS THAT LANGROCK AND HER CREW WERE BANISHED TO XEBEL, THE INTER-DIMENSIONAL AQUATIC PRISON KNOWN BY MANY AS THE BERMUDA TRIANGLE.
"THERE SHE PERISHED, ALONG WITH THE SECRET OF THE BLACK PEARL.
BREAKING INTO XEBEL TOOK EVERYTHING I HAD.
ONCE INSIDE, ALL I NEEDED WAS A GUIDE...
...YOUR MOTHER...

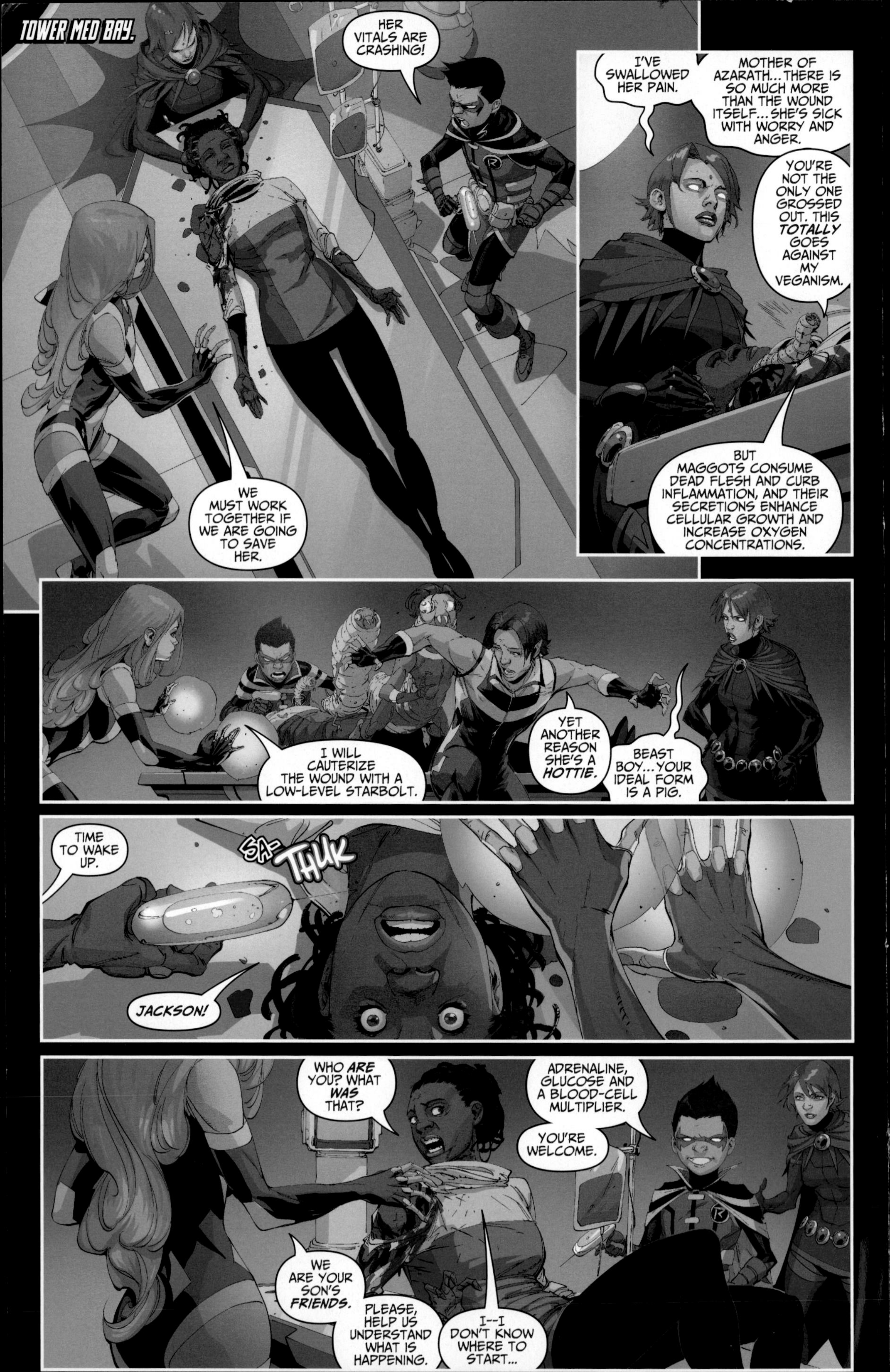
TOWER MED BAY.
HER VITALS ARE CRASHING!
WE MUST WORK TOGETHER IF WE ARE GOING TO SAVE HER.
I'VE SWALLOWED HER PAIN.
MOTHER OF AZARATH...THERE IS SO MUCH MORE THAN THE WOUND ITSELF...SHE'S SICK WITH WORRY AND ANGER.
YOU'RE NOT THE ONLY ONE GROSSED OUT. THIS TOTALLY GOES AGAINST MY VEGANISM.
BUT MAGGOTS CONSUME DEAD FLESH AND CURB INFLAMMATION, AND THEIR SECRETIONS ENHANCE CELLULAR GROWTH AND INCREASE OXYGEN CONCENTRATIONS.
I WILL CAUTERIZE THE WOUND WITH A LOW-LEVEL STARBOLT.
YET ANOTHER REASON SHE'S A HOTTIE.
BEAST BOY...YOUR IDEAL FORM IS A PIG.
TIME TO WAKE UP.
SA-THUK
JACKSON!
WHO ARE YOU? WHAT WAS THAT?
ADRENALINE, GLUCOSE AND A BLOOD-CELL MULTIPLIER.
YOU'RE WELCOME.
WE ARE YOUR SON'S FRIENDS.
PLEASE, HELP US UNDERSTAND WHAT IS HAPPENING.
I--I DON'T KNOW WHERE TO START...

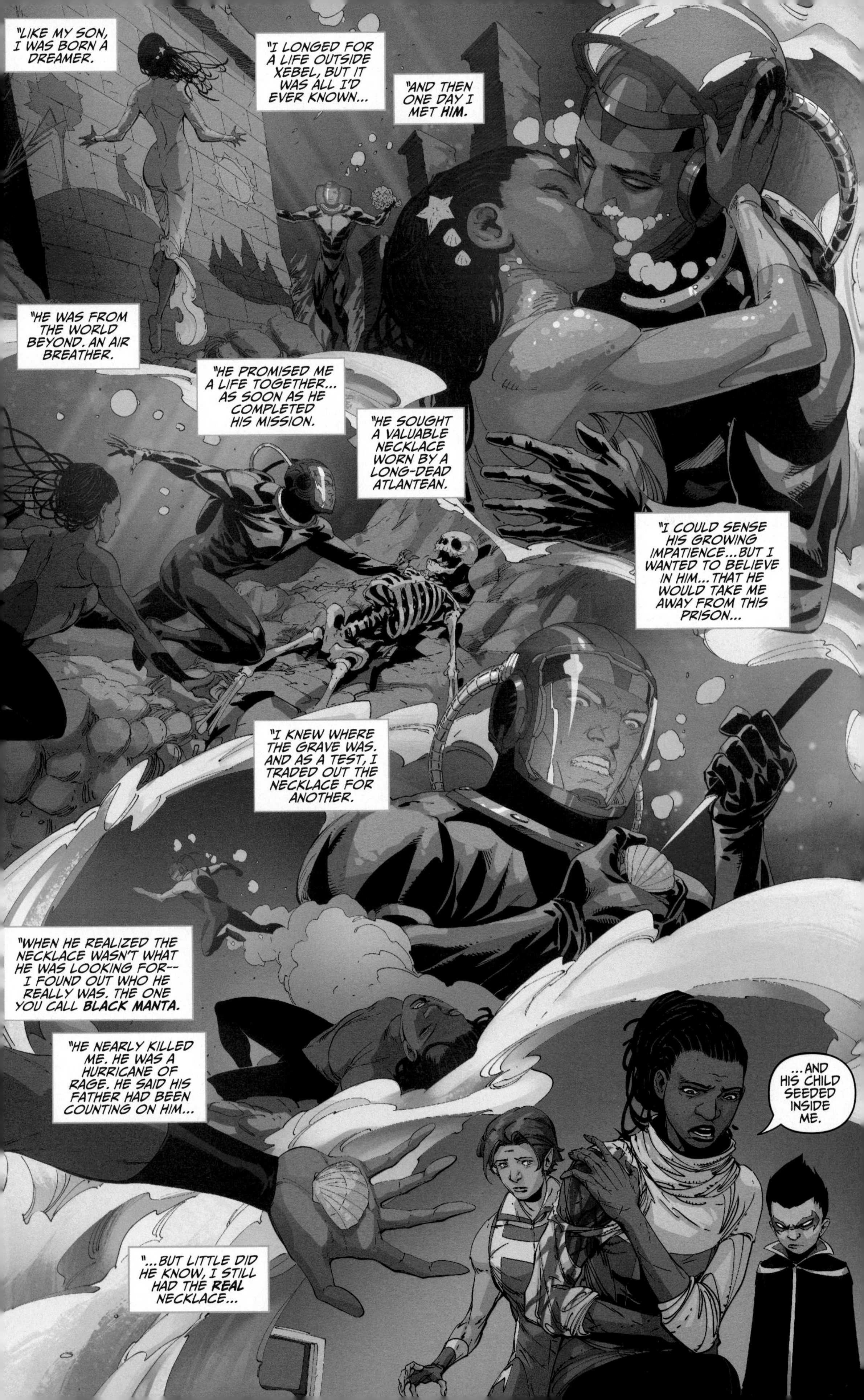
"LIKE MY SON, I WAS BORN A DREAMER.
"I LONGED FOR A LIFE OUTSIDE XEBEL, BUT IT WAS ALL I'D EVER KNOWN...
"AND THEN ONE DAY I MET HIM.
"HE WAS FROM THE WORLD BEYOND. AN AIR BREATHER.
"HE PROMISED ME A LIFE TOGETHER... AS SOON AS HE COMPLETED HIS MISSION.
"HE SOUGHT A VALUABLE NECKLACE WORN BY A LONG-DEAD ATLANTEAN.
"I COULD SENSE HIS GROWING IMPATIENCE...BUT I WANTED TO BELIEVE IN HIM...THAT HE WOULD TAKE ME AWAY FROM THIS PRISON...
"I KNEW WHERE THE GRAVE WAS. AND AS A TEST, I TRADED OUT THE NECKLACE FOR ANOTHER.
"WHEN HE REALIZED THE NECKLACE WASN'T WHAT HE WAS LOOKING FOR-- I FOUND OUT WHO HE REALLY WAS. THE ONE YOU CALL BLACK MANTA.
"HE NEARLY KILLED ME. HE WAS A HURRICANE OF RAGE. HE SAID HIS FATHER HAD BEEN COUNTING ON HIM...
"...BUT LITTLE DID HE KNOW, I STILL HAD THE REAL NECKLACE...
...AND HIS CHILD SEEDED INSIDE ME.

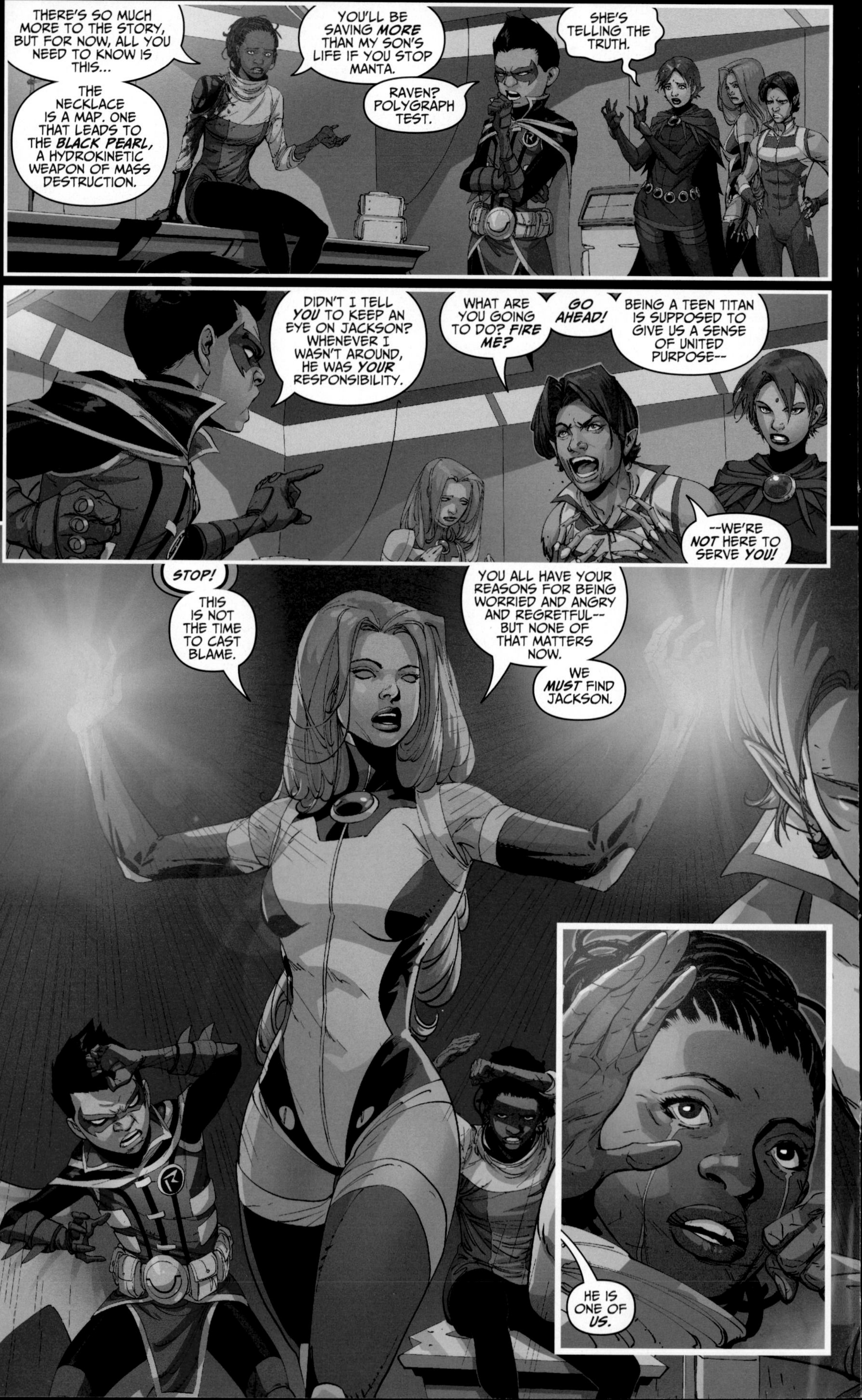
THERE'S SO MUCH MORE TO THE STORY, BUT FOR NOW, ALL YOU NEED TO KNOW IS THIS...
THE NECKLACE IS A MAP. ONE THAT LEADS TO THE BLACK PEARL, A HYDROKINETIC WEAPON OF MASS DESTRUCTION.
YOU'LL BE SAVING MORE THAN MY SON'S LIFE IF YOU STOP MANTA.
RAVEN? POLYGRAPH TEST.
SHE'S TELLING THE TRUTH.
DIDN'T I TELL YOU TO KEEP AN EYE ON JACKSON? WHENEVER I WASN'T AROUND, HE WAS YOUR RESPONSIBILITY.
WHAT ARE YOU GOING TO DO? FIRE ME?
GO AHEAD!
BEING A TEEN TITAN IS SUPPOSED TO GIVE US A SENSE OF UNITED PURPOSE--
--WE'RE NOT HERE TO SERVE YOU!
STOP!
THIS IS NOT THE TIME TO CAST BLAME.
YOU ALL HAVE YOUR REASONS FOR BEING WORRIED AND ANGRY AND REGRETFUL-- BUT NONE OF THAT MATTERS NOW.
WE MUST FIND JACKSON.
HE IS ONE OF US.

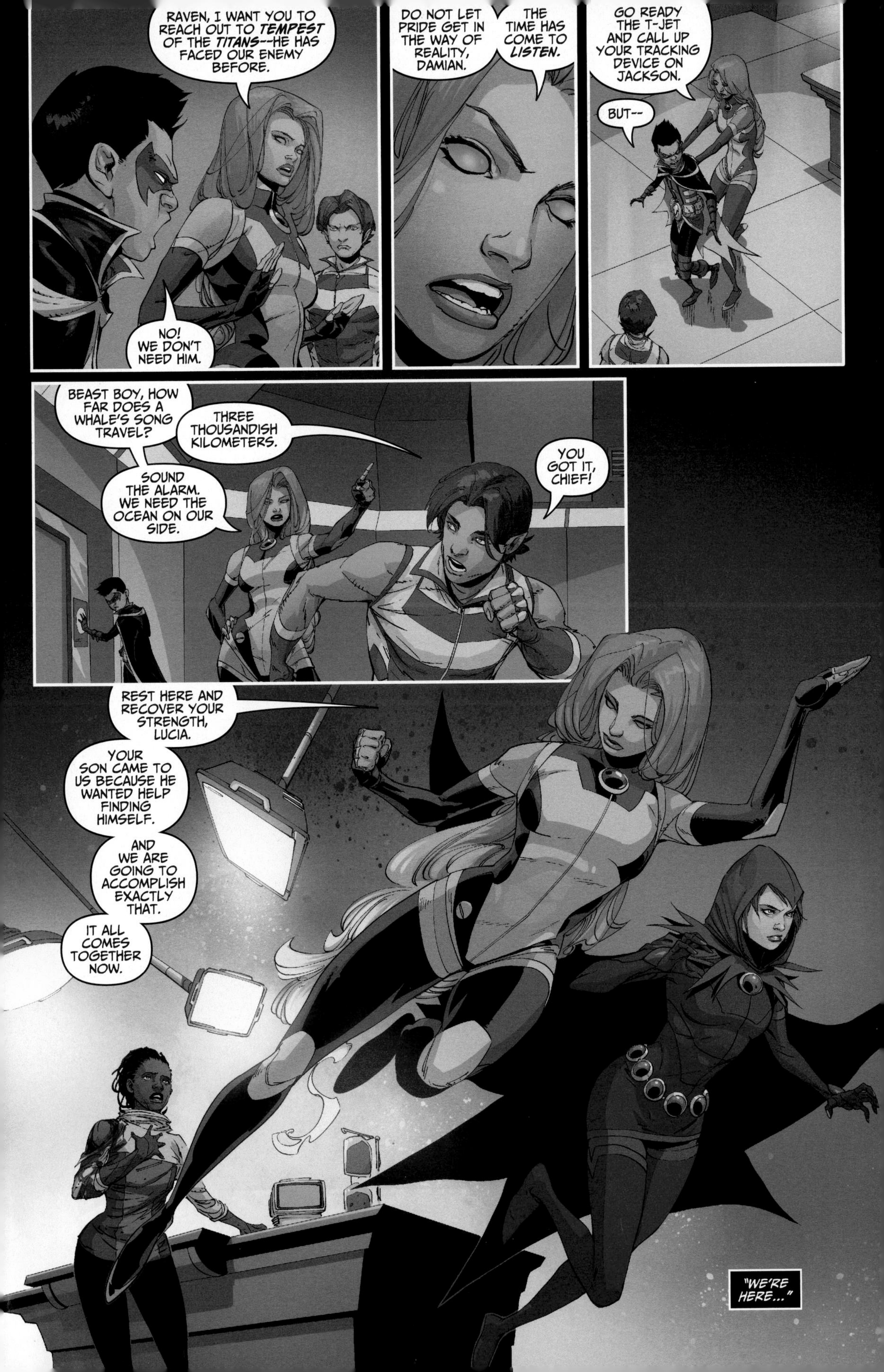
RAVEN, I WANT YOU TO REACH OUT TO TEMPEST OF THE TITANS--HE HAS FACED OUR ENEMY BEFORE.
NO! WE DON'T NEED HIM.
DO NOT LET PRIDE GET IN THE WAY OF REALITY, DAMIAN.
THE TIME HAS COME TO LISTEN.
GO READY THE T-JET AND CALL UP YOUR TRACKING DEVICE ON JACKSON.
BUT--
BEAST BOY, HOW FAR DOES A WHALE'S SONG TRAVEL?
THREE THOUSANDISH KILOMETERS.
SOUND THE ALARM. WE NEED THE OCEAN ON OUR SIDE.
YOU GOT IT, CHIEF!
REST HERE AND RECOVER YOUR STRENGTH, LUCIA.
YOUR SON CAME TO US BECAUSE HE WANTED HELP FINDING HIMSELF.
AND WE ARE GOING TO ACCOMPLISH EXACTLY THAT.
IT ALL COMES TOGETHER NOW.
"WE'RE HERE..."

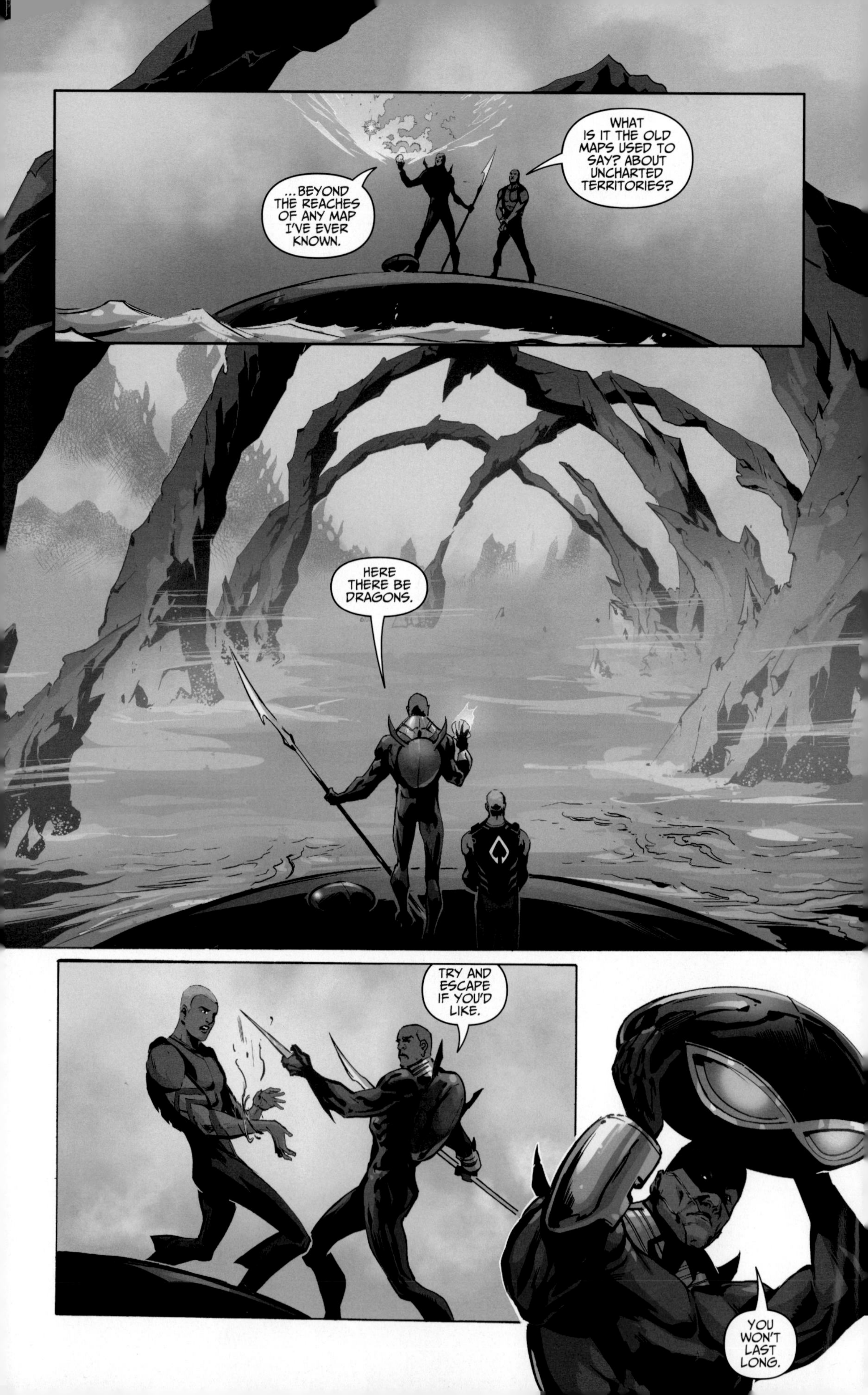
...BEYOND THE REACHES OF ANY MAP I'VE EVER KNOWN.
WHAT IS IT THE OLD MAPS USED TO SAY? ABOUT UNCHARTED TERRITORIES?
HERE THERE BE DRAGONS.
TRY AND ESCAPE IF YOU'D LIKE.
YOU WON'T LAST LONG.

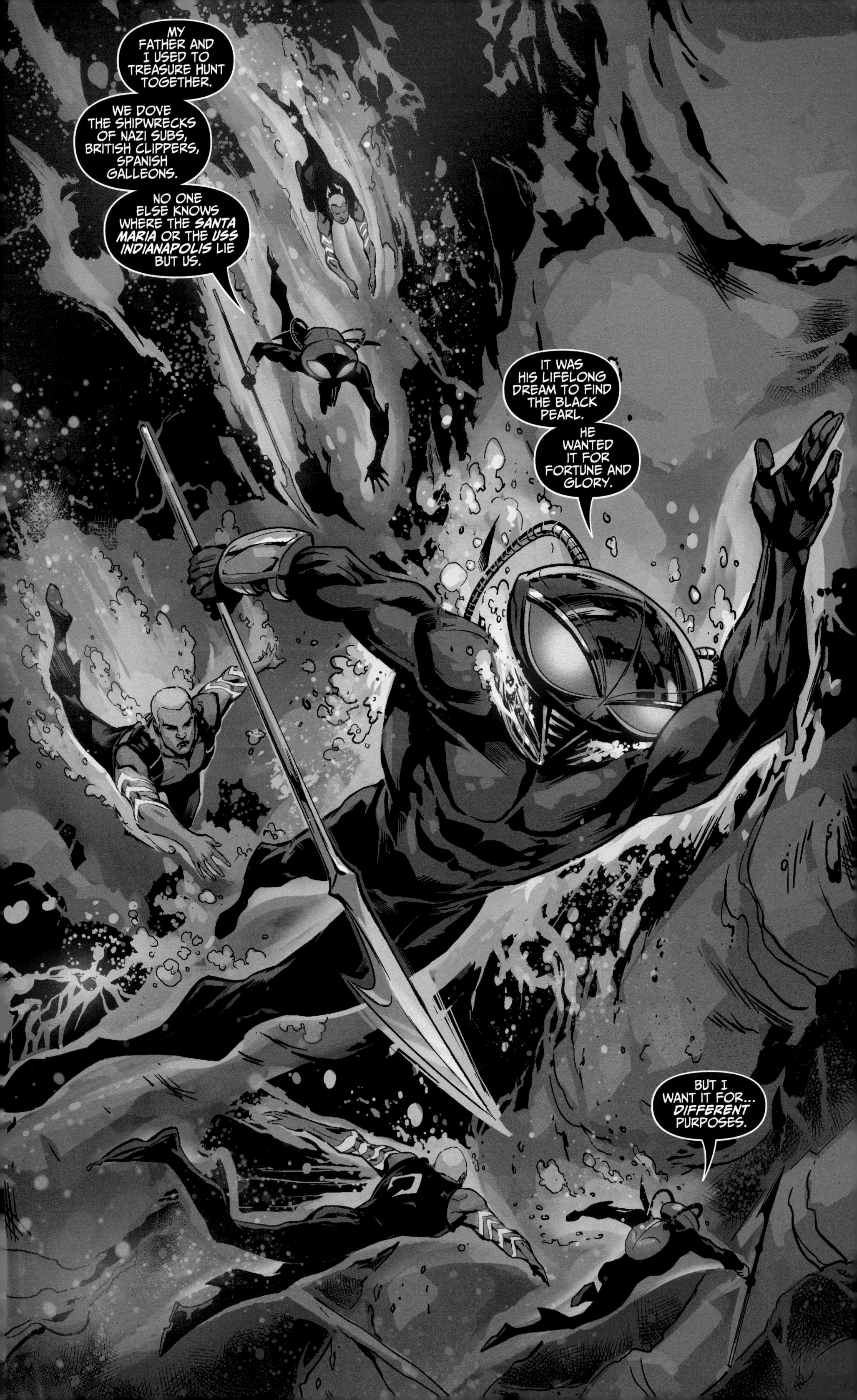
MY FATHER AND I USED TO TREASURE HUNT TOGETHER.
WE DOVE THE SHIPWRECKS OF NAZI SUBS, BRITISH CLIPPERS, SPANISH GALLEONS.
NO ONE ELSE KNOWS WHERE THE *SANTA MARIA* OR THE *USS INDIANAPOLIS* LIE BUT US.
IT WAS HIS LIFELONG DREAM TO FIND THE BLACK PEARL.
HE WANTED IT FOR FORTUNE AND GLORY.
BUT I WANT IT FOR... *DIFFERENT* PURPOSES.

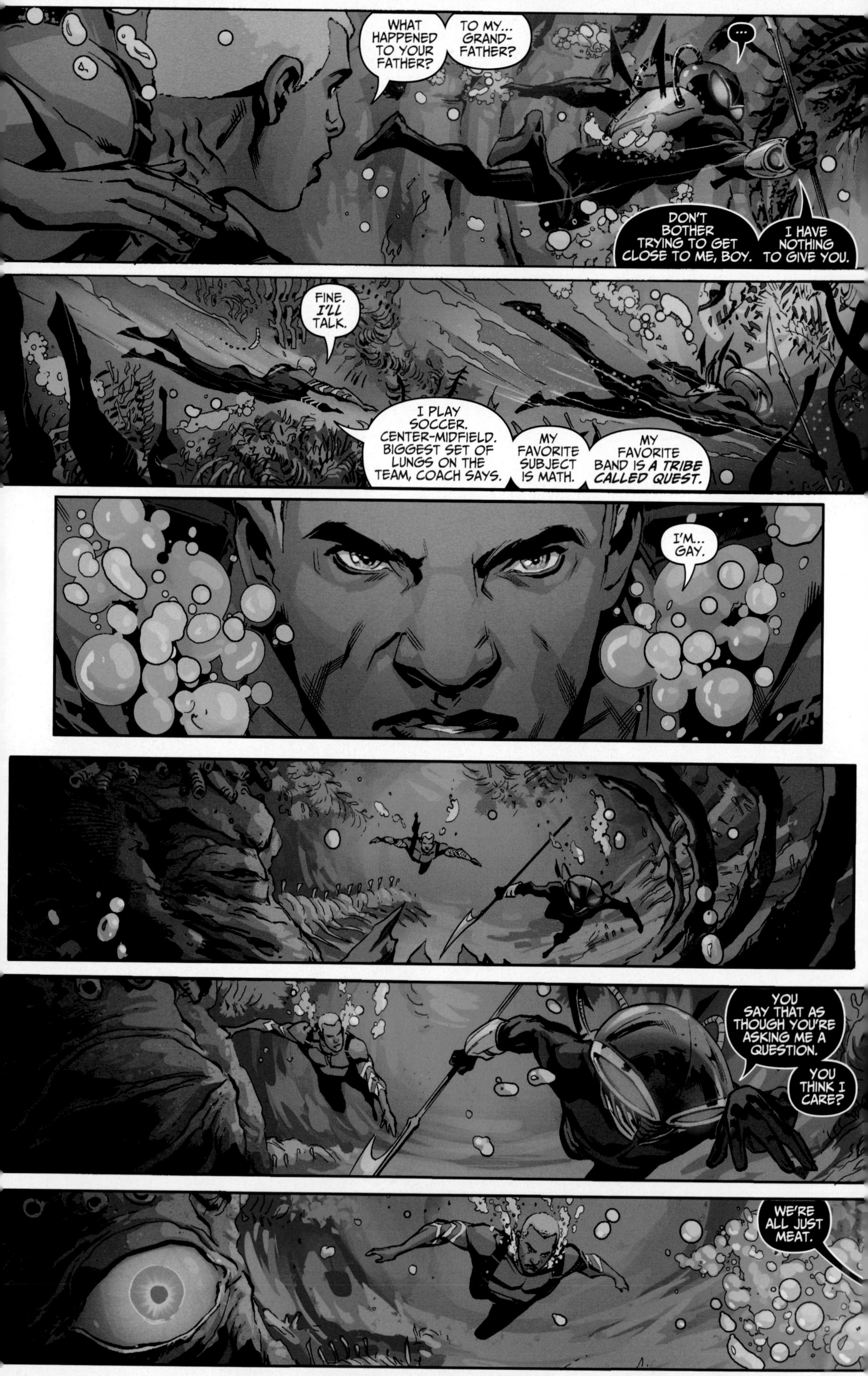
WHAT HAPPENED TO YOUR FATHER?
TO MY... GRAND-FATHER?
...
DON'T BOTHER TRYING TO GET CLOSE TO ME, BOY.
I HAVE NOTHING TO GIVE YOU.
FINE. I'LL TALK.
I PLAY SOCCER. CENTER-MIDFIELD. BIGGEST SET OF LUNGS ON THE TEAM, COACH SAYS.
MY FAVORITE SUBJECT IS MATH.
MY FAVORITE BAND IS A TRIBE CALLED QUEST.
I'M... GAY.
YOU SAY THAT AS THOUGH YOU'RE ASKING ME A QUESTION.
YOU THINK I CARE?
WE'RE ALL JUST MEAT.

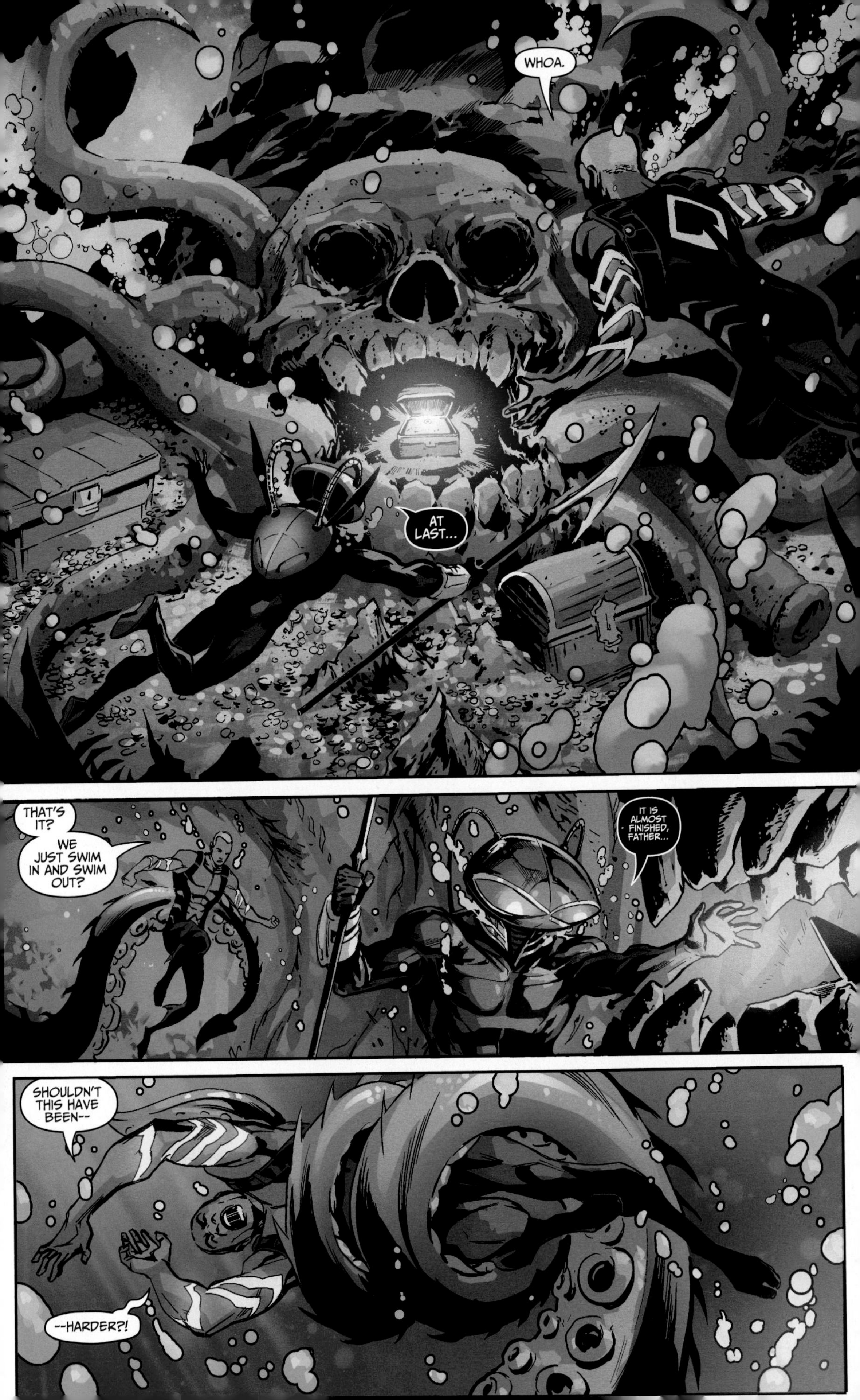
WHOA.
AT LAST...
THAT'S IT?
WE JUST SWIM IN AND SWIM OUT?
IT IS ALMOST FINISHED, FATHER...
SHOULDN'T THIS HAVE BEEN--
--HARDER?!

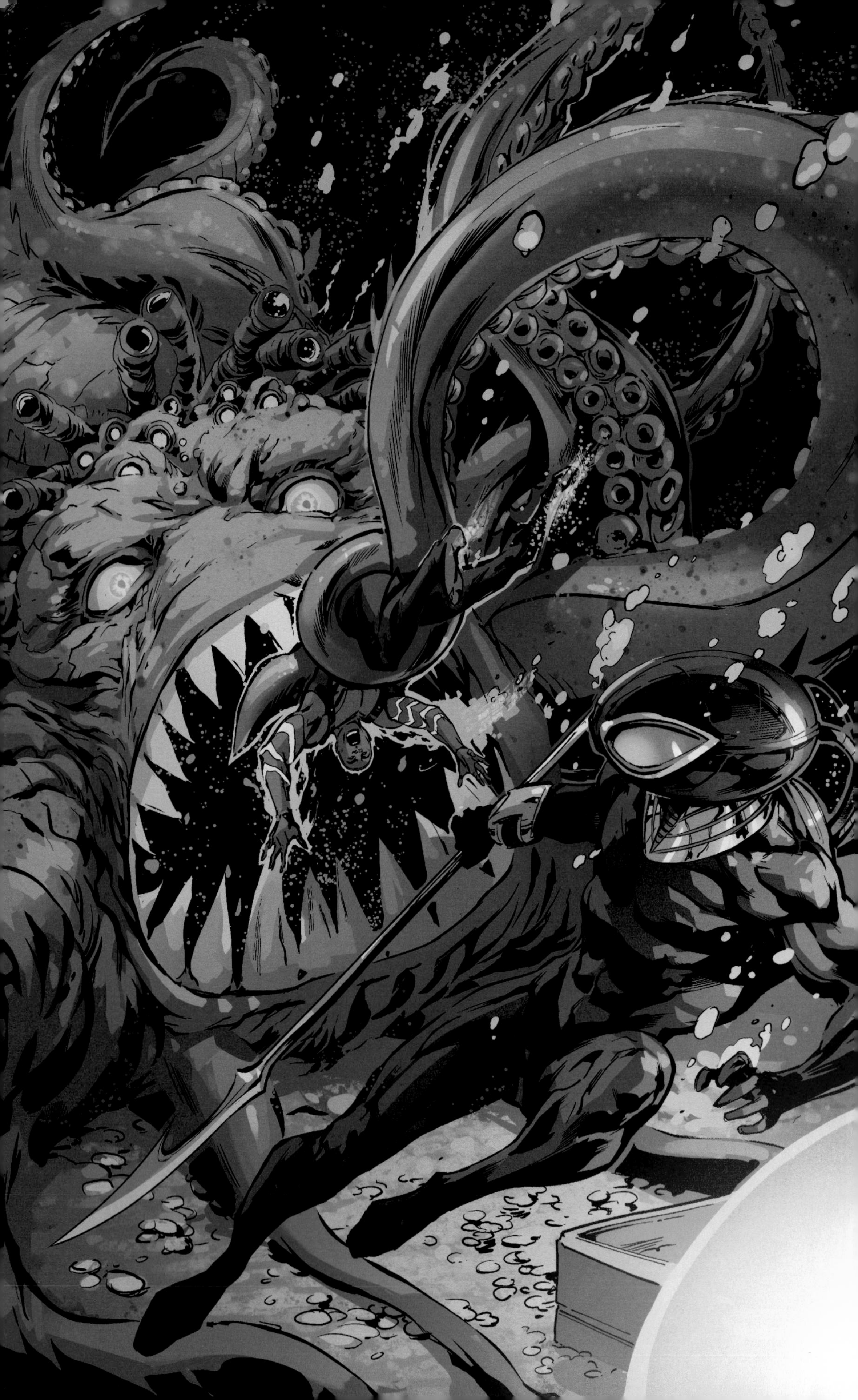

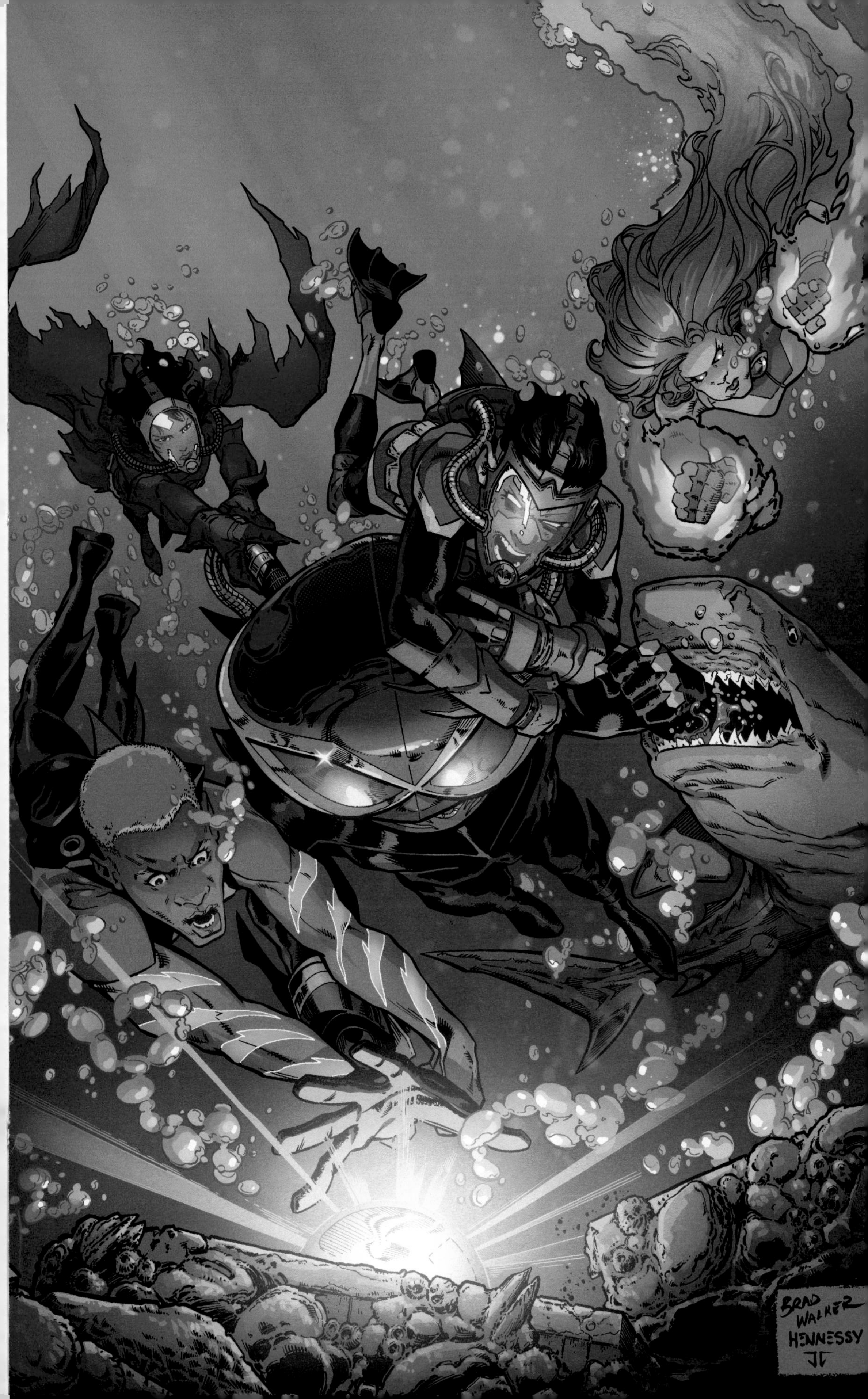
BRAD WALKER
HENNESSY
JL

DZZZzt

BLOOD OF THE MANTA FINALE

SON OF THE SEVEN SEAS!

FIGHT WITH ME, SON!

BENJAMIN PERCY *SCRIPT* • PHIL HESTER *BREAKDOWNS* • KHOI PHAM *PENCILS*
TREVOR SCOTT *INKS* • JIM CHARALAMPIDIS *COLORS* • COREY BREEN *LETTERS*
BRAD WALKER, ANDREW HENNESSY & JIM CHARALAMPIDIS *COVER*
CHAD HARDIN & ALEX SINCLAIR *VARIANT COVER* • BRITTANY HOLZHERR *ASSOCIATE EDITOR*
ALEX ANTONE *EDITOR* • MARIE JAVINS *GROUP EDITOR*

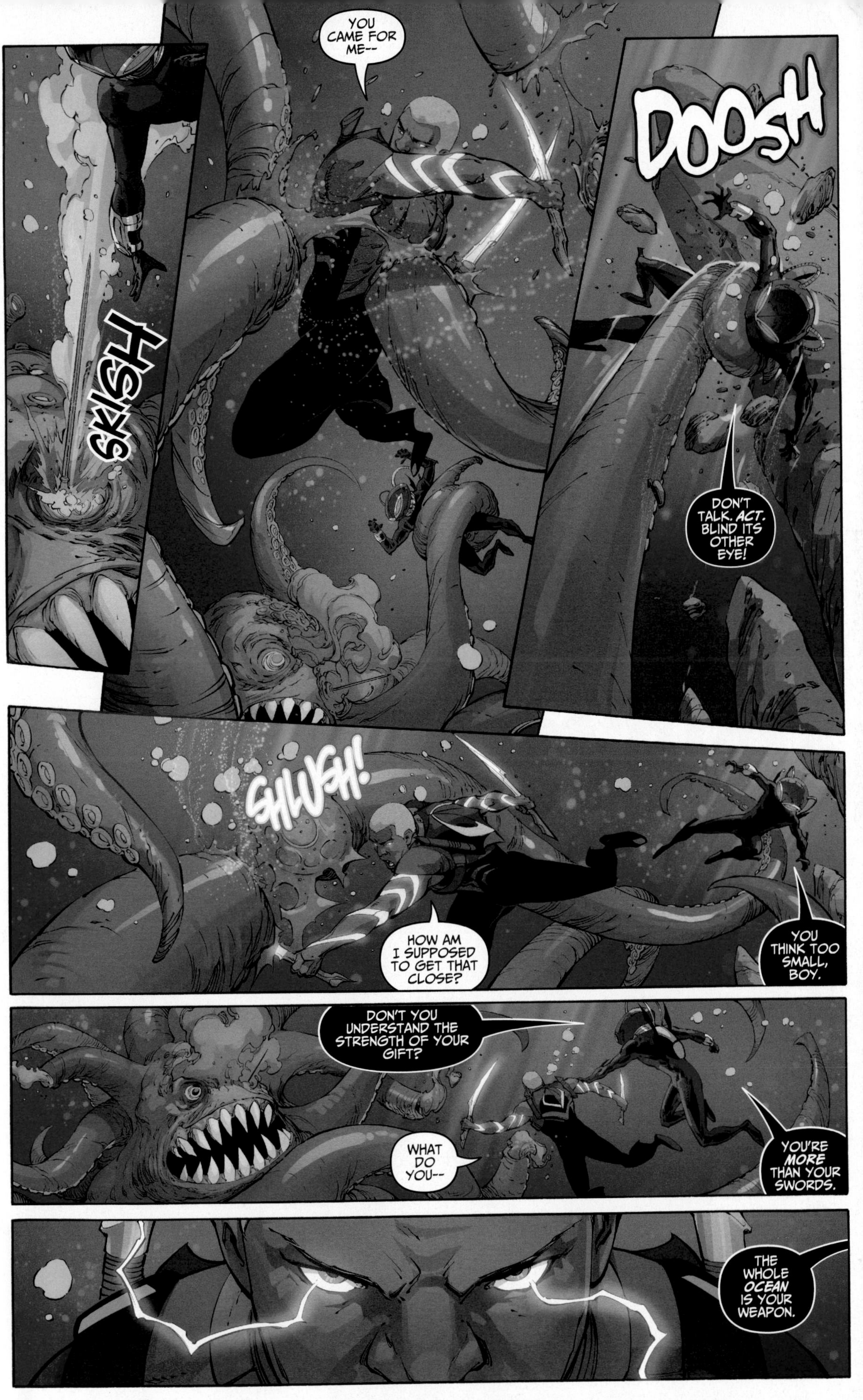
SKISH
YOU CAME FOR ME--
DOOSH
DON'T TALK. ACT. BLIND ITS OTHER EYE!
SHLUSH!
HOW AM I SUPPOSED TO GET THAT CLOSE?
YOU THINK TOO SMALL, BOY.
DON'T YOU UNDERSTAND THE STRENGTH OF YOUR GIFT?
WHAT DO YOU--
YOU'RE MORE THAN YOUR SWORDS.
THE WHOLE OCEAN IS YOUR WEAPON.

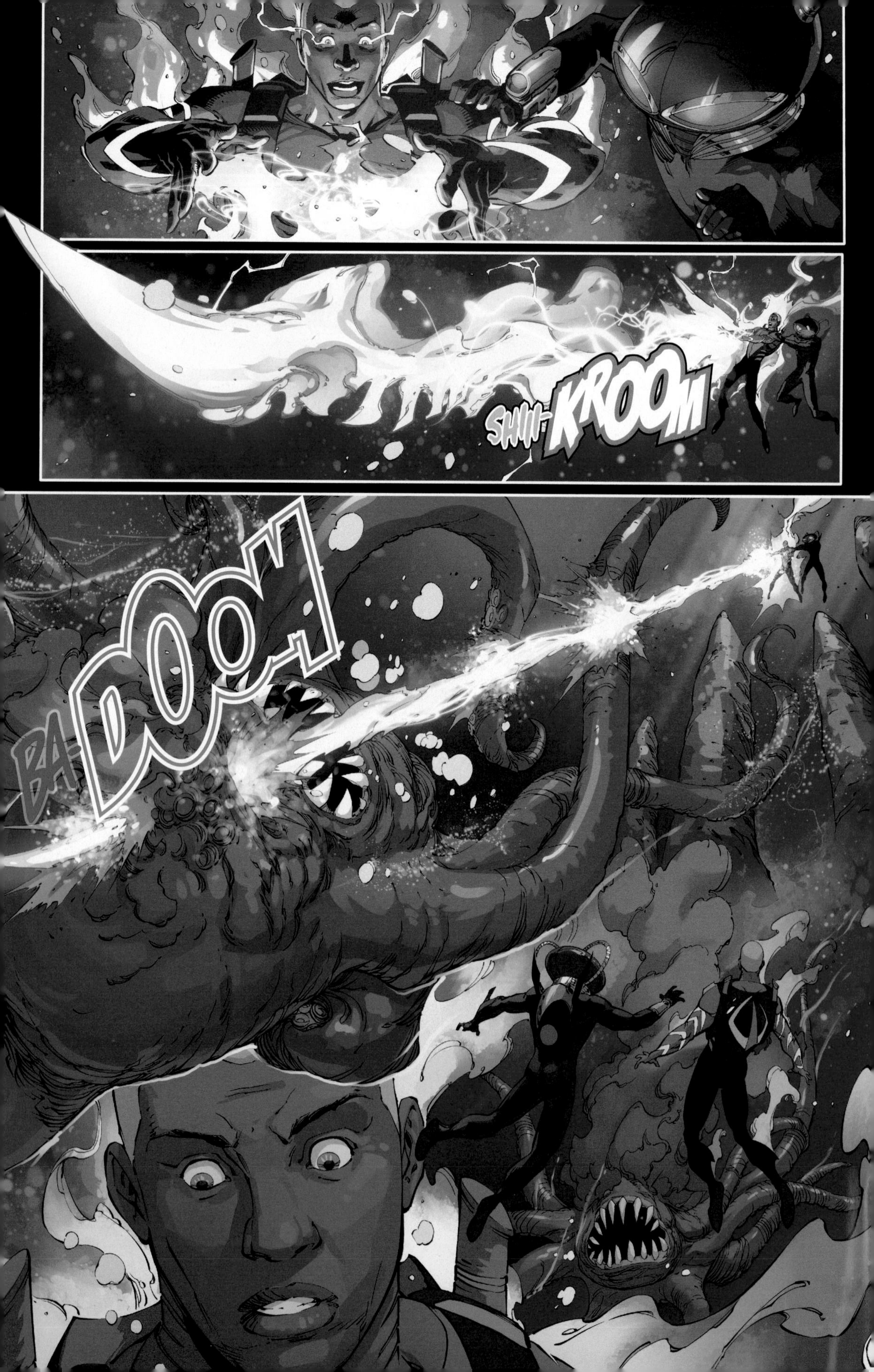

SHIIII-KROOM
BA-DOOOM

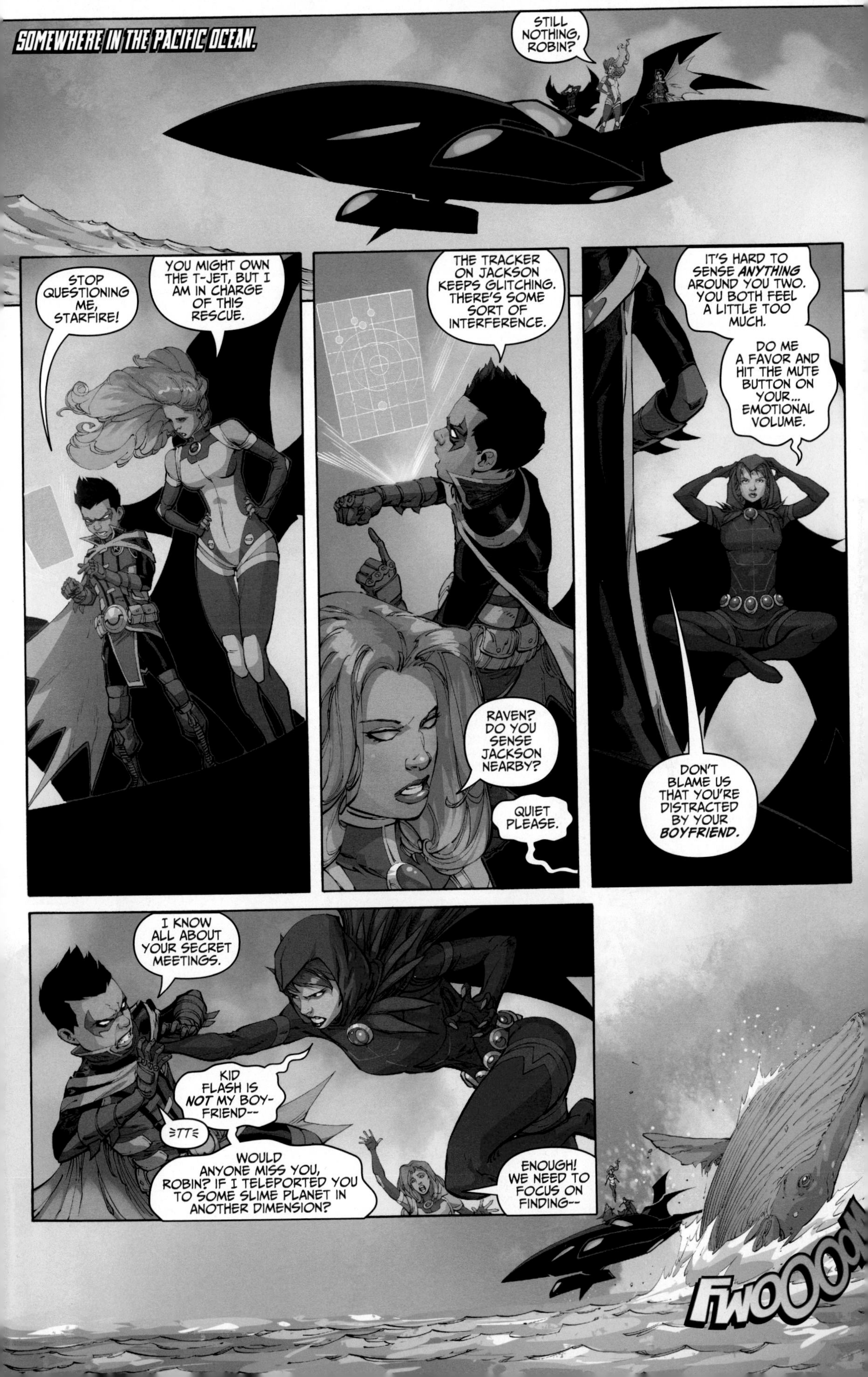
SOMEWHERE IN THE PACIFIC OCEAN.
STILL NOTHING, ROBIN?
STOP QUESTIONING ME, STARFIRE!
YOU MIGHT OWN THE T-JET, BUT I AM IN CHARGE OF THIS RESCUE.
THE TRACKER ON JACKSON KEEPS GLITCHING. THERE'S SOME SORT OF INTERFERENCE.
RAVEN? DO YOU SENSE JACKSON NEARBY?
QUIET PLEASE.
IT'S HARD TO SENSE ANYTHING AROUND YOU TWO. YOU BOTH FEEL A LITTLE TOO MUCH.
DO ME A FAVOR AND HIT THE MUTE BUTTON ON YOUR... EMOTIONAL VOLUME.
DON'T BLAME US THAT YOU'RE DISTRACTED BY YOUR BOYFRIEND.
I KNOW ALL ABOUT YOUR SECRET MEETINGS.
KID FLASH IS NOT MY BOY-FRIEND--
TT
WOULD ANYONE MISS YOU, ROBIN? IF I TELEPORTED YOU TO SOME SLIME PLANET IN ANOTHER DIMENSION?
ENOUGH! WE NEED TO FOCUS ON FINDING--
FWOOOOM

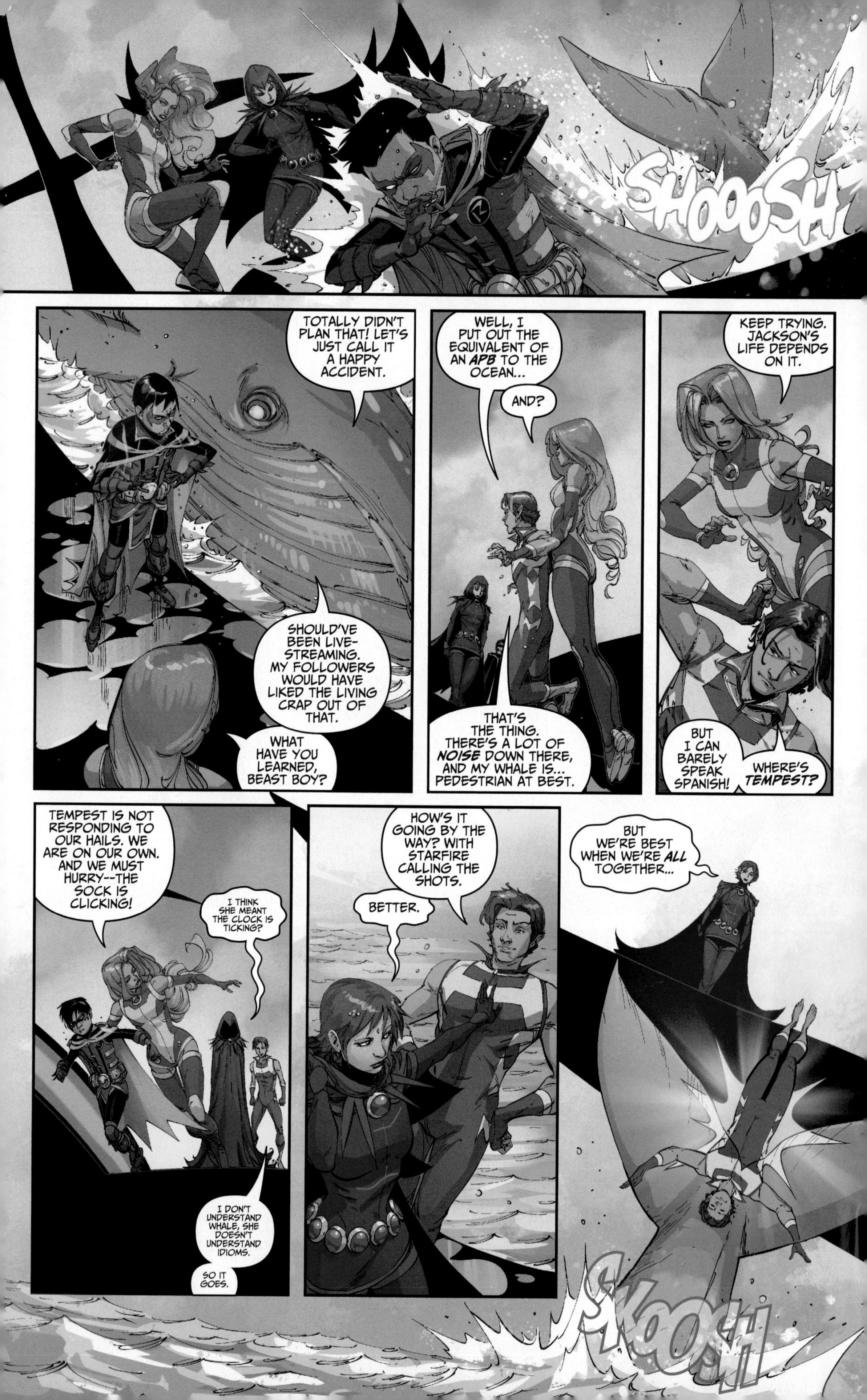
SHOOOSH
TOTALLY DIDN'T PLAN THAT! LET'S JUST CALL IT A HAPPY ACCIDENT.
SHOULD'VE BEEN LIVE-STREAMING. MY FOLLOWERS WOULD HAVE LIKED THE LIVING CRAP OUT OF THAT.
WHAT HAVE YOU LEARNED, BEAST BOY?
WELL, I PUT OUT THE EQUIVALENT OF AN APB TO THE OCEAN...
AND?
THAT'S THE THING. THERE'S A LOT OF NOISE DOWN THERE, AND MY WHALE IS... PEDESTRIAN AT BEST.
KEEP TRYING. JACKSON'S LIFE DEPENDS ON IT.
BUT I CAN BARELY SPEAK SPANISH!
WHERE'S TEMPEST?
TEMPEST IS NOT RESPONDING TO OUR HAILS. WE ARE ON OUR OWN. AND WE MUST HURRY--THE SOCK IS CLICKING!
I THINK SHE MEANT THE CLOCK IS TICKING?
I DON'T UNDERSTAND WHALE, SHE DOESN'T UNDERSTAND IDIOMS.
SO IT GOES.
HOW'S IT GOING BY THE WAY? WITH STARFIRE CALLING THE SHOTS.
BETTER.
BUT WE'RE BEST WHEN WE'RE ALL TOGETHER...
SKOOSH

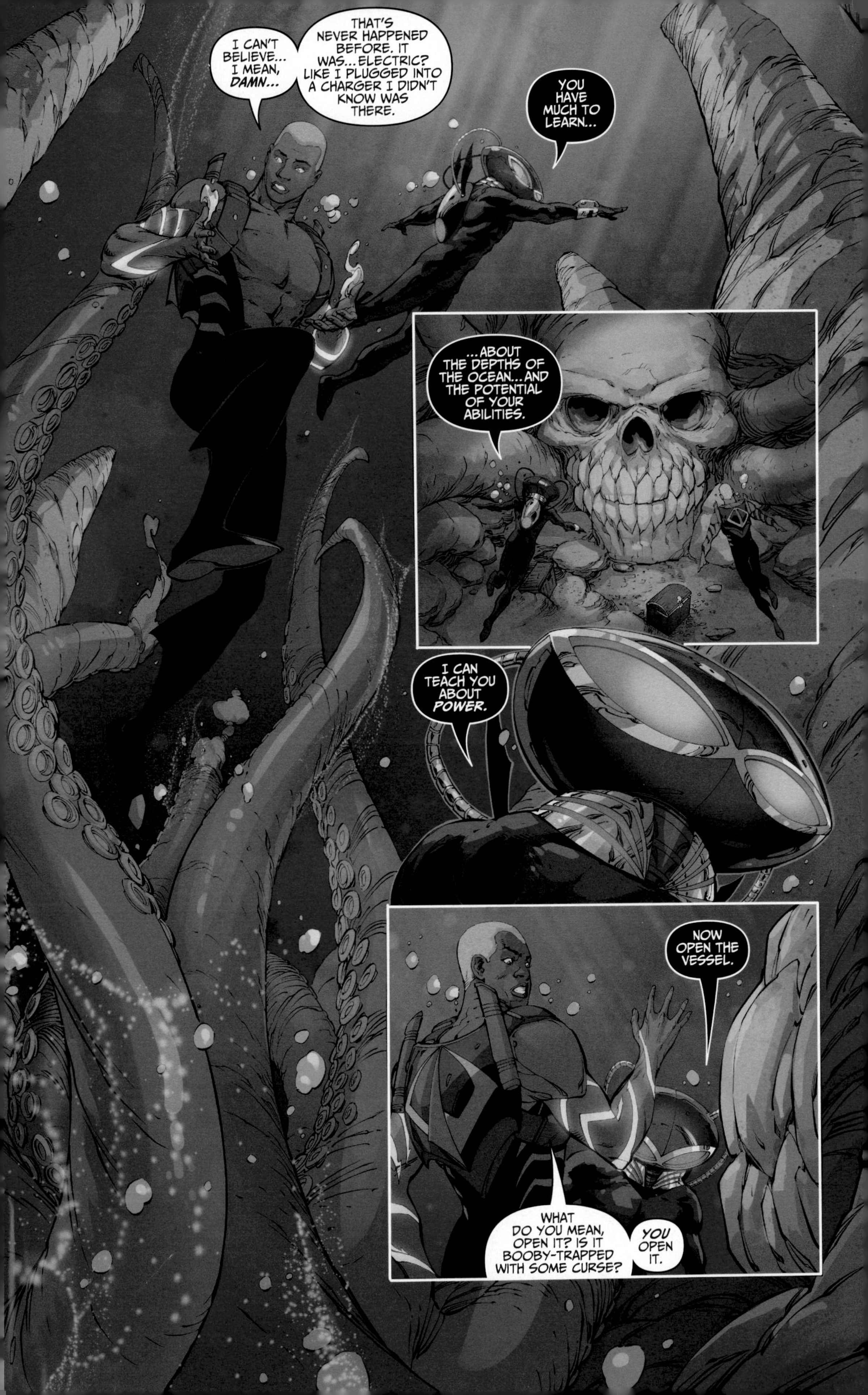
I CAN'T BELIEVE... I MEAN, DAMN...
THAT'S NEVER HAPPENED BEFORE. IT WAS...ELECTRIC? LIKE I PLUGGED INTO A CHARGER I DIDN'T KNOW WAS THERE.
YOU HAVE MUCH TO LEARN...
...ABOUT THE DEPTHS OF THE OCEAN...AND THE POTENTIAL OF YOUR ABILITIES.
I CAN TEACH YOU ABOUT POWER.
NOW OPEN THE VESSEL.
WHAT DO YOU MEAN, OPEN IT? IS IT BOOBY-TRAPPED WITH SOME CURSE?
YOU OPEN IT.

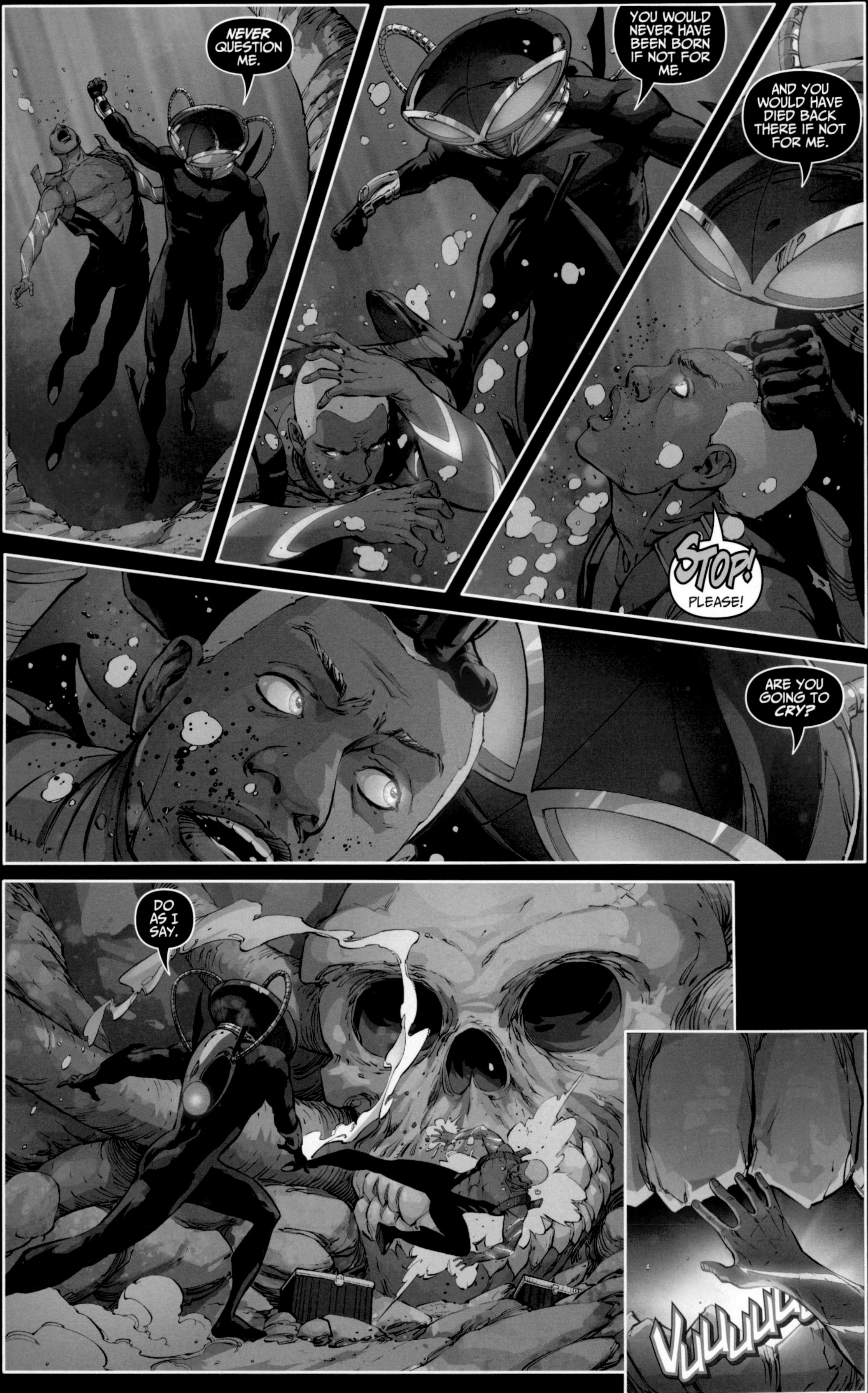
NEVER QUESTION ME.
YOU WOULD NEVER HAVE BEEN BORN IF NOT FOR ME.
AND YOU WOULD HAVE DIED BACK THERE IF NOT FOR ME.
STOP! PLEASE!
ARE YOU GOING TO CRY?
DO AS I SAY.
VUUUUU

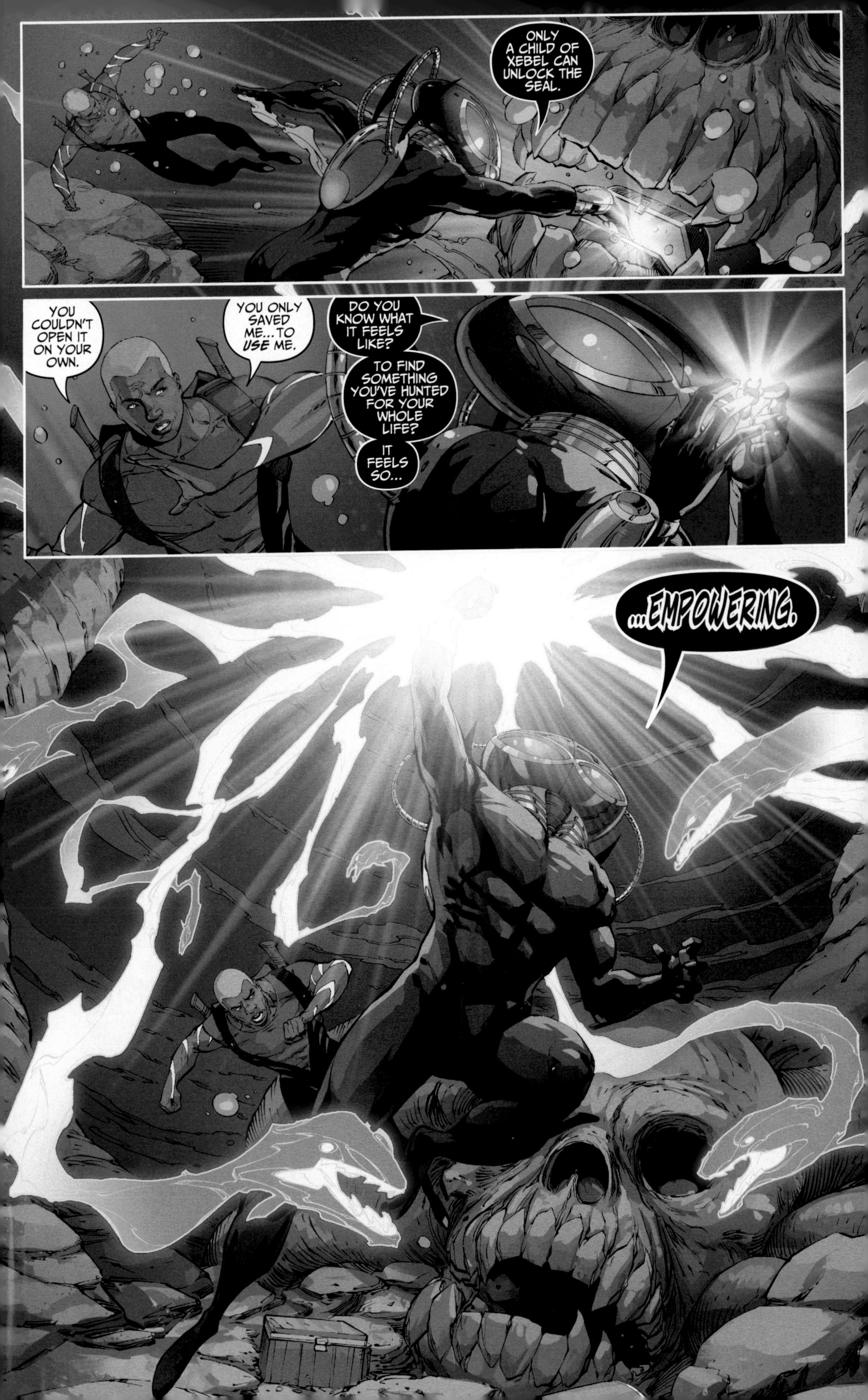
ONLY A CHILD OF XEBEL CAN UNLOCK THE SEAL.
YOU COULDN'T OPEN IT ON YOUR OWN.
YOU ONLY SAVED ME... TO USE ME.
DO YOU KNOW WHAT IT FEELS LIKE?
TO FIND SOMETHING YOU'VE HUNTED FOR YOUR WHOLE LIFE?
IT FEELS SO...
...EMPOWERING.

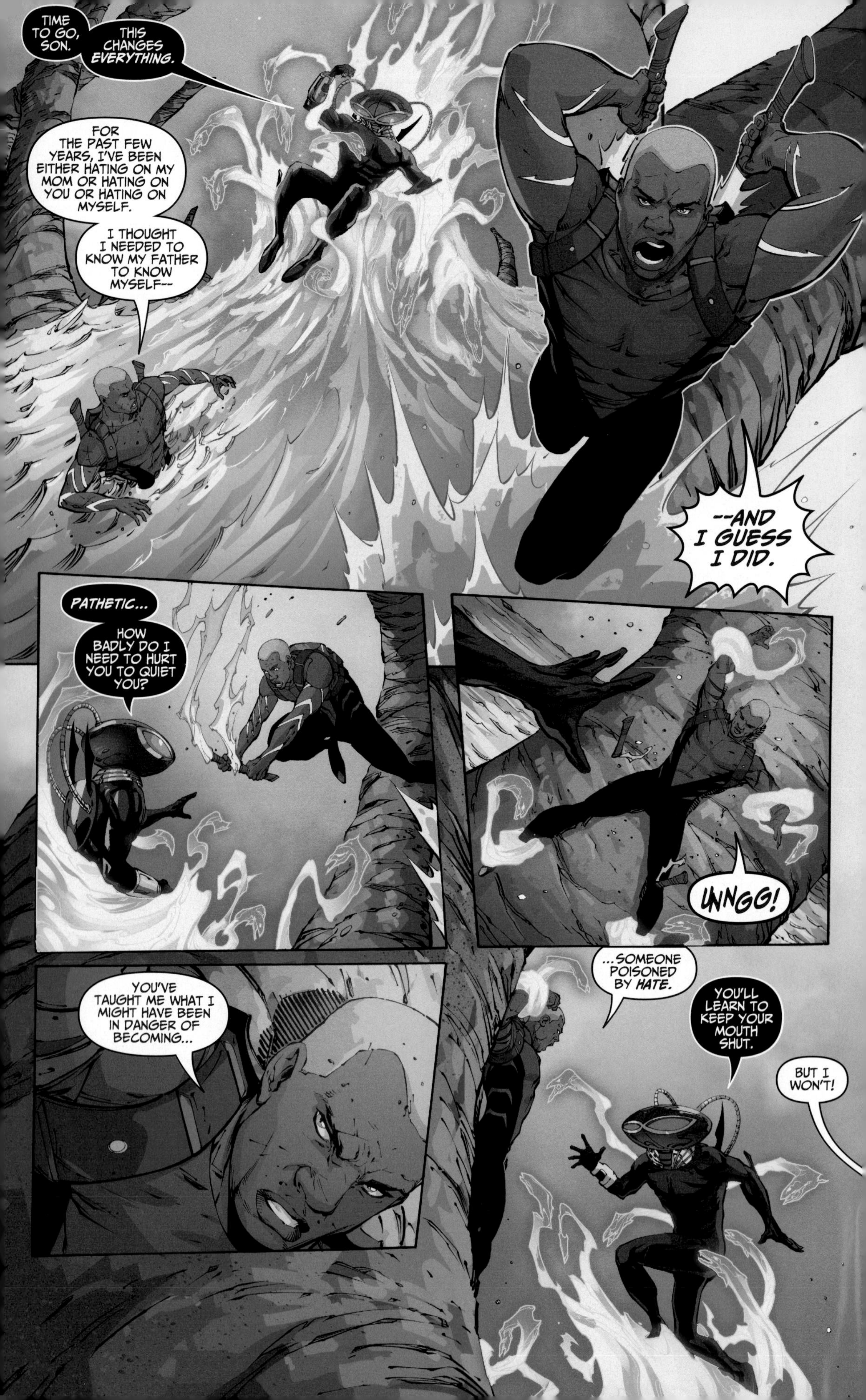
TIME TO GO, SON.
THIS CHANGES EVERYTHING.
FOR THE PAST FEW YEARS, I'VE BEEN EITHER HATING ON MY MOM OR HATING ON YOU OR HATING ON MYSELF.
I THOUGHT I NEEDED TO KNOW MY FATHER TO KNOW MYSELF--
--AND I GUESS I DID.
PATHETIC...
HOW BADLY DO I NEED TO HURT YOU TO QUIET YOU?
UNNGG!
YOU'VE TAUGHT ME WHAT I MIGHT HAVE BEEN IN DANGER OF BECOMING...
...SOMEONE POISONED BY HATE.
YOU'LL LEARN TO KEEP YOUR MOUTH SHUT.
BUT I WON'T!

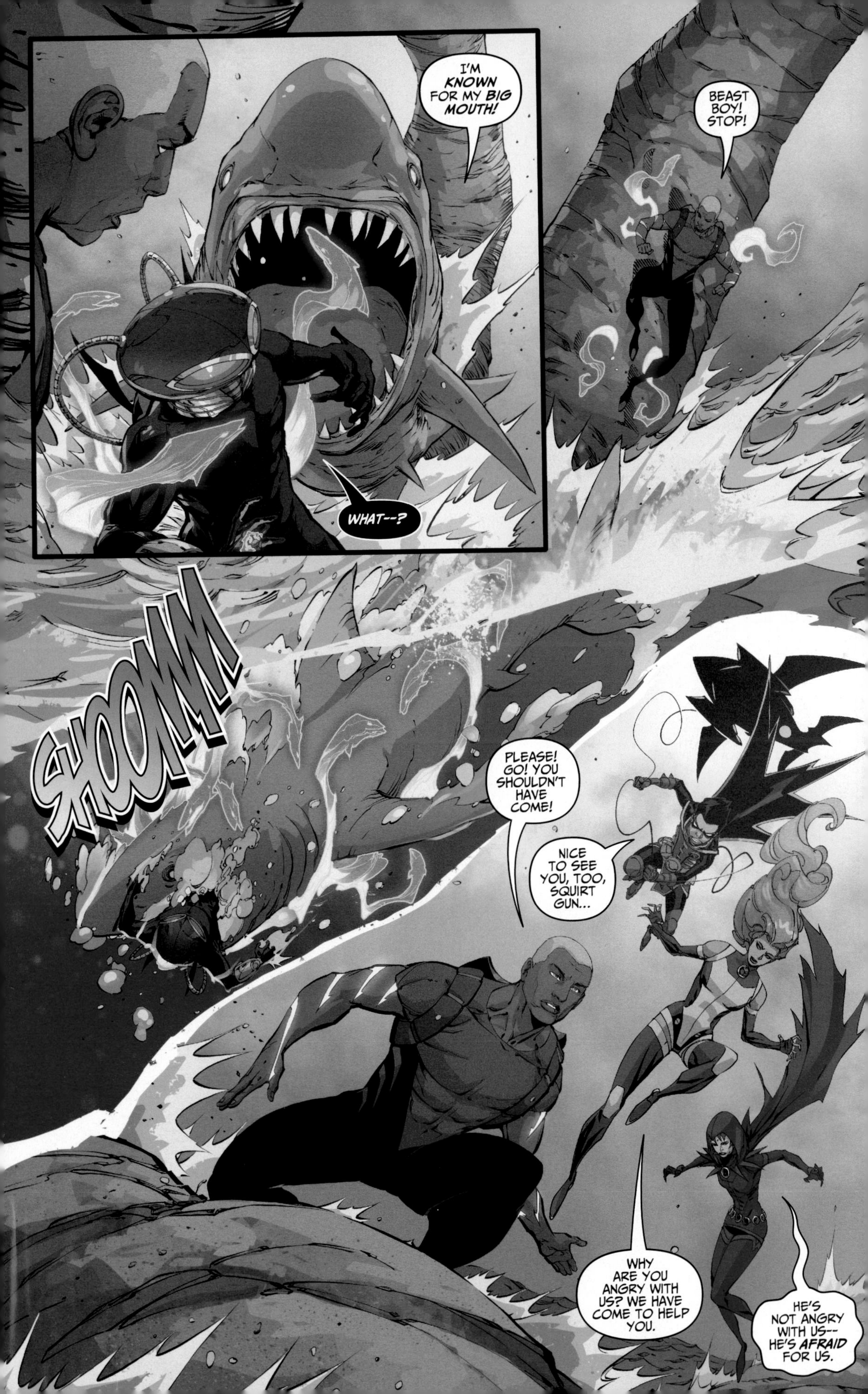
I'M KNOWN FOR MY BIG MOUTH!
BEAST BOY! STOP!
WHAT--?
SHOOMM
PLEASE! GO! YOU SHOULDN'T HAVE COME!
NICE TO SEE YOU, TOO, SQUIRT GUN...
WHY ARE YOU ANGRY WITH US? WE HAVE COME TO HELP YOU.
HE'S NOT ANGRY WITH US-- HE'S AFRAID FOR US.

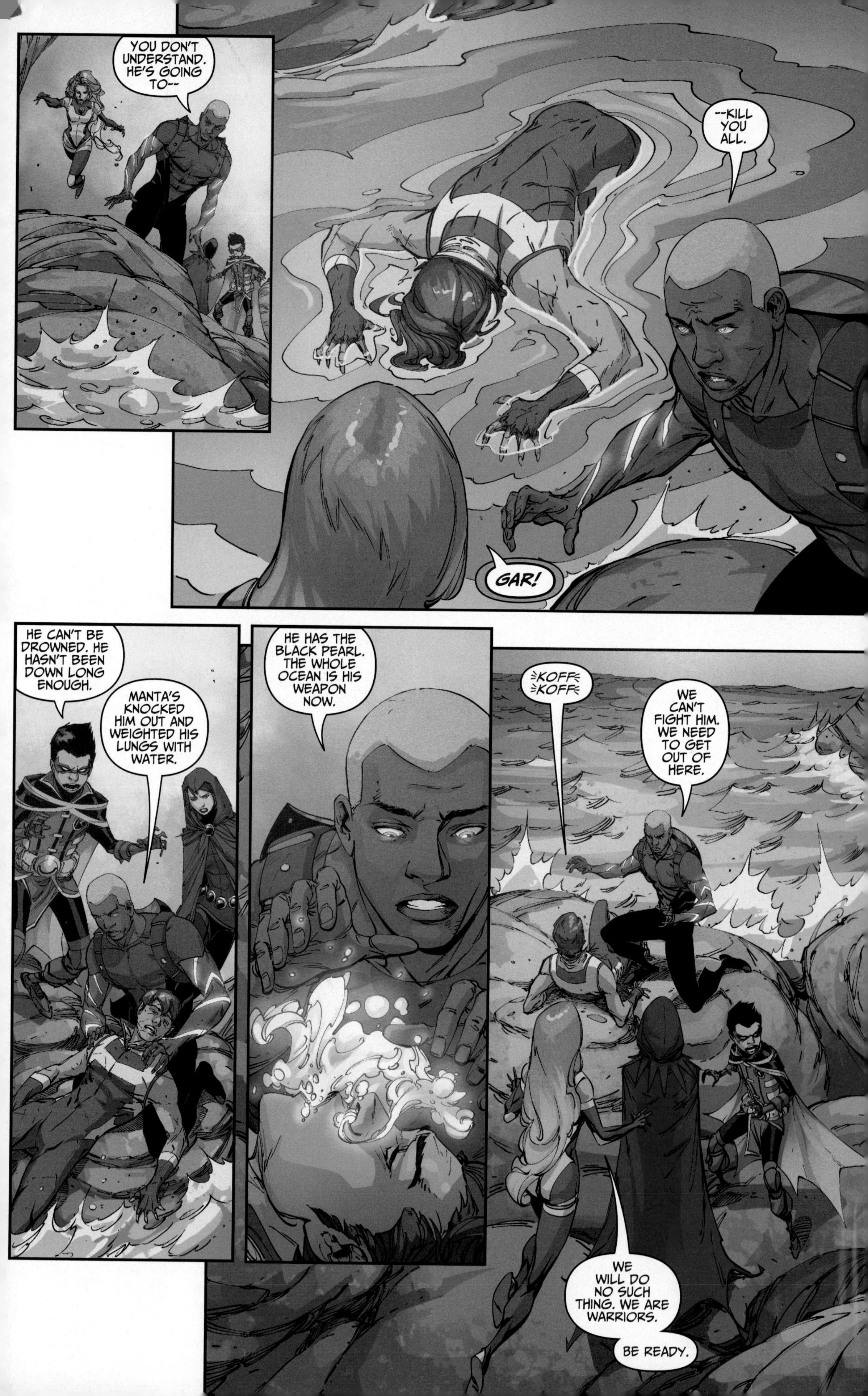
YOU DON'T UNDERSTAND. HE'S GOING TO--
--KILL YOU ALL.
GAR!
HE CAN'T BE DROWNED. HE HASN'T BEEN DOWN LONG ENOUGH.
MANTA'S KNOCKED HIM OUT AND WEIGHTED HIS LUNGS WITH WATER.
HE HAS THE BLACK PEARL. THE WHOLE OCEAN IS HIS WEAPON NOW.
KOFF KOFF
WE CAN'T FIGHT HIM. WE NEED TO GET OUT OF HERE.
WE WILL DO NO SUCH THING. WE ARE WARRIORS.
BE READY.

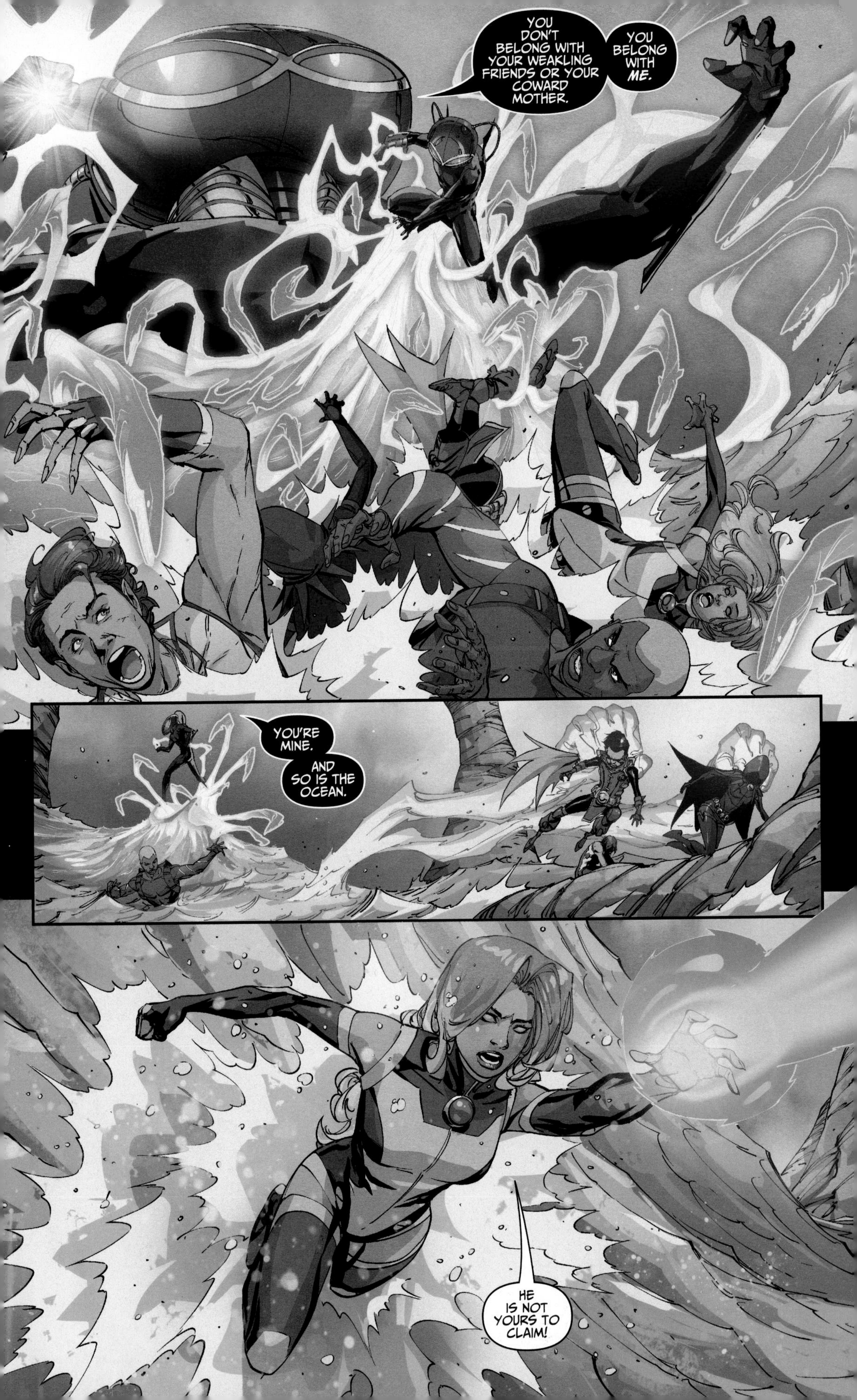
YOU DON'T BELONG WITH YOUR WEAKLING FRIENDS OR YOUR COWARD MOTHER.
YOU BELONG WITH *ME.*
YOU'RE MINE.
AND SO IS THE OCEAN.
HE IS NOT YOURS TO CLAIM!

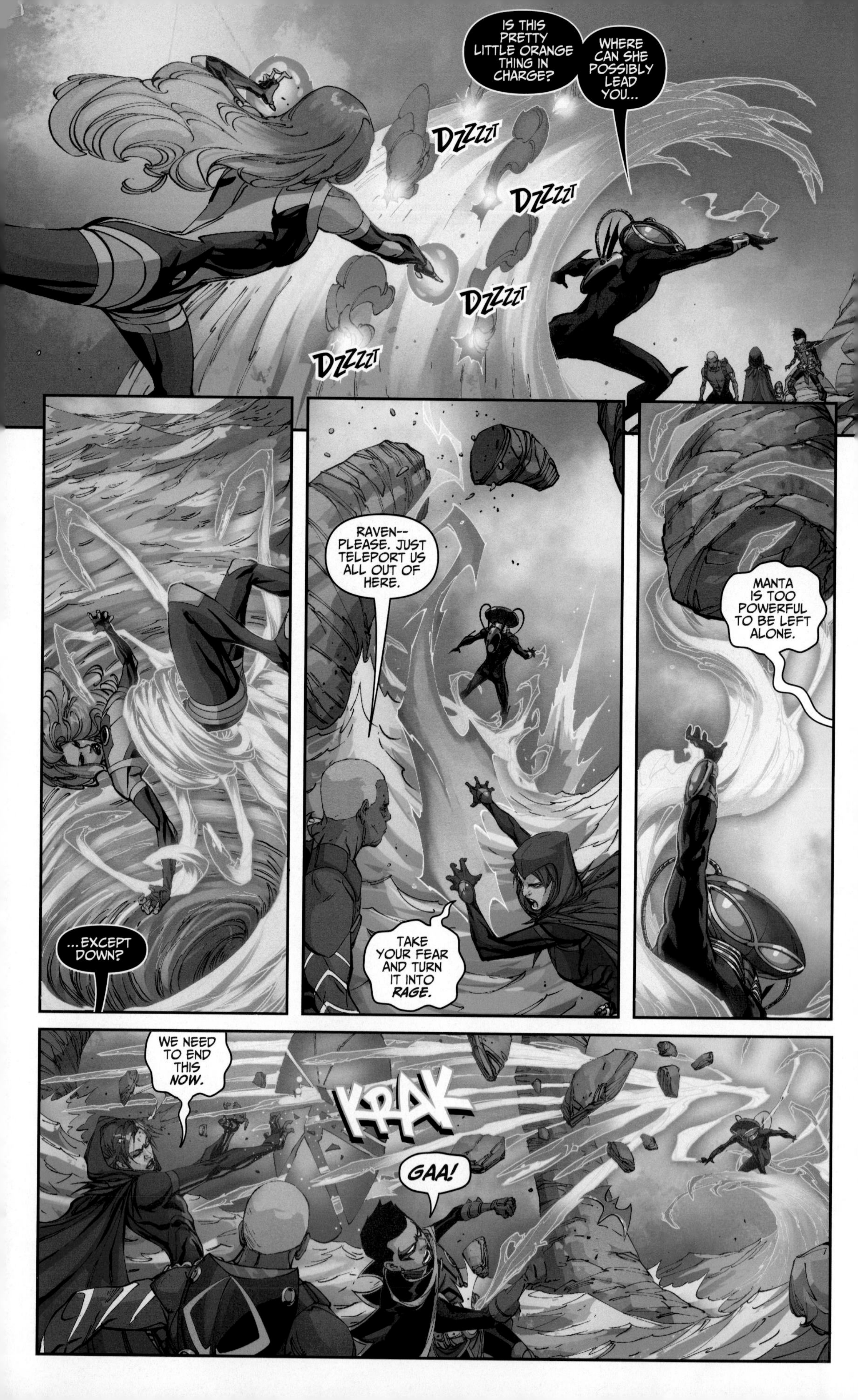
IS THIS PRETTY LITTLE ORANGE THING IN CHARGE?
WHERE CAN SHE POSSIBLY LEAD YOU...
DZZZZT
DZZZZT
DZZZZT
DZZZZT
...EXCEPT DOWN?
RAVEN-- PLEASE. JUST TELEPORT US ALL OUT OF HERE.
TAKE YOUR FEAR AND TURN IT INTO RAGE.
MANTA IS TOO POWERFUL TO BE LEFT ALONE.
WE NEED TO END THIS NOW.
KRAK
GAA!

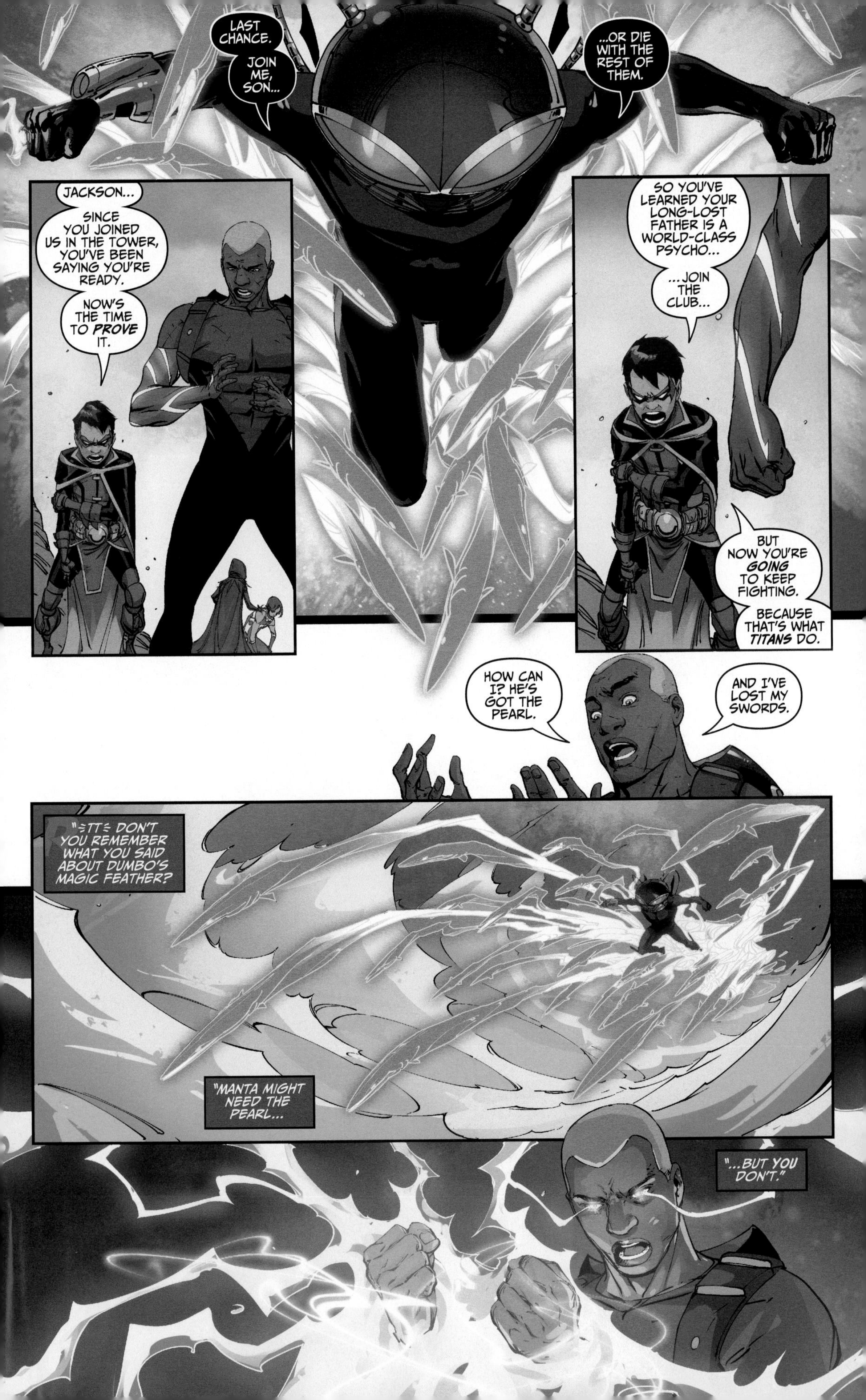
LAST CHANCE.
JOIN ME, SON...
...OR DIE WITH THE REST OF THEM.
JACKSON...
SINCE YOU JOINED US IN THE TOWER, YOU'VE BEEN SAYING YOU'RE READY.
NOW'S THE TIME TO PROVE IT.
SO YOU'VE LEARNED YOUR LONG-LOST FATHER IS A WORLD-CLASS PSYCHO...
...JOIN THE CLUB...
BUT NOW YOU'RE GOING TO KEEP FIGHTING.
BECAUSE THAT'S WHAT TITANS DO.
HOW CAN I? HE'S GOT THE PEARL.
AND I'VE LOST MY SWORDS.
"TT DON'T YOU REMEMBER WHAT YOU SAID ABOUT DUMBO'S MAGIC FEATHER?
"MANTA MIGHT NEED THE PEARL...
"...BUT YOU DON'T."

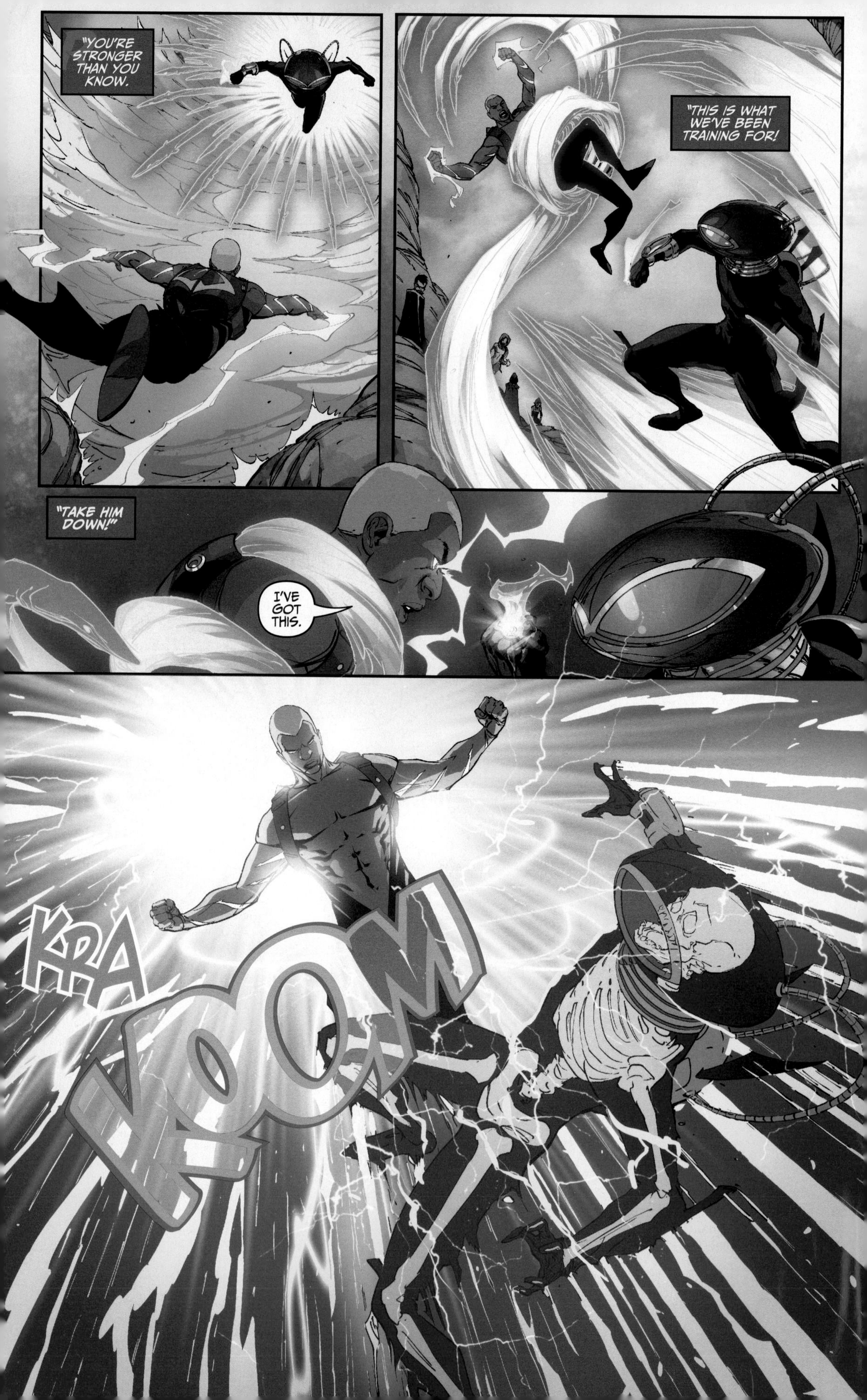
"YOU'RE STRONGER THAN YOU KNOW.
"THIS IS WHAT WE'VE BEEN TRAINING FOR!
"TAKE HIM DOWN!"
I'VE GOT THIS.
KRA KOOM

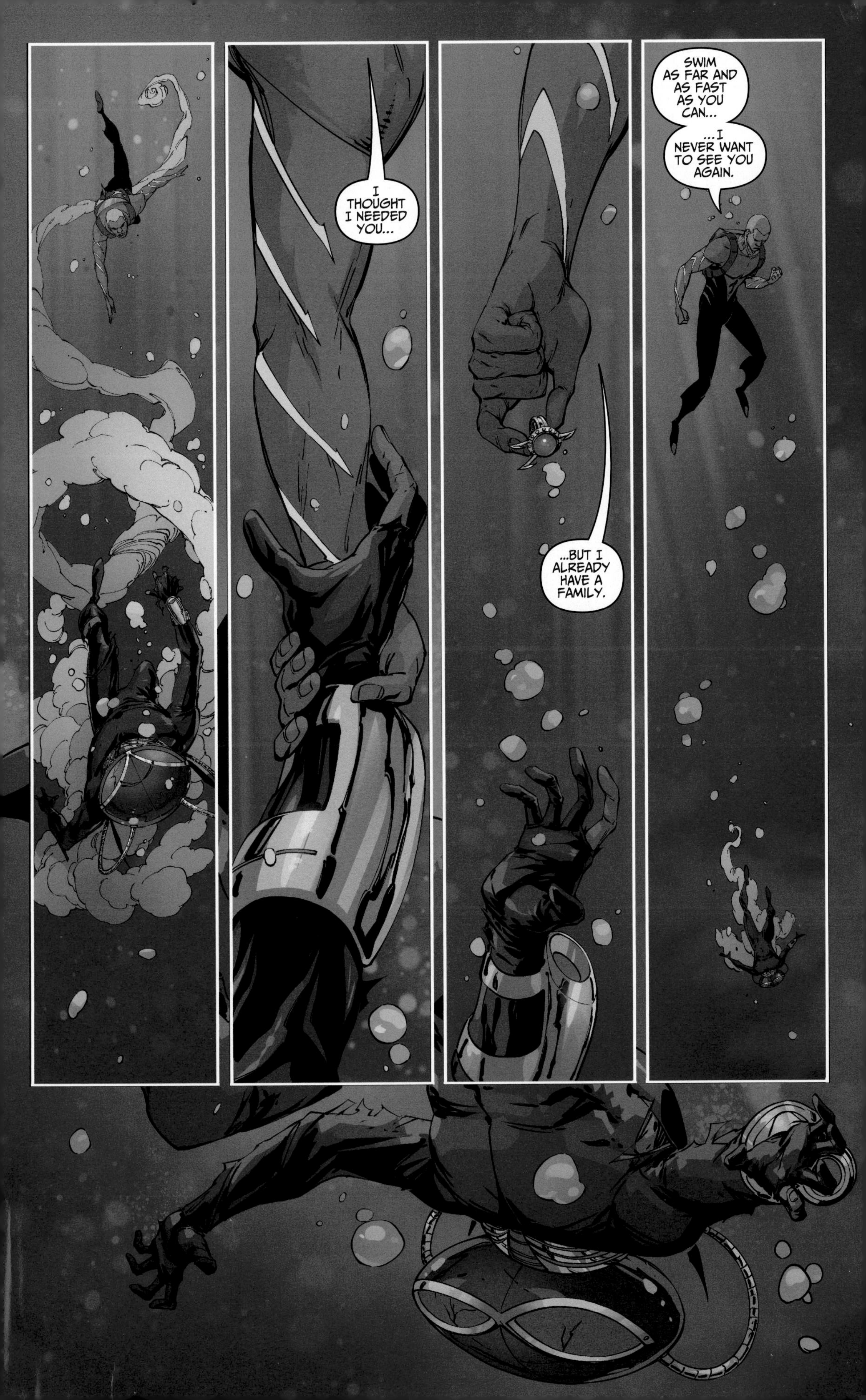
I THOUGHT I NEEDED YOU...
...BUT I ALREADY HAVE A FAMILY.
SWIM AS FAR AND AS FAST AS YOU CAN...
...I NEVER WANT TO SEE YOU AGAIN.

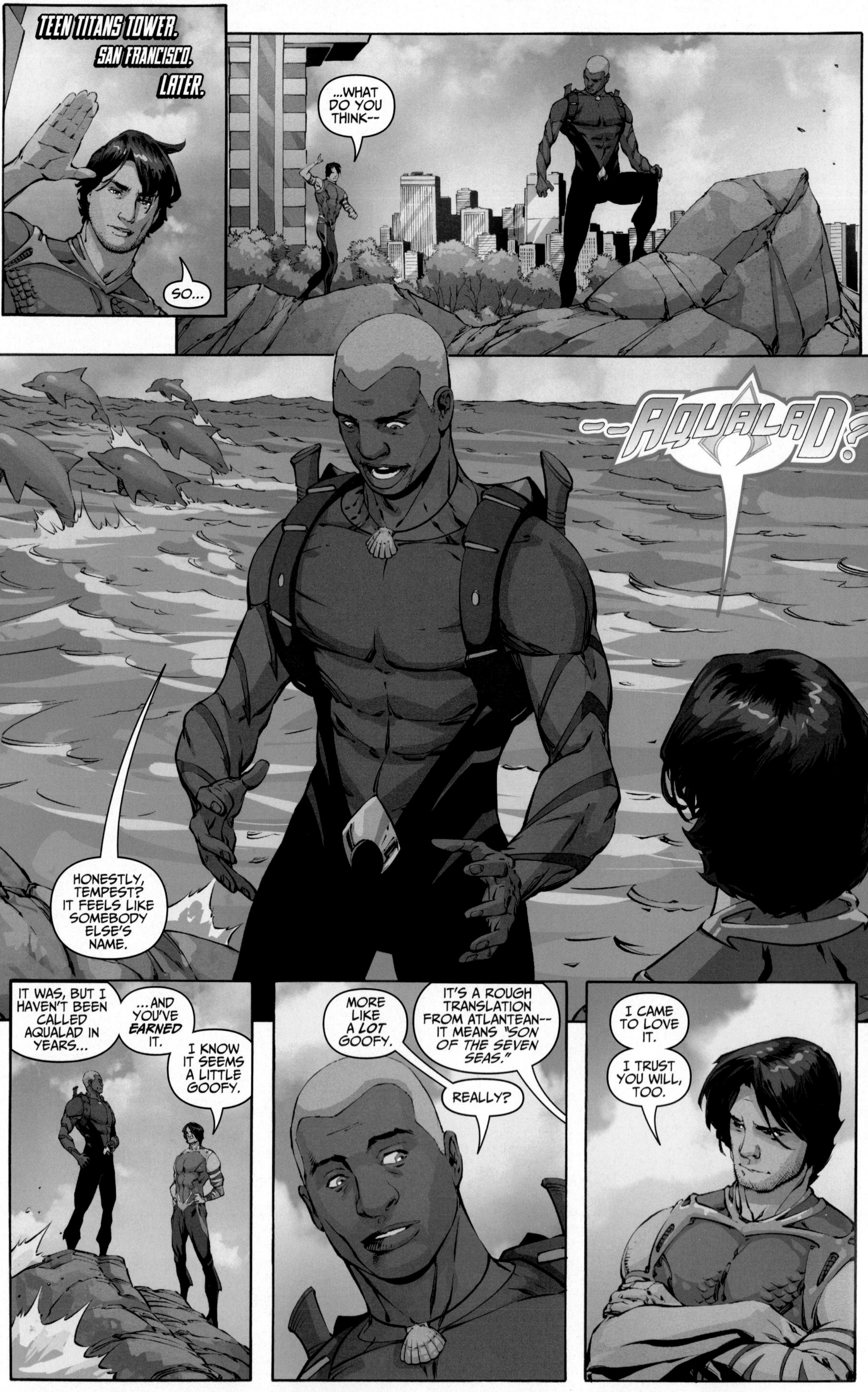
TEEN TITANS TOWER.
SAN FRANCISCO.
LATER.
SO...
...WHAT DO YOU THINK--
--AQUALAD?
HONESTLY, TEMPEST? IT FEELS LIKE SOMEBODY ELSE'S NAME.
IT WAS, BUT I HAVEN'T BEEN CALLED AQUALAD IN YEARS...
...AND YOU'VE EARNED IT.
I KNOW IT SEEMS A LITTLE GOOFY.
MORE LIKE A LOT GOOFY.
IT'S A ROUGH TRANSLATION FROM ATLANTEAN-- IT MEANS "SON OF THE SEVEN SEAS."
REALLY?
I CAME TO LOVE IT.
I TRUST YOU WILL, TOO.

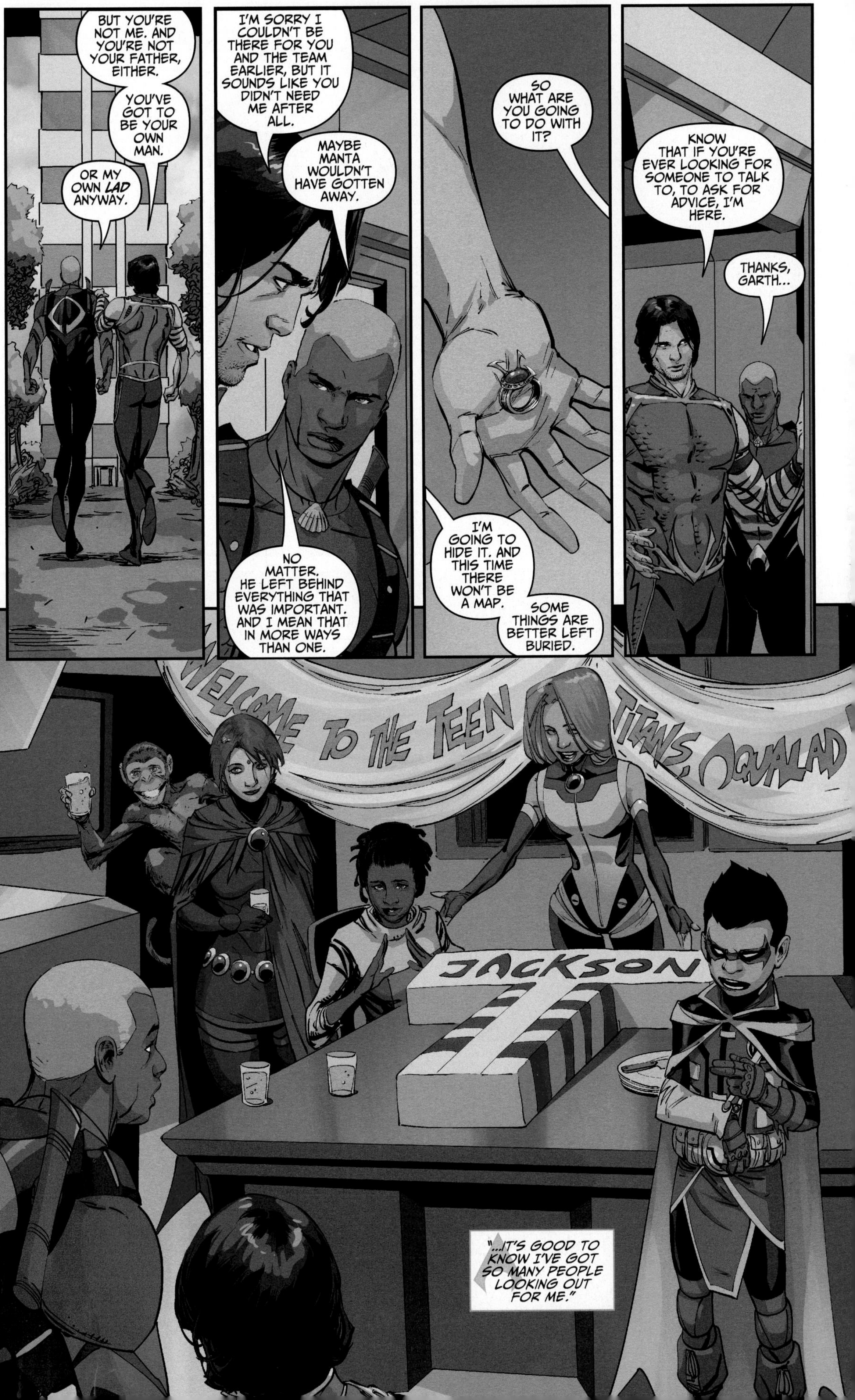
BUT YOU'RE NOT ME. AND YOU'RE NOT YOUR FATHER, EITHER.
YOU'VE GOT TO BE YOUR OWN MAN.
OR MY OWN LAD ANYWAY.
I'M SORRY I COULDN'T BE THERE FOR YOU AND THE TEAM EARLIER, BUT IT SOUNDS LIKE YOU DIDN'T NEED ME AFTER ALL.
MAYBE MANTA WOULDN'T HAVE GOTTEN AWAY.
NO MATTER. HE LEFT BEHIND EVERYTHING THAT WAS IMPORTANT. AND I MEAN THAT IN MORE WAYS THAN ONE.
SO WHAT ARE YOU GOING TO DO WITH IT?
I'M GOING TO HIDE IT. AND THIS TIME THERE WON'T BE A MAP.
SOME THINGS ARE BETTER LEFT BURIED.
KNOW THAT IF YOU'RE EVER LOOKING FOR SOMEONE TO TALK TO, TO ASK FOR ADVICE, I'M HERE.
THANKS, GARTH...
WELCOME TO THE TEEN TITANS, AQUALAD
JACKSON
"...IT'S GOOD TO KNOW I'VE GOT SO MANY PEOPLE LOOKING OUT FOR ME."

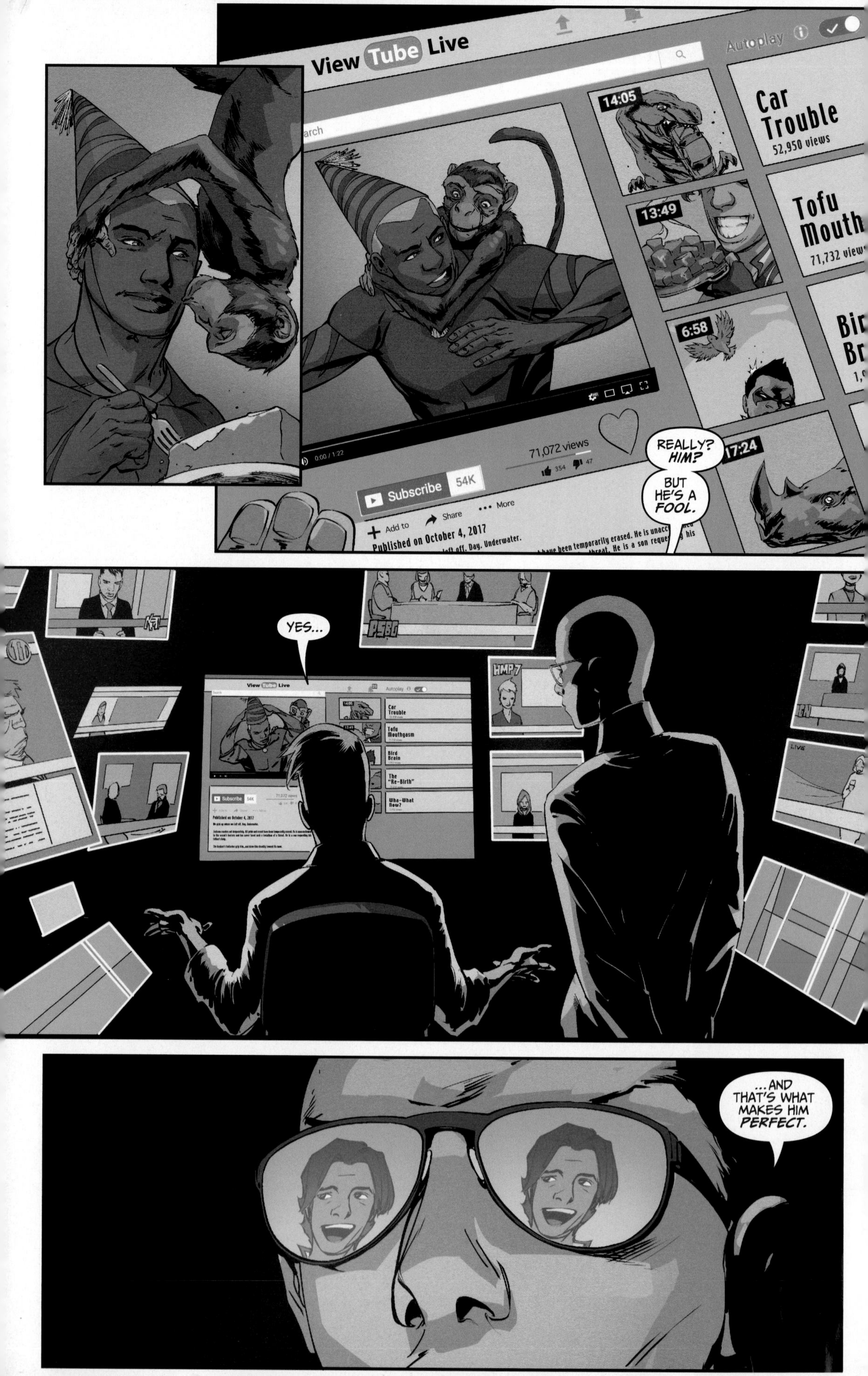
View Tube Live
Autoplay
14:05
Car Trouble
52,950 views
13:49
6:58
17:24
0:00 / 1:22
71,072 views
354
47
Subscribe
54K
Add to
Share
More
Published on October 4, 2017
REALLY? *HIM?*
BUT HE'S A *FOOL.*
YES...
...AND THAT'S WHAT MAKES HIM *PERFECT.*

TEEN TITANS

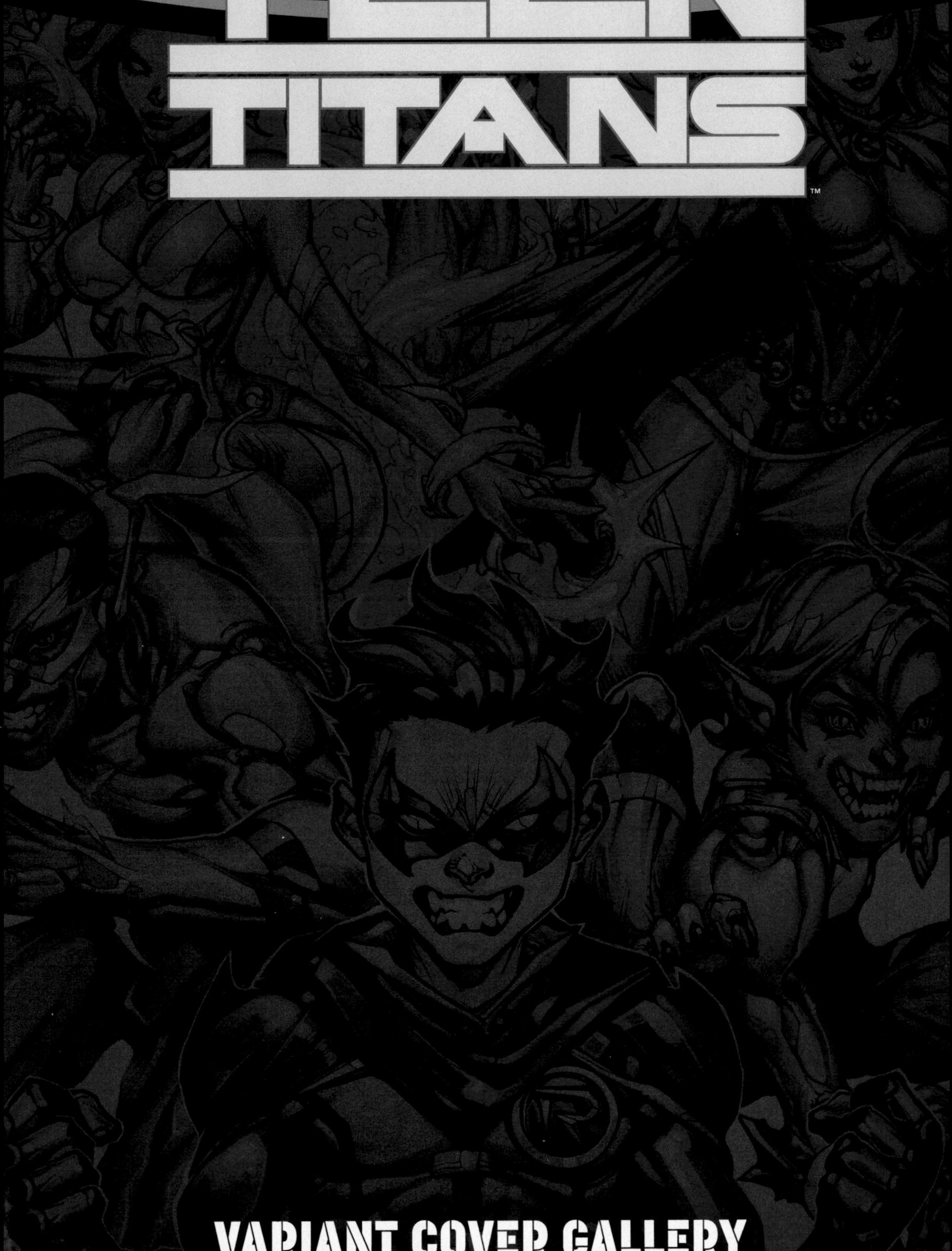

VARIANT COVER GALLERY

TEEN TITANS #6 variant cover by CHRIS BURNHAM
and NATHAN FAIRBAIRN

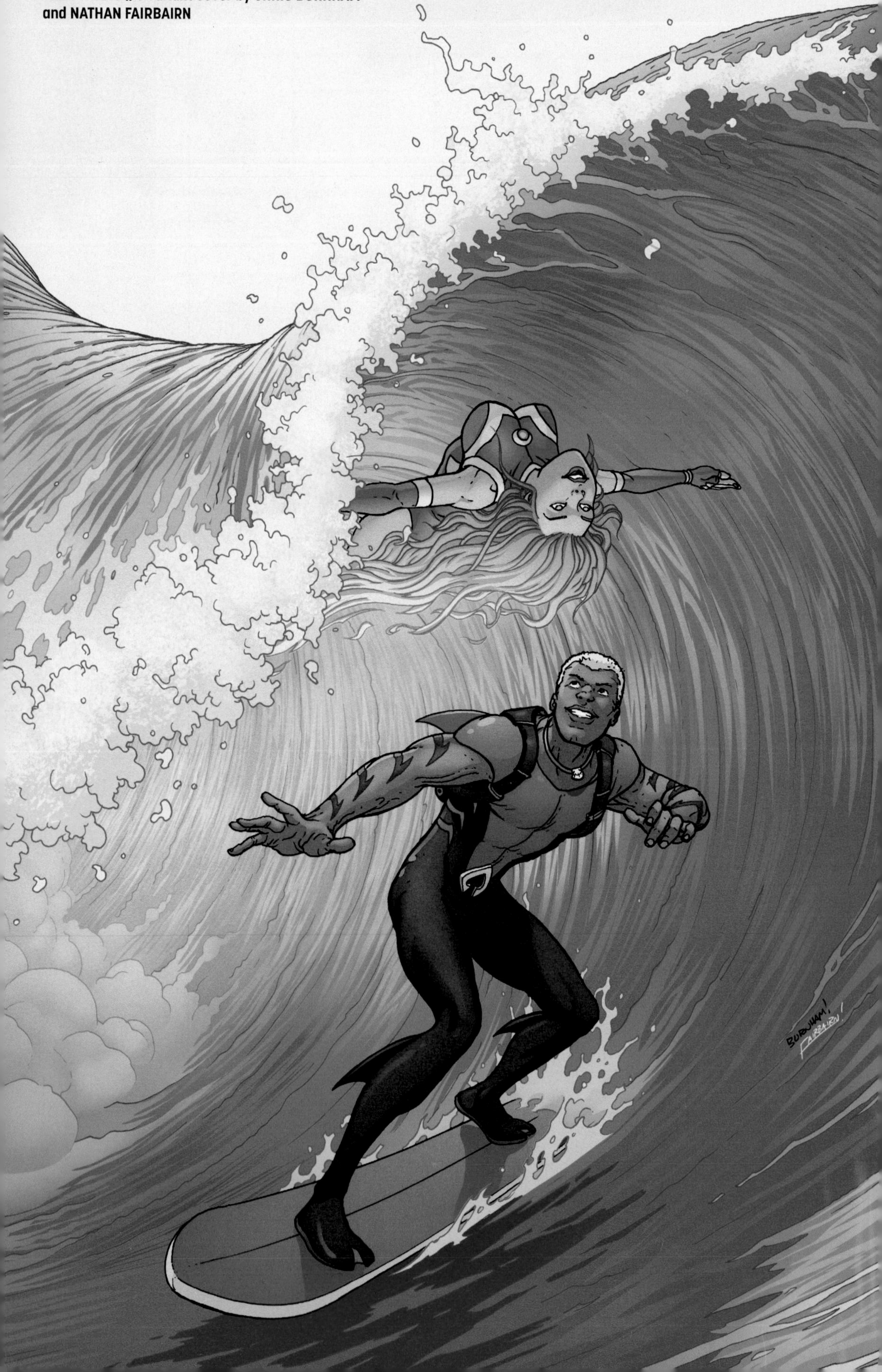
BURNHAM!
FAIRBAIRN!

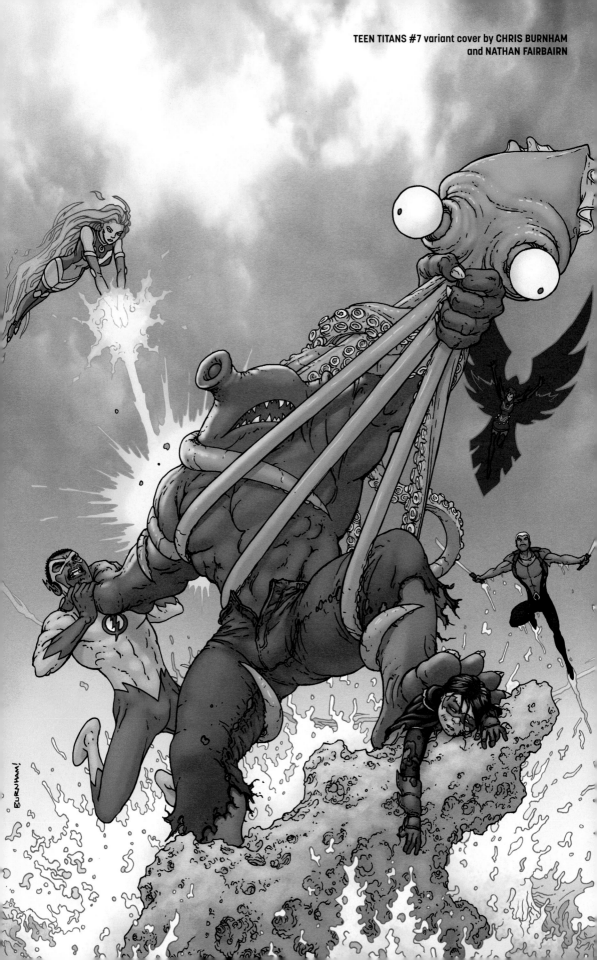

TEEN TITANS #7 variant cover by CHRIS BURNHAM
and NATHAN FAIRBAIRN

TEEN TITANS #9 variant cover by PAOLO PANTALENA and ARIF PRIANTO

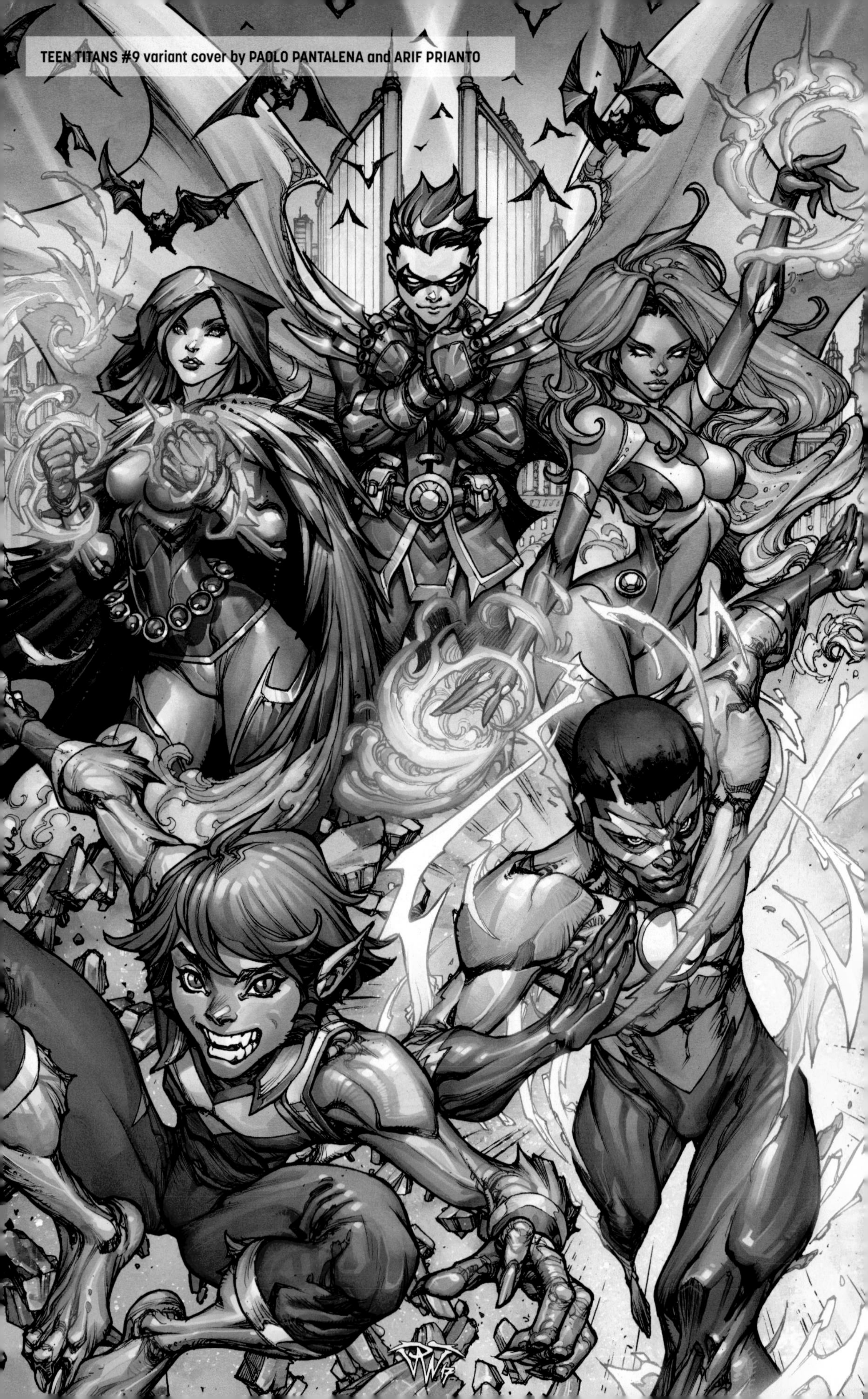

TEEN TITANS #10 variant cover by PAOLO PANTALENA and ARIF PRIANTO

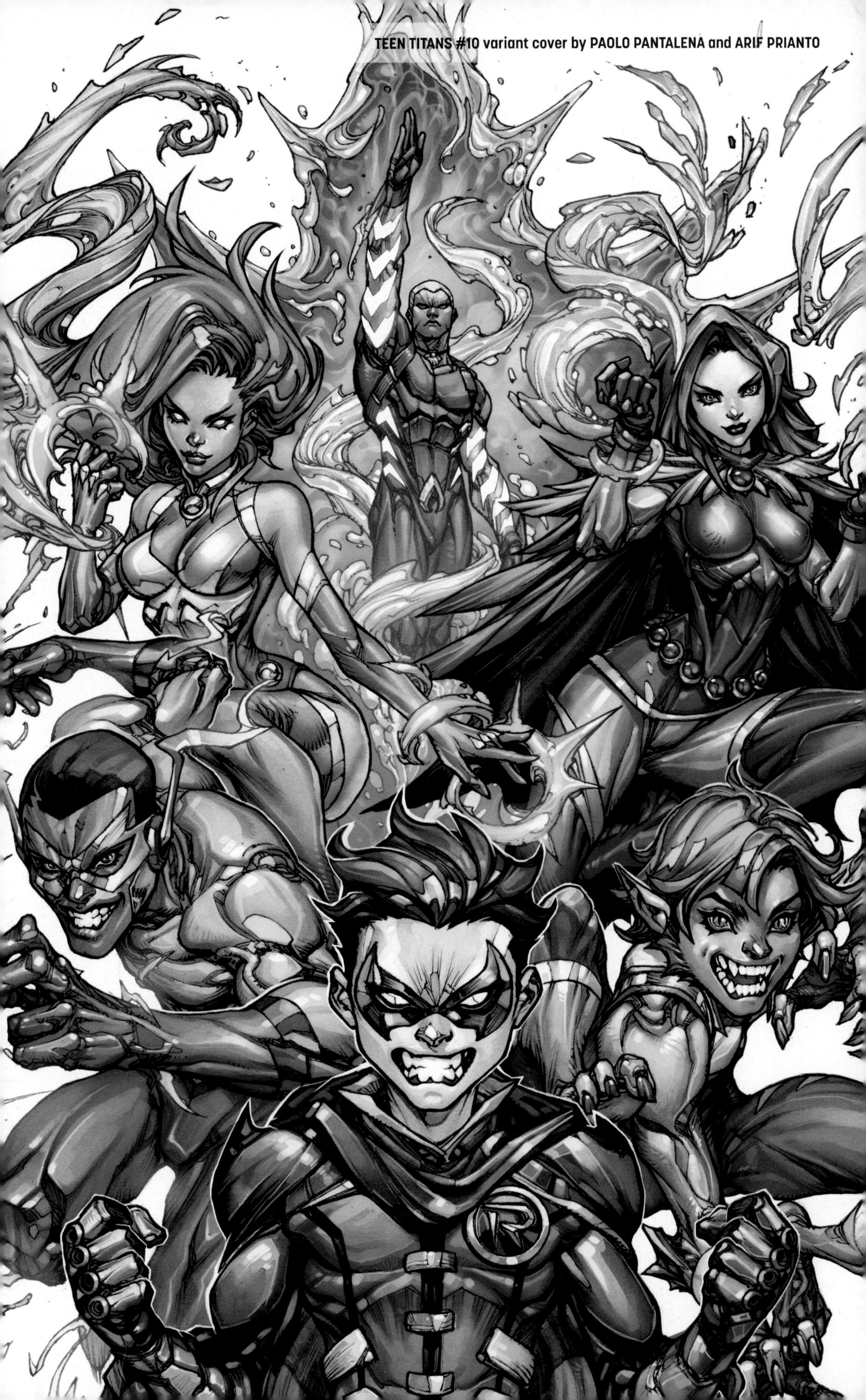

TEEN TITANS #11 variant cover by CHAD HARDIN and ALEX SINCLAIR

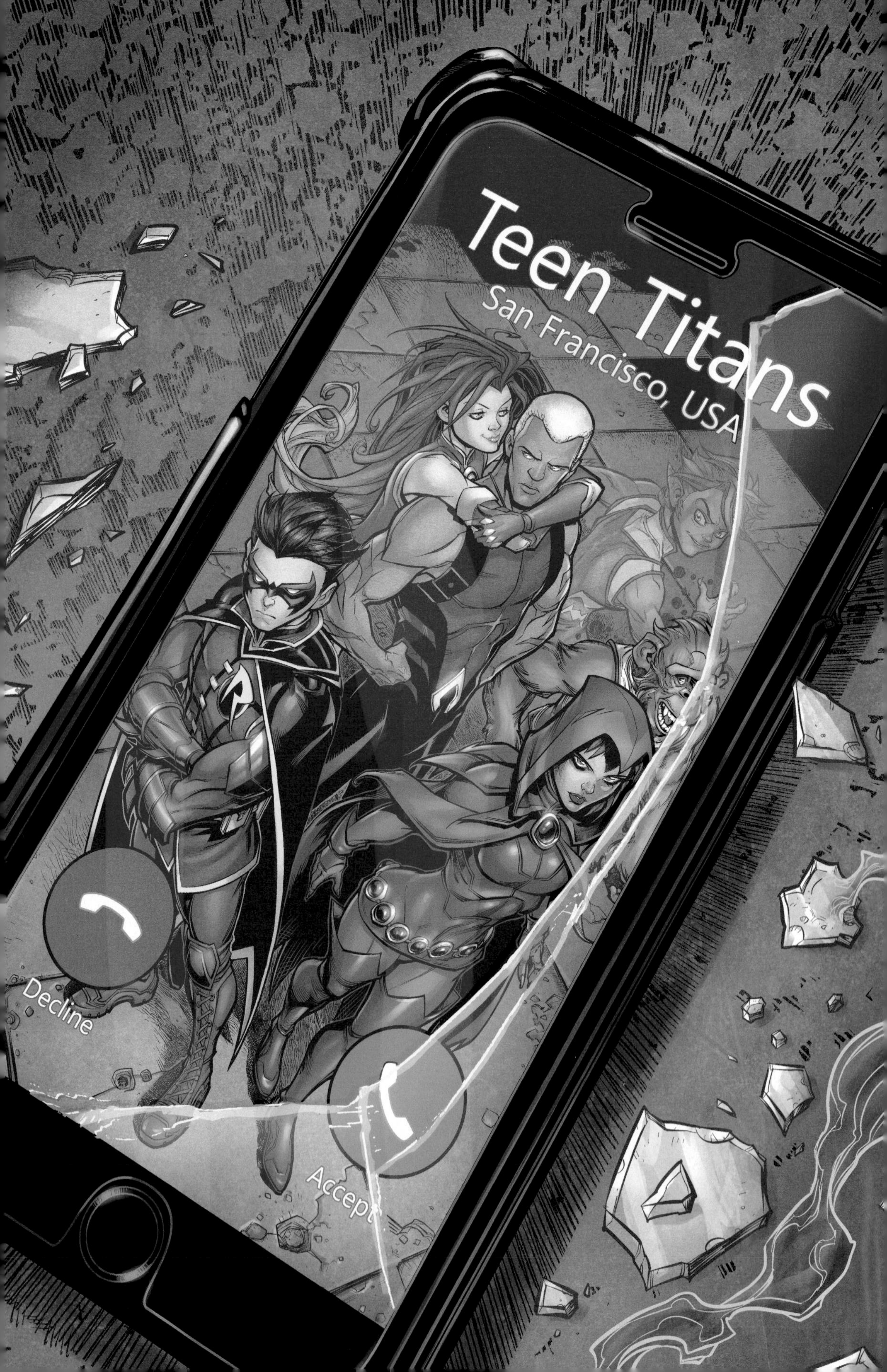
Teen Titans
San Francisco, USA
Decline
Accept

AQUALAD DESIGN
by KHOI PHAM

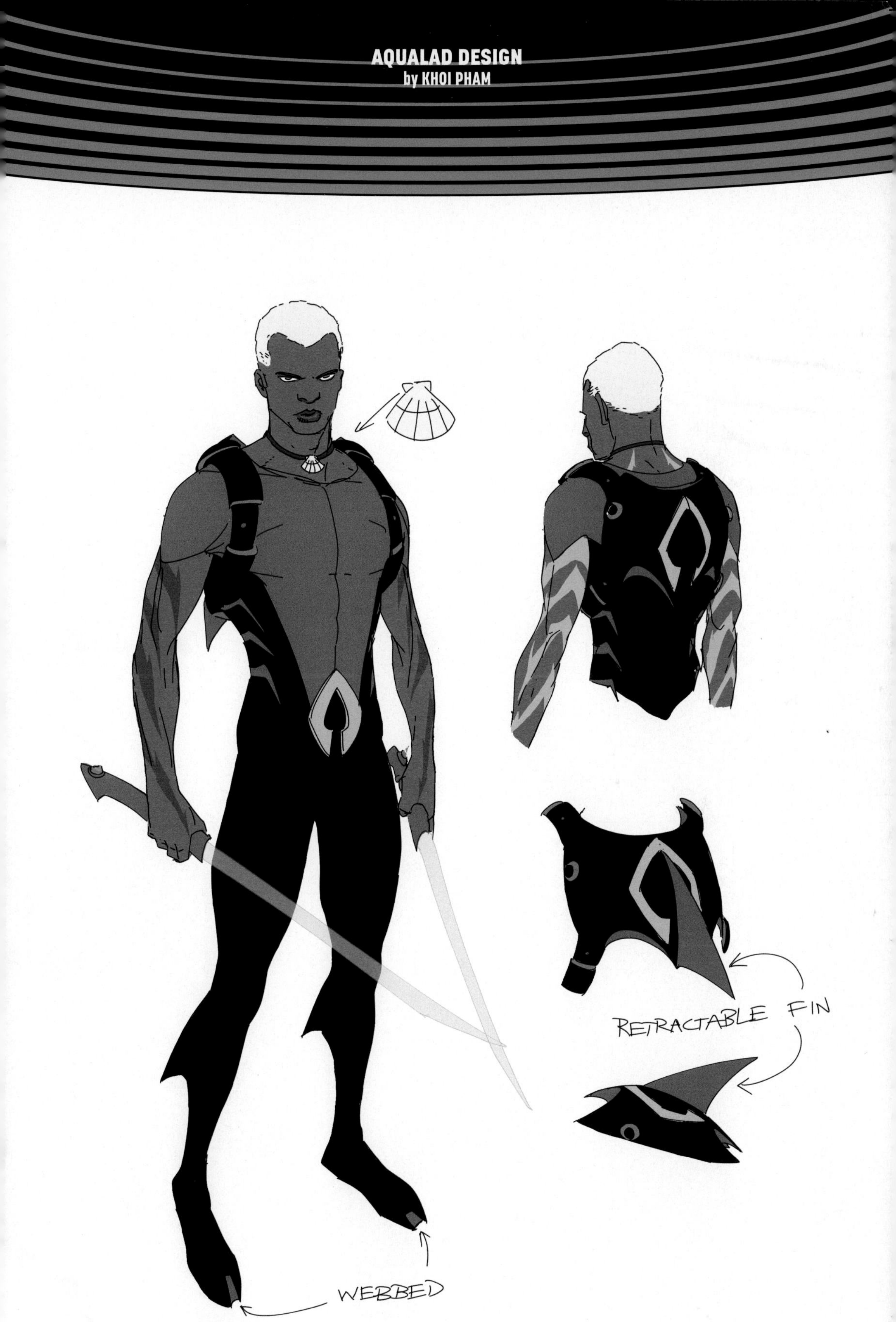

RETRACTABLE FIN
WEBBED

PAGE LAYOUTS FOR TEEN TITANS #9

by PHIL HESTER

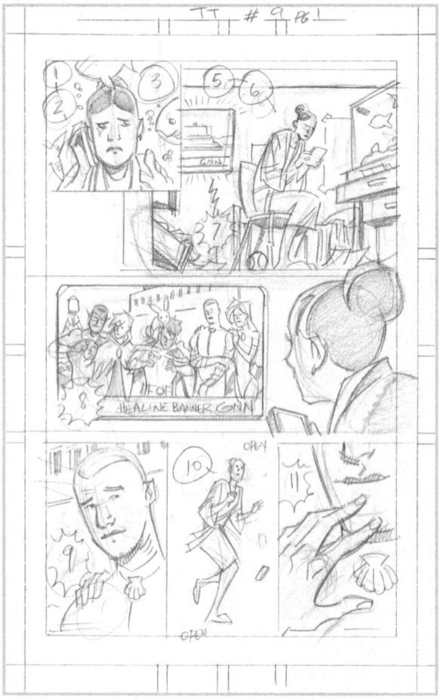
TT # 9 PG 1
GNN

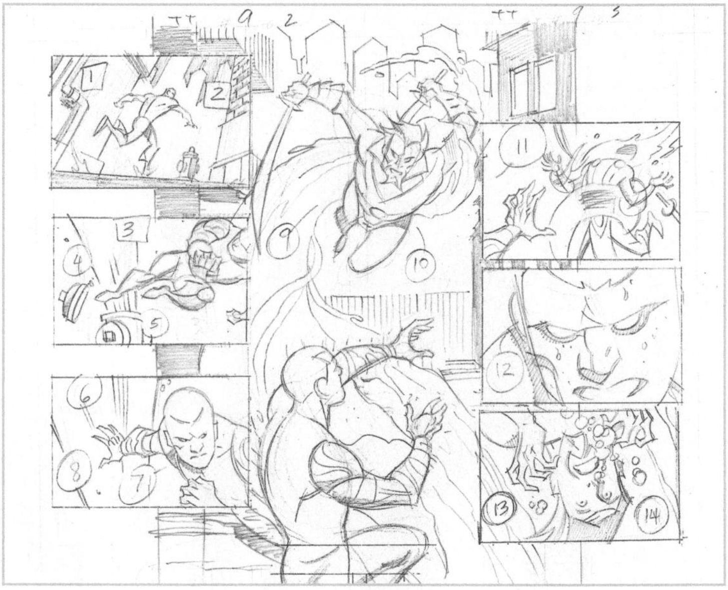

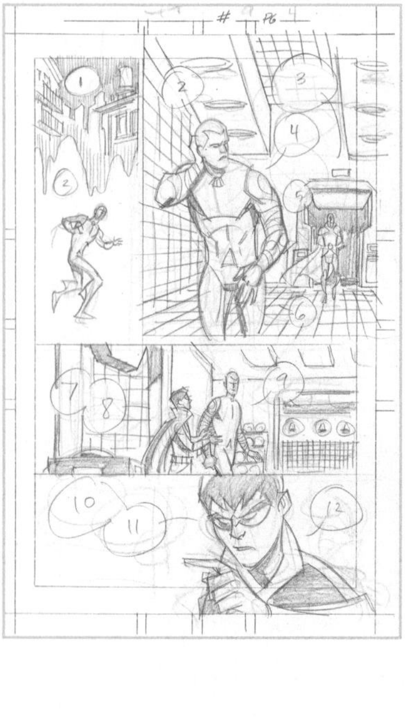

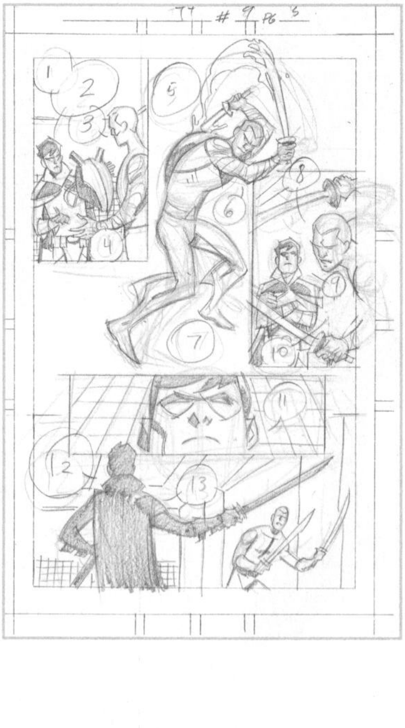

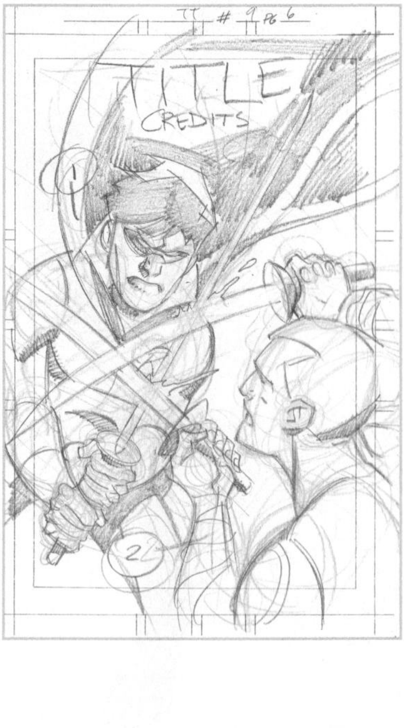
TT # 9 PG 6
TITLE
CREDITS

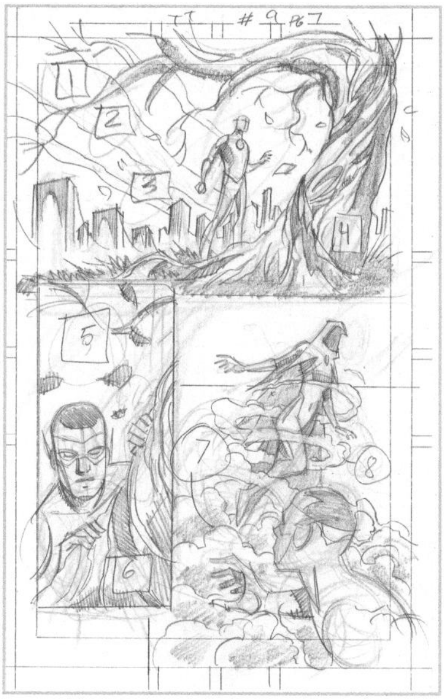
9 PG 7

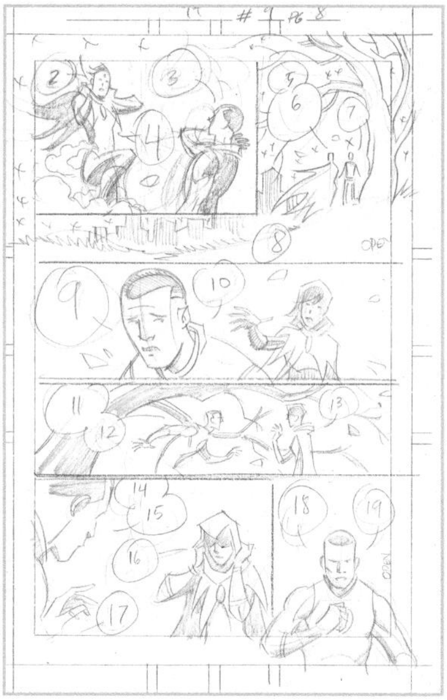
9 PG 8
OPEN

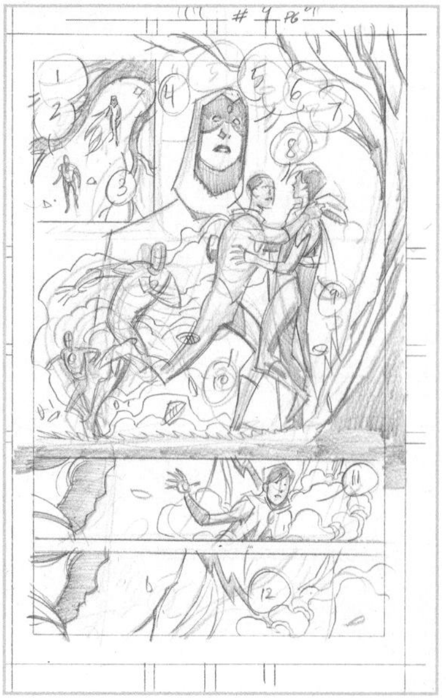
9 PG 9

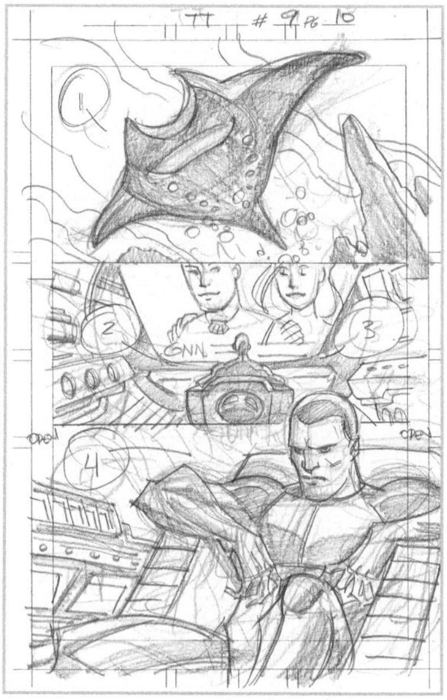
9 PG 10
GNN
OPEN
OPEN

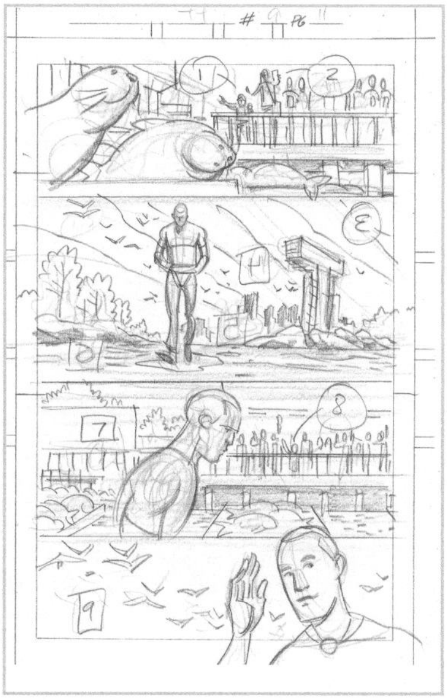
9 PG 11

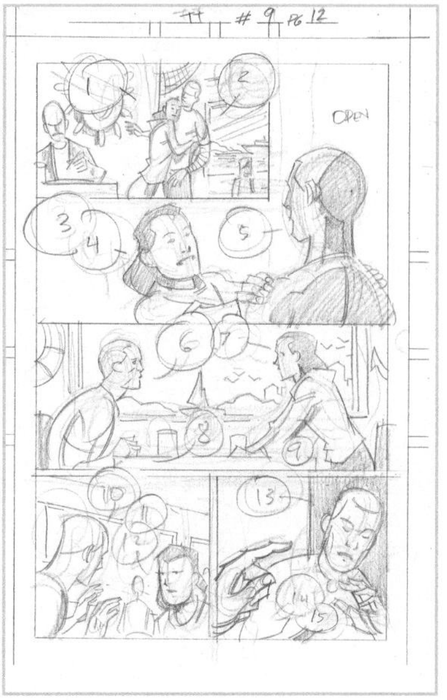
9 PG 12
OPEN

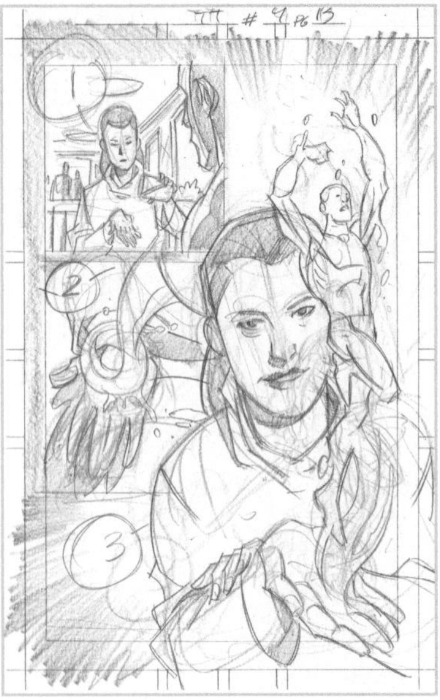
TT # 9 PG 13

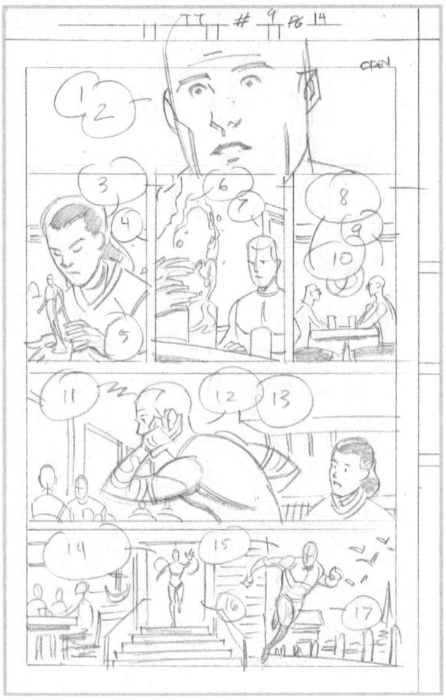
TT # 9 PG 14

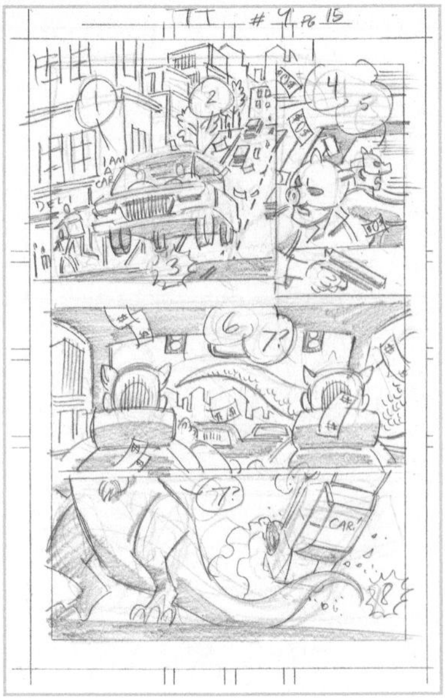
TT # 9 PG 15

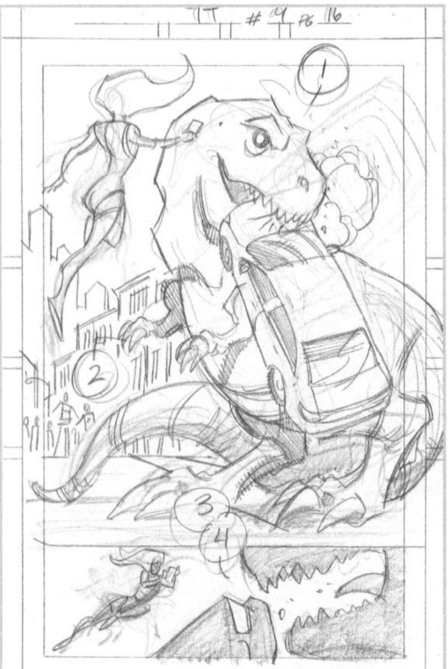
TT # 9 PG 16

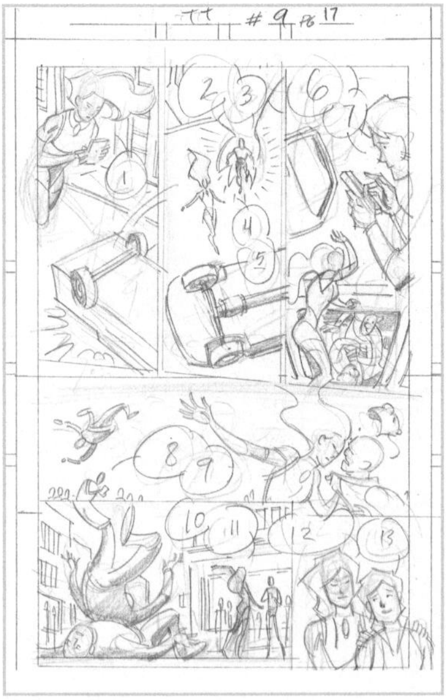
TT # 9 PG 17

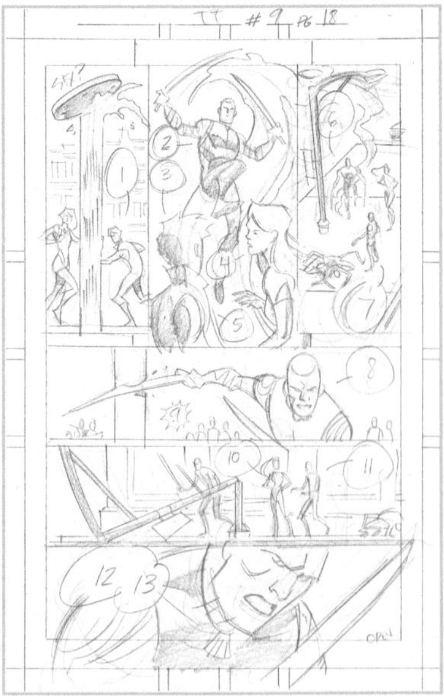
TT # 9 PG 18

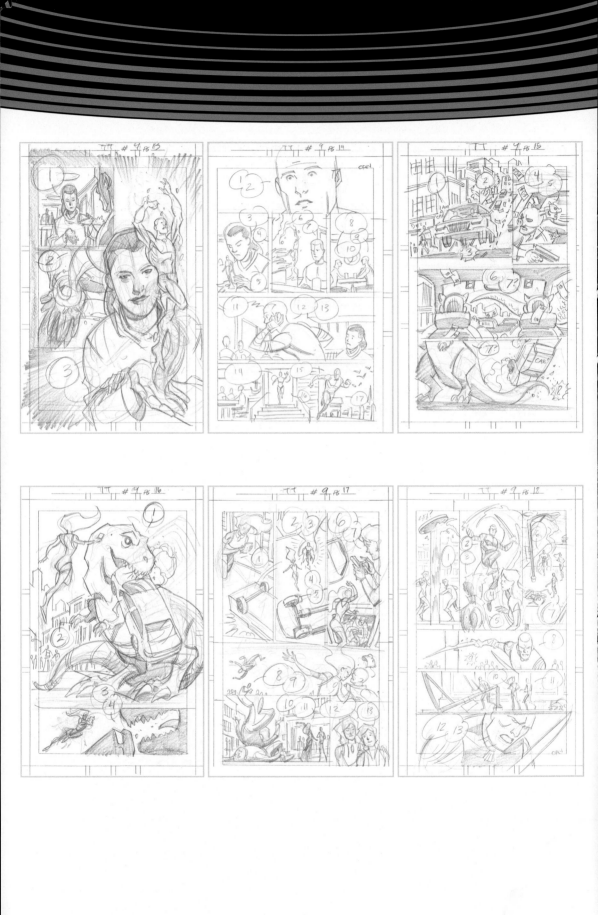

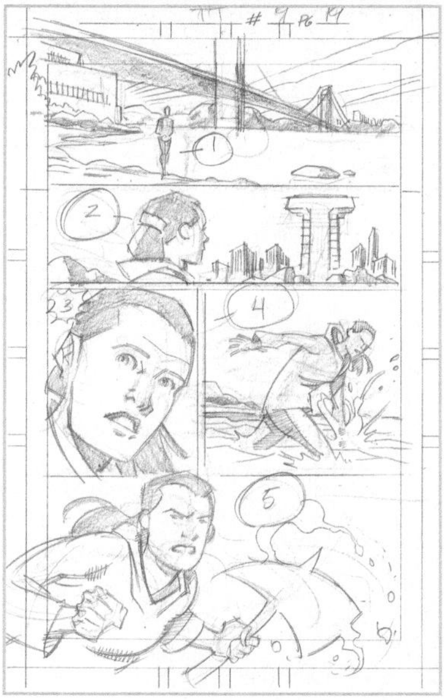
#9 PG 19

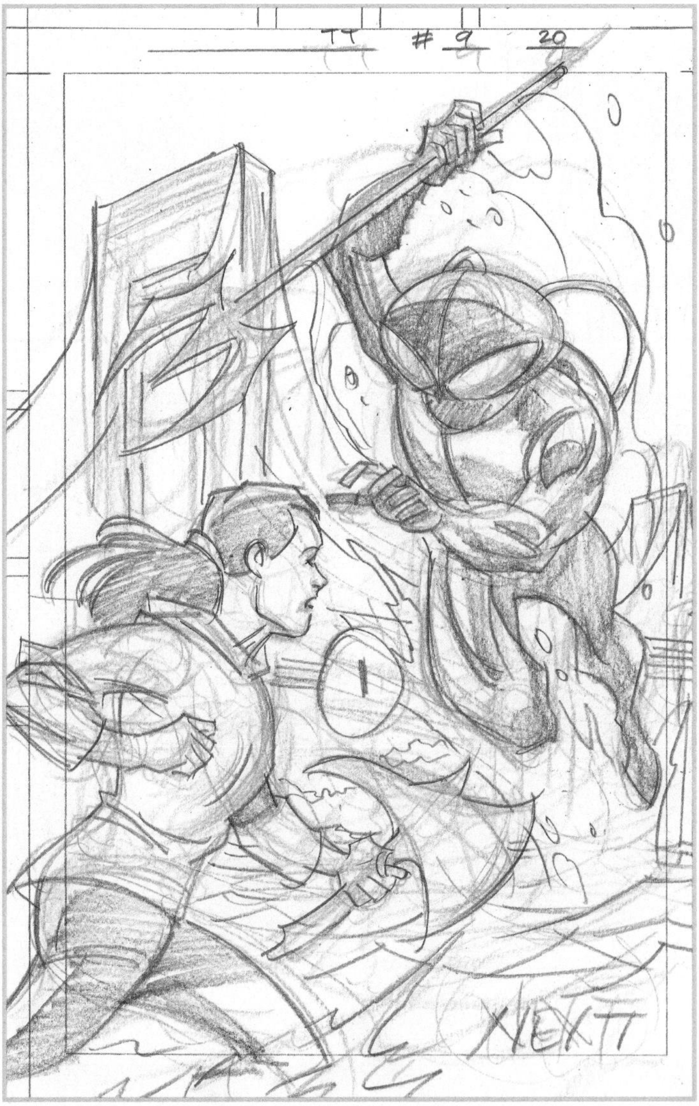
#9 20
NEXT!

"Brilliantly executed."
–IGN

"Morrison and Quitely have the magic touch that makes any book they collaborate on stand out from the rest."
–MTV's Splash Page

GRANT MORRISON
with FRANK QUITELY & PHILIP TAN

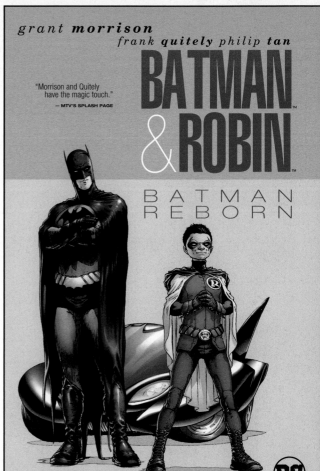

grant morrison
frank quitely philip tan

BATMAN & ROBIN

BATMAN REBORN

"Morrison and Quitely have the magic touch."
— MTV'S SPLASH PAGE

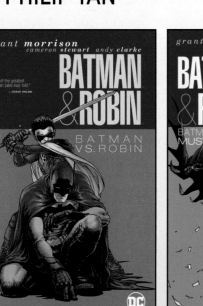

VOL. 2:
BATMAN VS. ROBIN

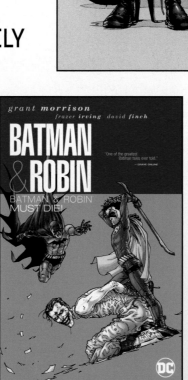

VOL. 3:
BATMAN & ROBIN MUST DIE!

"Thrilling and invigorating... Gotham City that has never looked this good, felt this strange, or been this deadly."
–Comic Book Resources

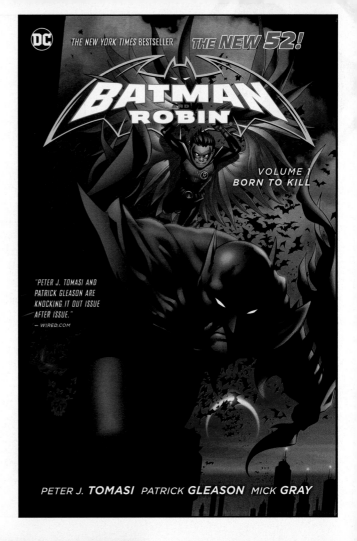

"Rock solid."
– IGN

"This is the kind of Batman story I like to read: an
actual mystery with an emotional hook."
– THE ONION / AV CLUB

BATMAN & ROBIN

VOL. 1: BORN TO KILL
PETER J. TOMASI
with PATRICK GLEASON

**BATMAN & ROBIN VOL. 2:
PEARL**

**BATMAN & ROBIN VOL. 3:
DEATH OF THE FAMILY**

READ THE ENTIRE EPIC!

BATMAN & ROBIN VOL. 4:
REQUIEM FOR DAMIAN

BATMAN & ROBIN VOL. 5:
THE BIG BURN

BATMAN & ROBIN VOL. 6:
THE HUNT FOR ROBIN

BATMAN & ROBIN VOL. 7:
ROBIN RISES

TEEN TITANS

VOL. 1: IT'S OUR RIGHT TO FIGHT
SCOTT LOBDELL
with BRETT BOOTH

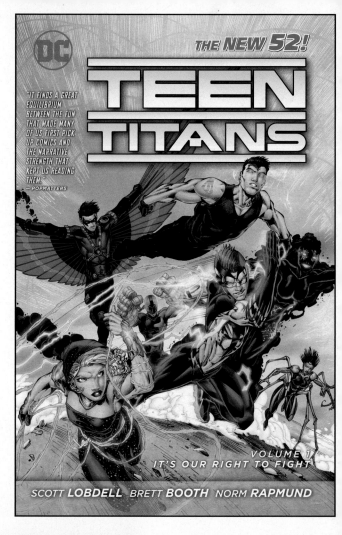

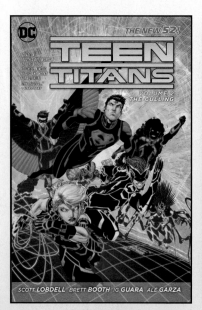

TEEN TITANS
VOL. 2: THE CULLING

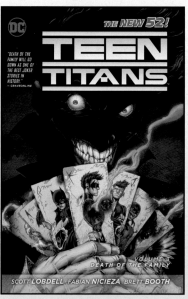

TEEN TITANS
VOL. 3: DEATH OF THE FAMILY

READ THE ENTIRE EPIC!

Teen Titans
VOL. 4: LIGHT AND DARK

TEEN TITANS
VOL. 5: THE TRIAL OF KID FLASH